IMAGES
of America

ROCKY HILL

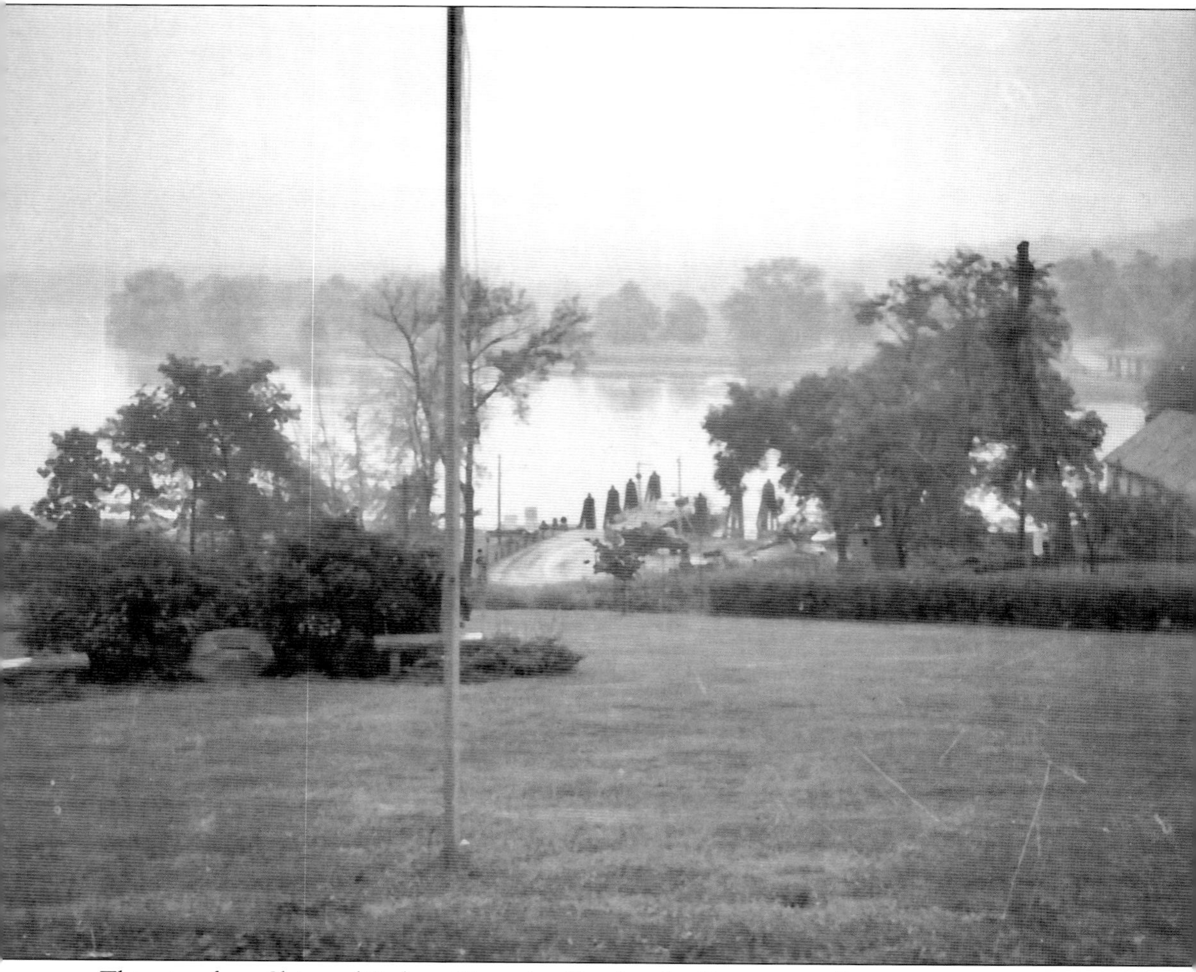

This view from Shipyard Park on Riverview Road to the Connecticut River is a town treasure. In the 18th and 19th centuries, one would have seen an active shipyard with as many as six sloops, schooners, or brigs under construction on the blocks. The historic ferry might be seen approaching the landing or a steamboat passing by. To the left, crops could be seen growing in the meadows. On the right was the industrial and commercial area that began as shops, chandleries, and more and evolved to the foundry property, whose remains and future are the subject of much planning and discussion. Along Riverview Road are the historic homes of sea captains. It is an ideal spot for sunrise services or simply for sitting in quiet reflection. (Courtesy of Rocky Hill Historical Society.)

On the Cover: Since Rocky Hill–Glastonbury Ferry began service in 1655, many types of boats have plied the Connecticut River. The tug-and-barge combination shown here loads children on the Glastonbury side on the Connecticut River. Rocky Hill is on the opposite side. (Courtesy of Rocky Hill Historical Society.)

IMAGES
of America

ROCKY HILL

Robert C. Herron with Mike Martino

ARCADIA
PUBLISHING

ISBN 978-1-4671-0422-7

Published by Arcadia Publishing
Charleston, South Carolina

Printed in the United States of America

Library of Congress Control Number: 2019943776

For all general information, please contact Arcadia Publishing:
Telephone 843-853-2070
Fax 843-853-0044
E-mail sales@arcadiapublishing.com
For customer service and orders:
Toll-Free 1-888-313-2665

Visit us on the Internet at www.arcadiapublishing.com

In developing this book, we uncovered many interesting facts about our town's history. We're sure there are many more to be discovered. We invite you to share your stories and photographs. You can do this by contacting us at thistorian@rockyhillct.gov.

Contents

ACKNOWLEDGMENTS

Many thanks to Rocky Hill Historical Society president Ed Chiucarello and the historical society's executive board for access to their photograph collection and research materials. Unless otherwise noted, the photographs in this book are from the Rocky Hill Historical Society's photograph collection.

The Rocky Hill Town Clerk's Office and Assessor's Office provided substantial support and were exceptionally tolerant of the author's perpetual presence and questions.

Thanks to the book's expert readers, Wendell and Susan Coogan, Maureen Mullen, Linda Nadeau, John Serra, and Martin Smith, for their proofreading, fact-checking, and readability comments.

Jennifer Duff at jenniferduffcreations@gmail.com provided the maps and line drawings used in this book.

Lewis Nedell provided insights concerning use of land records and other town documents.

Thanks to Bob McDougall of the Portland Historical Society and Michelle Tom of the Windsor Historical Society, who were involved in creating their towns' Images of America books, for their help and pointers.

Thanks also to Barbara Austen of the Connecticut State Library for providing scanned files of many historic Rocky Hill houses; Laura Smith, archivist at the University of Connecticut, for scans of Rocky Hill quarry photographs; Louisa Watrous of Mystic Seaport for maritime pictures; and Curtiss Hoffman of the Massachusetts Archaeological Society for the Lone Pine photographs.

Introduction

Rocky Hill lies on the west bank of the Connecticut River about eight miles south of Hartford. It was originally the land of the Wangunk tribe. Settlers from Wethersfield began to populate this area in 1650. The town is named for a trap rock ridge (called "a rockie hill" in old texts) that rises in the northeast section of town. European settlers overwhelmed the land of the Wangunks, and after the hostilities of King Phillip's War, the Wangunk, along with other tribes, were moved downriver to Middletown and then to western Connecticut as part of the Schaghticoke tribe. When the English forced them out of there, they moved west to settle among the Mohawks in New York. After the American Revolution, they were driven west to Wisconsin.

In 1962, as stone was being removed from the Rocky Hill quarry to serve as a roadbed for the new Interstate 91, the earth-moving activities began to uncover points, knives, scrapers, and other artifacts of indigenous people. This pre-European settlement acquired the name Lone Pine Site from an ancient pine tree that marked it.

The Great Meadows, covering 1,000 acres along the Connecticut River on the northern Rocky Hill riverfront, were farmed by indigenous people as early as the 11th century. The Morgan State Archeological Site, located in the Great Meadows, is an 11th–14th century settlement excavated in the early 1980s. The site's excellent preservation yielded tens of thousands of recovered artifacts.

Rocky Hill was recognized as a district of Wethersfield called Stepney Parish in 1722. Its location on the Connecticut River made it a natural port for Wethersfield and an early center for shipbuilding, agriculture, and trade. Flooding around 1700 changed the river's course, and Rocky Hill became Wethersfield's principal port. The Connecticut River and its maritime trade have figured prominently in Rocky Hill's history. The Rocky Hill–Glastonbury Ferry, which began operations in 1655, is the country's oldest continuously operating ferry. The ferry landing and riverfront were busy marine centers from the 1750s through the mid-19th century. Trade was extensive with New York City, the Southern colonies, the West Indies, and possibly Europe and Africa. Privateers sailed from Rocky Hill during the Revolutionary War and the War of 1812. Many old-time Rocky Hill sea captains' houses still stand. Rocky Hill became an independent town in 1843. As steam power emerged and navigation on the Connecticut River improved, the town's maritime tradition ebbed, and farming assumed a more prominent role in its economy.

The coming of the railroad in 1871 enabled easier commuting to neighboring cities. In 1909, a trolley made commuting to Hartford and Middletown commonplace. The completion of the Silas Deane Highway in 1930 made automobile and bus commuting to Hartford a reality. In 1963, Interstate 91 arrived and changed the nature of the town from agricultural to residential.

With each advance in transportation, the population of Rocky Hill has grown. In the late 1950s, in anticipation of Interstate 91, tract housing mushroomed. By 1970, it had replaced most of the town's farmlands. By the late 20th century, Rocky Hill's available space, central location, and easy access from Connecticut's major highways fast-tracked commuting and provided a home for businesses and industries, including WFSB television (Connecticut's CBS affiliate), the Connecticut State Health Lab, the Burris Logistics Truck Depot, and several commercial enterprises in the Capitol Boulevard complex.

The rocky hill that gave the town its name became a trap rock quarry that opened in 1898, providing material for roadbeds, railroad beds, and river embankments. It provided work for immigrants. Many ancestors of Italian Americans now form an important part of the Rocky Hill community. The quarry closed in 1957.

In 1932, a supply farm opened in Rocky Hill to provide food for the Fitch Home for Veterans and Orphans at Noroton Heights, near Darien, Connecticut. A large influx of World War I veterans during the Great Depression put a strain on the antiquated Noroton Heights site. The veterans home was moved to Rocky Hill, where it operates today as the Connecticut Veterans Home and Hospital.

As the population grew, the town changed. For example, in the early 20th century, there was no high school in Rocky Hill. The town paid tuition for students to attend Middletown High School. Wealthier students paid higher tuition to attend Hartford Public High School. From 1930 through 1958, students attended Wethersfield High School. By 1958, the town had grown sufficiently to erect its own high school. Growth brought other changes. For most of its history, the town was governed by three selectmen and traditional New England town meetings. By 1967, the town had grown so much that the government had to change to a mayor, town manager, and town council with supporting specialized boards.

Rocky Hill maintains its heritage with dedicated open space and parks, a proposed riverfront redevelopment project, and several working farms. The town has taken measures to protect farms and open space, particularly in the Great Meadows. Entry gates have been installed to prevent the destructive effects of motorized vehicles and vandals doing harm to the crops.

There are several places of special interest in Rocky Hill. Dinosaur State Park is a nationally known tourist destination with thousands of dinosaur footprints and other attractions. The footprints were discovered in 1966 and are now on display along with related exhibits, hiking trails, and other features. The Rocky Hill–Glastonbury Ferry continues to traverse the river after almost 400 years. The Dividend Pond Trails and Archaeological District is made up of 68 acres with three miles of marked trails along Dividend Brook. In the 18th and 19th centuries, this was a booming industrial area. Quarry Park is a state-owned, town-managed park that was once the trap rock quarry.

The National Register of Historic Places recognizes three historic districts in Rocky Hill. The Ferry District spans the Connecticut River and includes parts of Rocky Hill and Glastonbury; the Rocky Hill part includes the Ferry Landing, Meadow Road, and parts of Glastonbury Avenue, Riverview Road, and Pratt Street; and the Center District includes Old Main Street, Church Street, Center Green, Center Cemetery, and parts of Riverview Road, Glastonbury Avenue, and Pratt Street. The Elm Street District runs from the intersection of Elm Street and the Silas Deane Highway west to Grimes Road.

One

Rocky Hill's Uniqueness

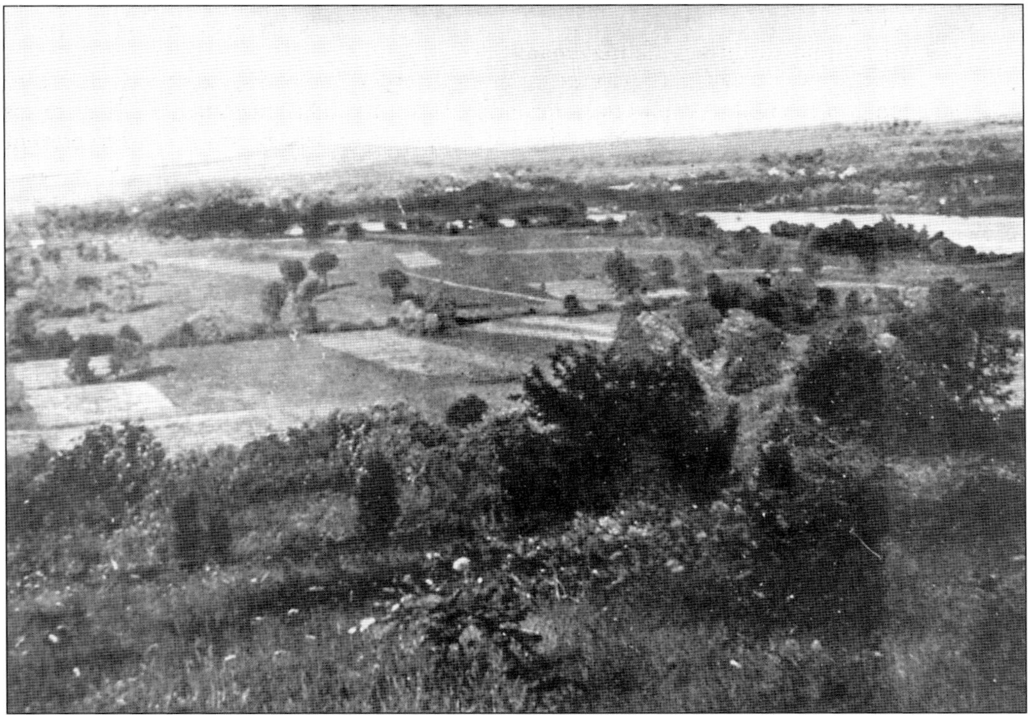

In many ways, Rocky Hill is like most New England towns. Its roots go back to the 17th century and conservative New Englanders. The Congregational Church was once the state-sanctioned church, public issues were settled at town meetings, and the locals' world was rooted in agriculture and, for a time, in maritime trade. As time passed, people from various cultures came, creating the rich cultural mix the town enjoys today. There are some things that make Rocky Hill unique. Among them are its experience on the Connecticut River, its ocean-going maritime history, the Connecticut Veterans Home, ancient relics left by indigenous people, and dinosaurs. The first grant of land in Rocky Hill was made by Wethersfield proprietors to Samuel Boardman in 1649–1650 in what was then south Wethersfield on the banks of the Connecticut River. It consisted of 20 acres on the southeast side of the "rockie hill." In 1661, Thomas Williams got a grant north of Hog Brook. In 1667, Joseph Smith was given a grant north of the Shipyard Grant.

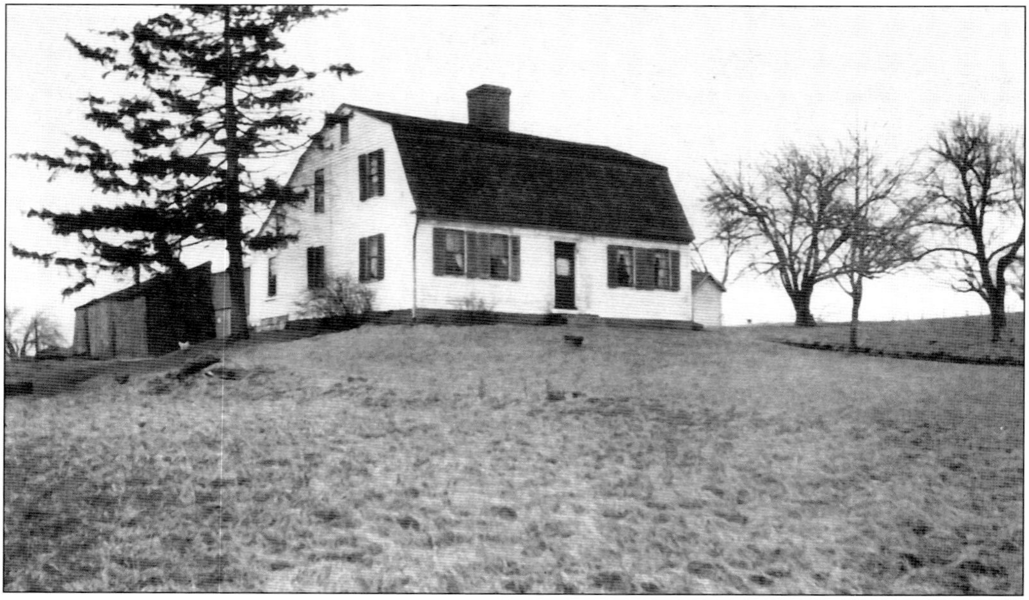

Phillip Goffe was the town crier of Wethersfield in the mid-17th century. He built the Goffe House at what is now 74 Old Main Street in 1655. There is some conjecture that the current house was built in 1700 or 1790 and replaced the original. This is viewed as the oldest house in Rocky Hill.

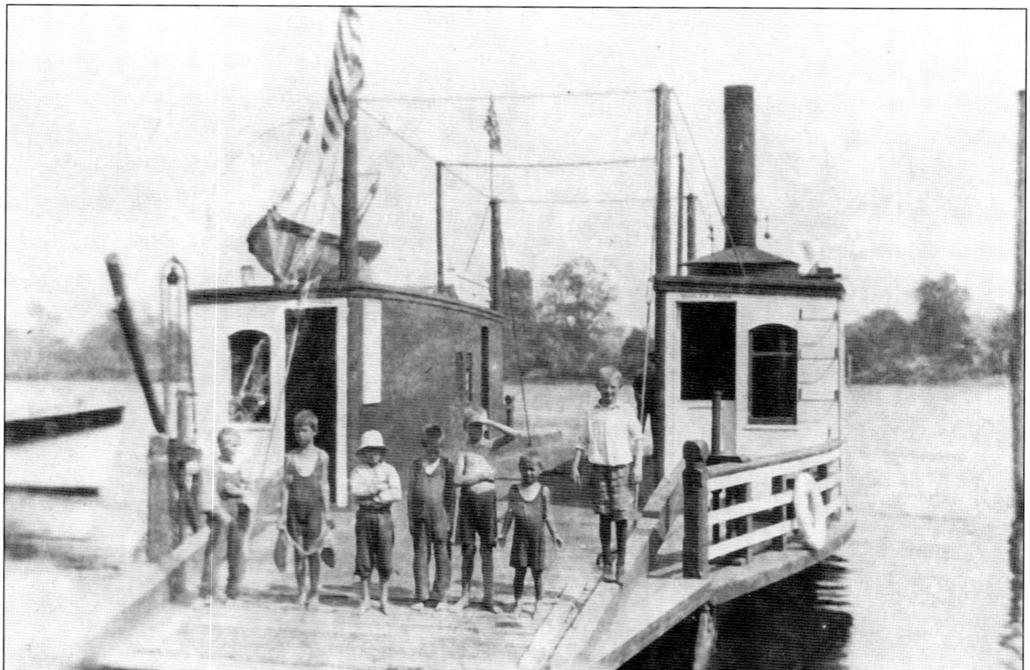

As early as 1650, farmers were crossing the Connecticut River to get to the fertile alluvial fields on the Glastonbury side. Ferry service developed as soon as the need arose, although the first legislative approval of a ferry was not recorded until 1673. At various times, the ferry has been powered by sails, sweeps (oars), poles, a horse on a treadmill, and steam. The steam ferry *Nayaug* (pictured) operated around 1900.

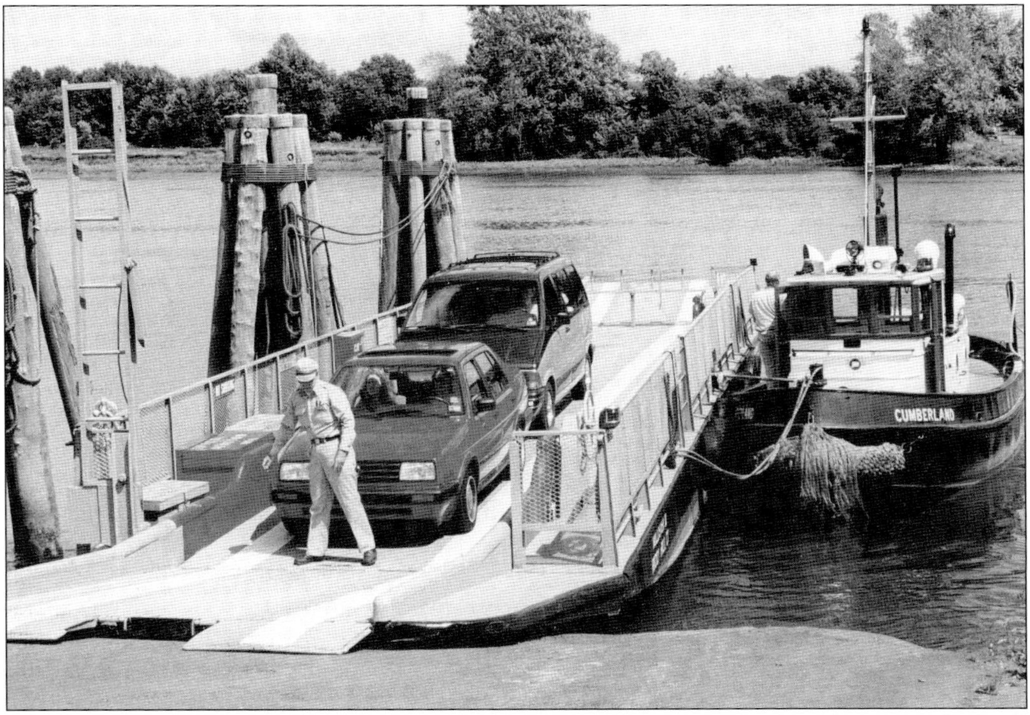

Today's ferry comprises the three-car barge *Hollister III* and the diesel tugboat *Cumberland*. Authority over the Rocky Hill–Glastonbury Ferry has changed several times, and today it is operated by the State of Connecticut. This is the oldest ferry in continuous operation in the United States. (Courtesy of Mike Martino.)

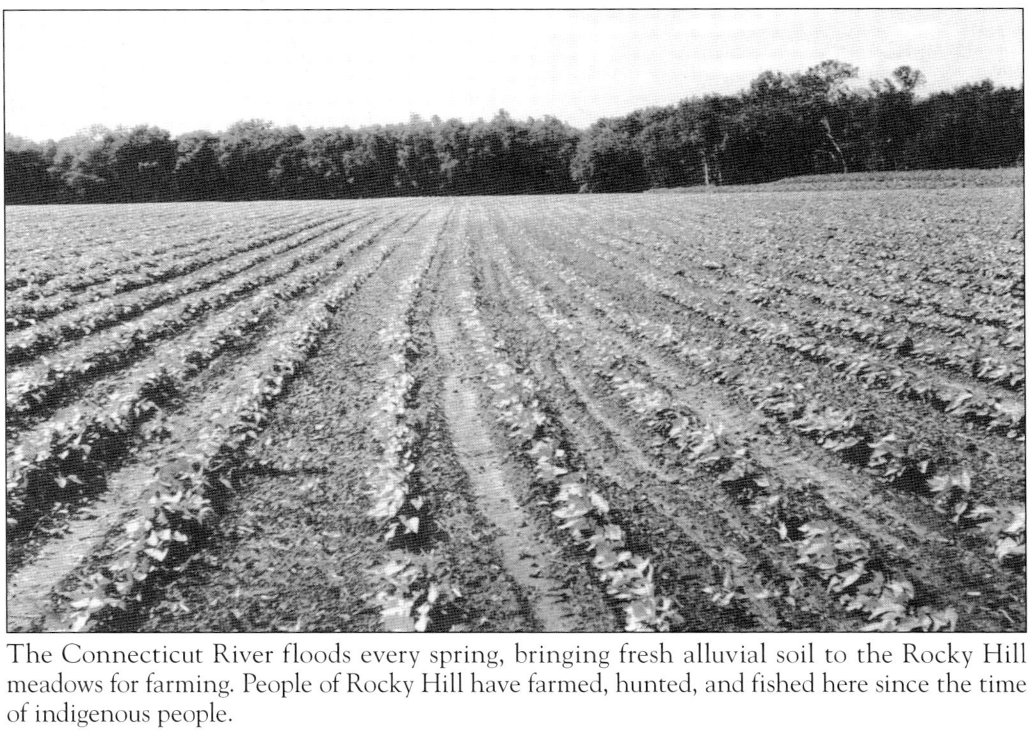

The Connecticut River floods every spring, bringing fresh alluvial soil to the Rocky Hill meadows for farming. People of Rocky Hill have farmed, hunted, and fished here since the time of indigenous people.

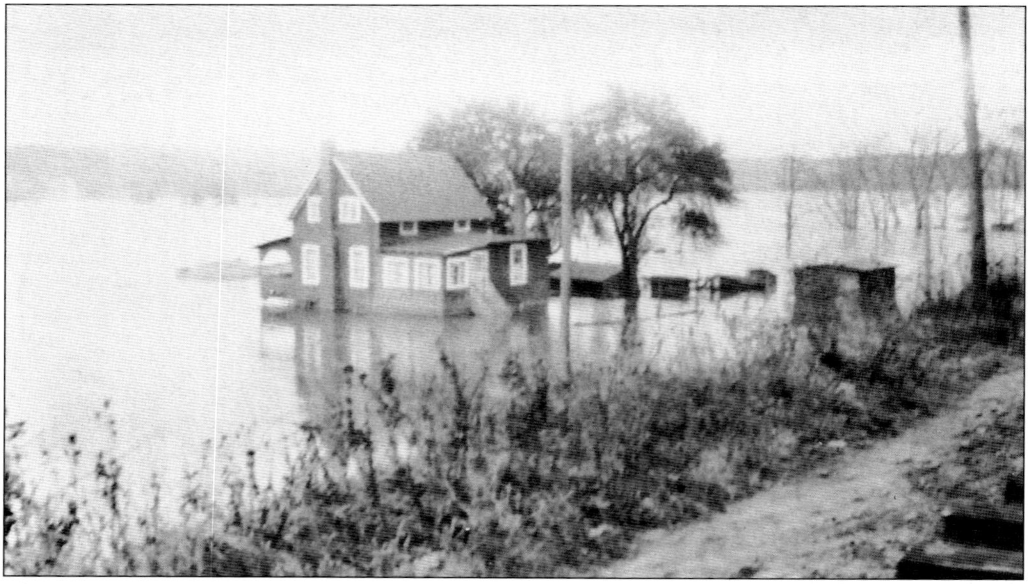

The price of the rich resources the Connecticut River brings is sometimes catastrophic flooding. The spring freshets, resulting from snow melt up north, can be anticipated. Other times, the river brings unexpected flooding. The March 1936 flood, pictured here, was particularly devastating. This was the Joseph Martino house near Hog Brook after the flood.

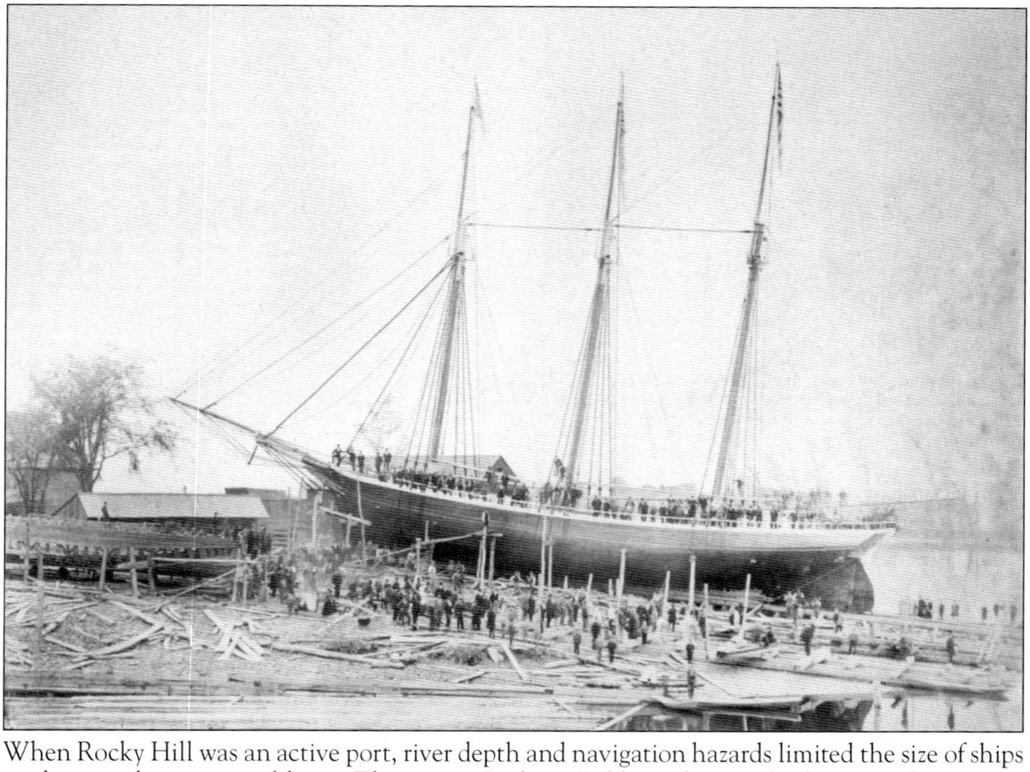

When Rocky Hill was an active port, river depth and navigation hazards limited the size of ships to sloops, schooners, and brigs. This was a Seabury Belden schooner built at Dutch Point in Hartford. It was similar to the *Henry H. Grant*, the last seagoing sailing ship launched by Seabury Belden in Rocky Hill in the 1880s. (Courtesy of Mystic Seaport.)

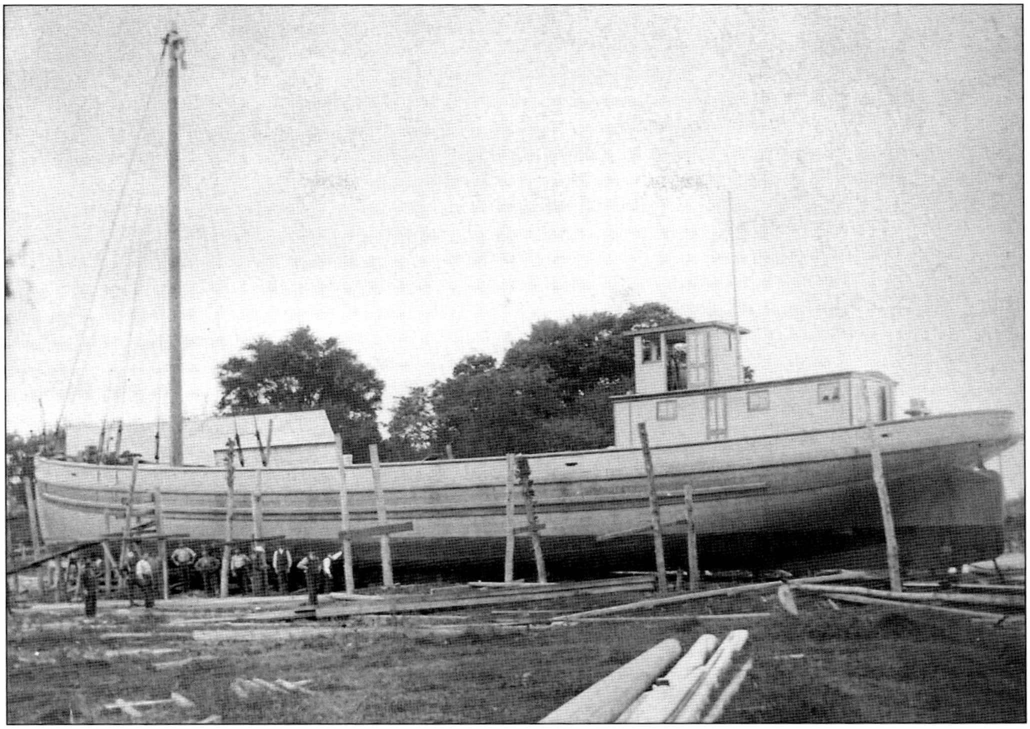

The heyday of shipbuilding in Rocky Hill lasted from about 1750 to around 1820, although ships and boats continued to be built until the 1890s. The last boats built in Rocky Hill were tugs like the one pictured here, barges, and construction craft built at the Belden Shipyard north of Hog Brook.

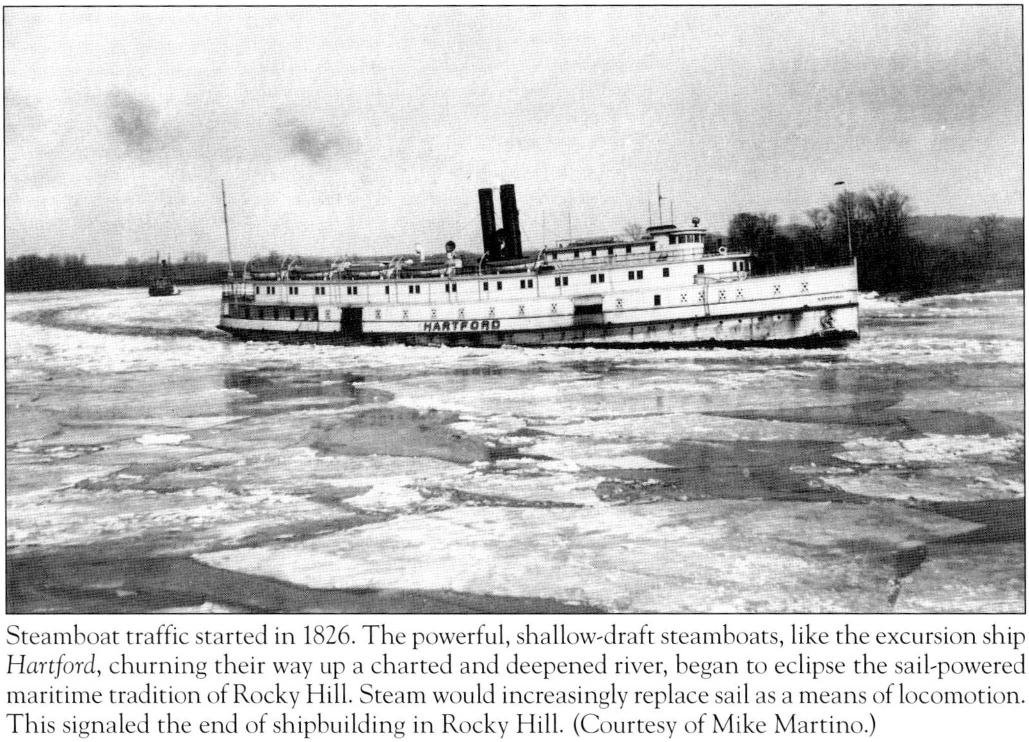

Steamboat traffic started in 1826. The powerful, shallow-draft steamboats, like the excursion ship *Hartford*, churning their way up a charted and deepened river, began to eclipse the sail-powered maritime tradition of Rocky Hill. Steam would increasingly replace sail as a means of locomotion. This signaled the end of shipbuilding in Rocky Hill. (Courtesy of Mike Martino.)

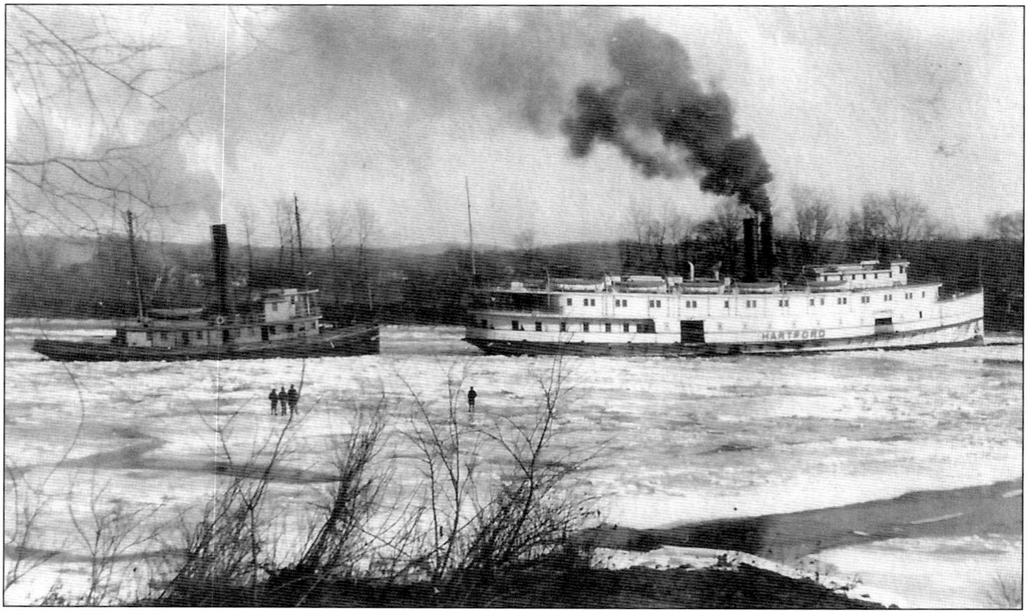

In the first half of the 20th century, the Connecticut River routinely froze solid in winter. Icebreakers like the *Spartan*, shown here passing the Rocky Hill ferry landing, would clear a path in the river for the twin excursion ships *Hartford* (pictured) and *Middletown*. Both were retired in 1931. They stopped at Rocky Hill when low water barred passage to Hartford. (Courtesy of Mike Martino.)

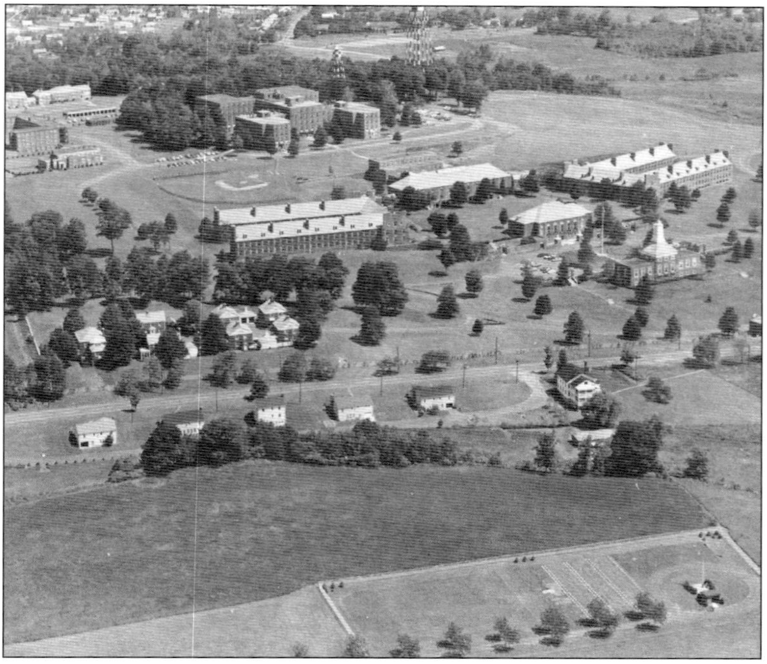

In 1932, a Rocky Hill facility opened to supplement the Fitch Home for Veterans and Orphans in Noroton Heights. An influx of World War I veterans entered the system during the Great Depression, and most took up residence in the Rocky Hill home. By 1940, it was decided to close the Fitch home and move all the veterans to Rocky Hill. This photograph was taken around 1969.

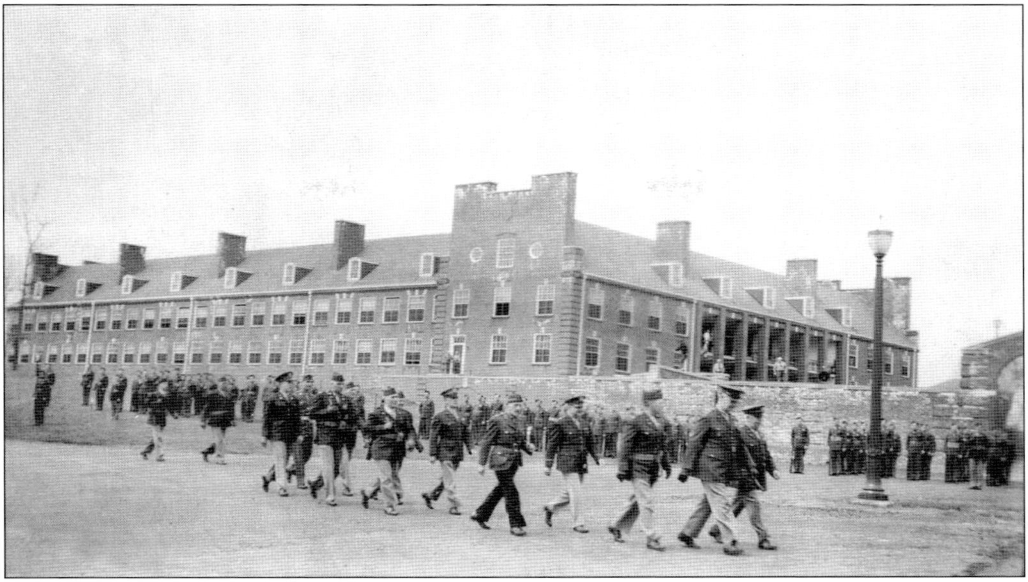

Operations of the Connecticut Veterans Home relocated to Rocky Hill from Noroton Heights on August 28, 1940. This photograph of soldiers marching on the grounds of the home was taken in 1944. (Courtesy of Mike Martino.)

In 1962, as stone was being removed from a hill in the Rocky Hill quarry to serve as a roadbed for Interstate 91, earth-movers began to uncover points, knives, scrapers, and other artifacts. The site was named Lone Pine after a large pine tree located there. Two well-defined cultural periods are discernible at this site. One, the Late Archaic Period (8000 BC to 1000 BC), was discovered in the Lower Zone (or Stone Bowl Zone).

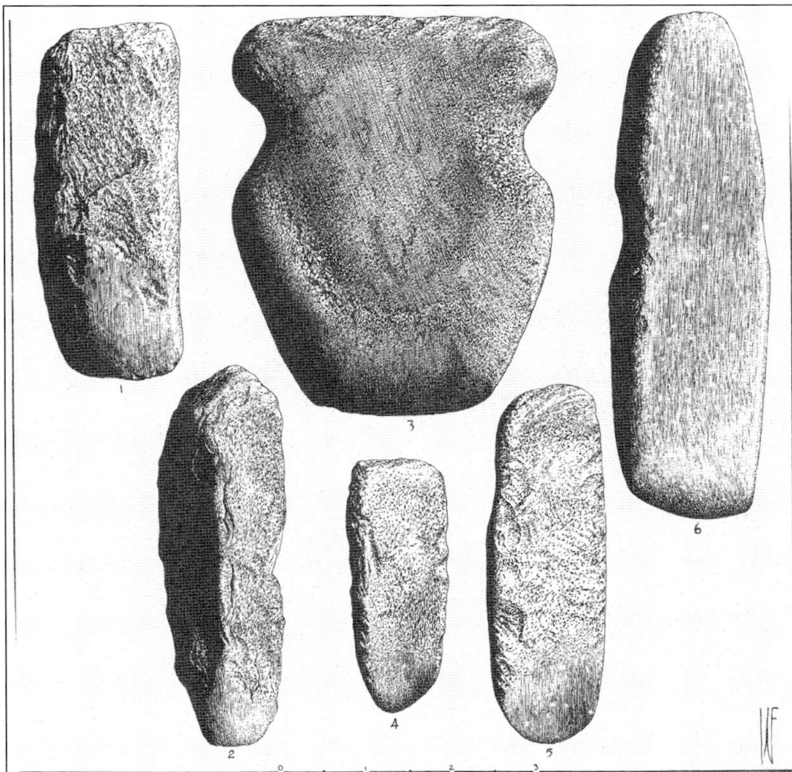

Fig. 11. LARGE IMPLEMENTS FROM LOWER ZONE, Lone Pine Site. 1,2,Celt; 3,Full Grooved Ax; 4,5,Grooved Gouge; 6,Grooved Adz.

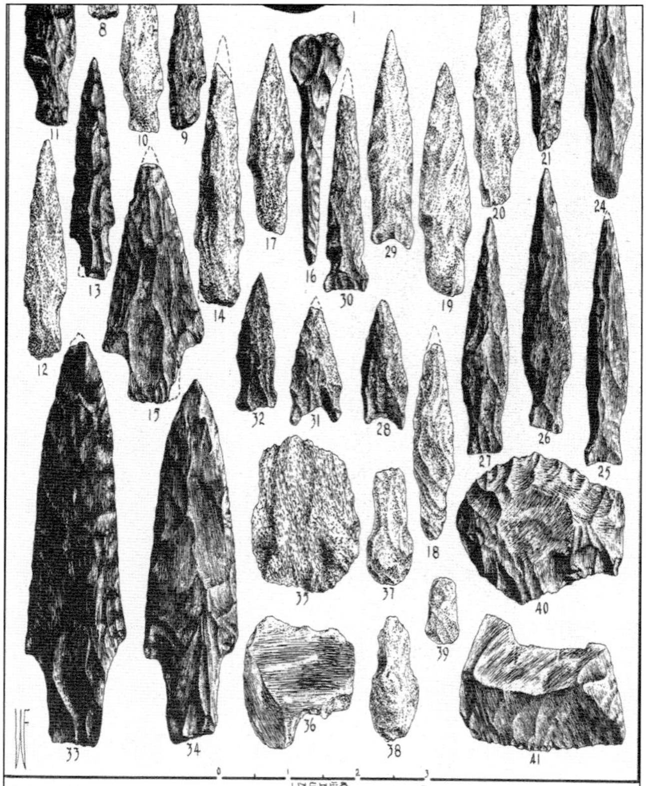

Fig. 10. ARTIFACTS FROM LOWER ZONE, Lone Pine Site. 1,Stone Bowl;2,3,Small Trangular#4, 4-10,17,Small Stem, 11-14,Side-notched#5, 15,Side-notched#1, 18-24,Corner-removed#3, 25-27,Side-notched#6, 28-32,Eared, 33,34,Corner-removed#7 Projectile Points; 16,T-base Drill; 35-39,Stem scraper; 40,Stem Knife; 41,Flake Knife.

Artifacts from the Early Ceramic Period (600 BC to 1,000 CE, also known as the Woodland Period) were found in the Upper Zone. (Reprinted from the *Bulletin of the Massachusetts Archaeological Society*, vol. 32, with permission of the Massachusetts Archaeological Society.)

In 1977, David Cooke, an amateur archaeologist and native of Rocky Hill, was hunting pheasants in the Rocky Hill meadows with his wife, June. While she was bending to recover a fallen pheasant, she picked up a piece of handsomely decorated pottery. She was an accomplished archaeologist in her own right and called David to look at what she had found.

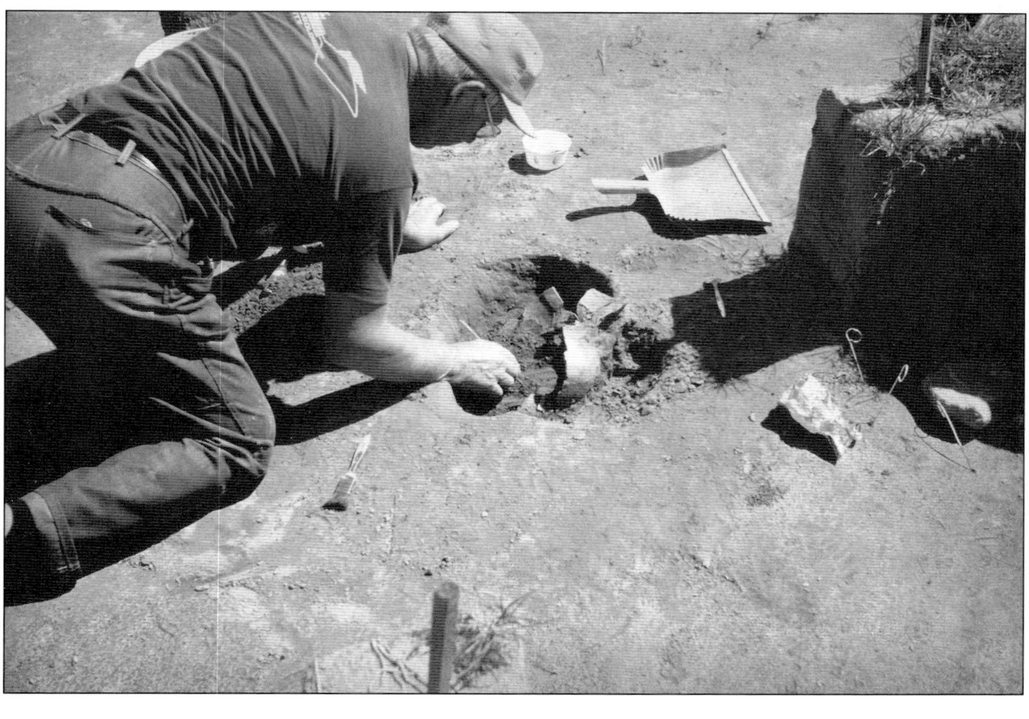

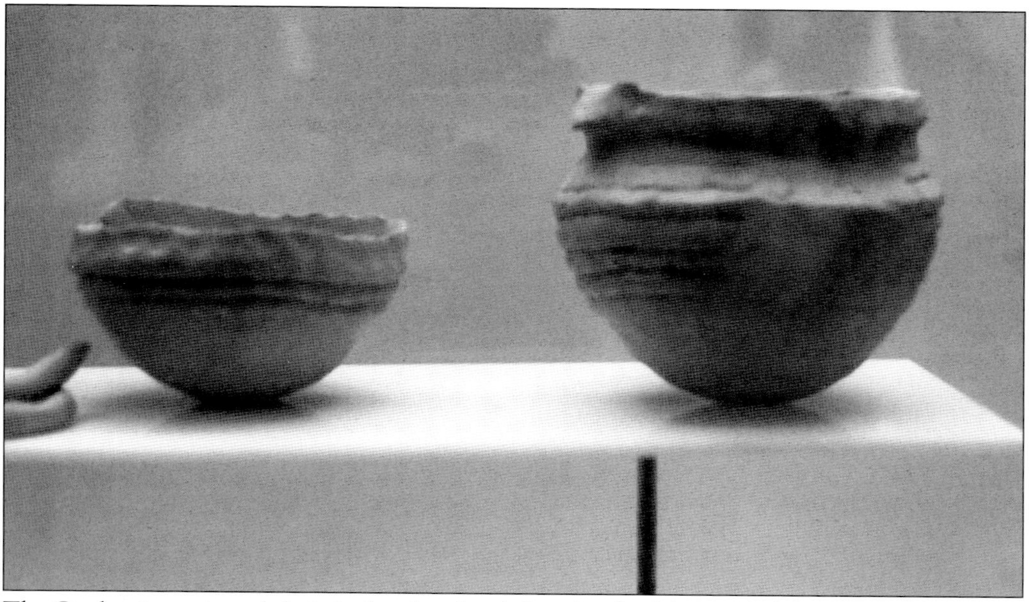

The Cookes investigated their find and realized that they had discovered the site of a significant Woodland Indian settlement. This led to the Morgan Site archaeological dig. Many ancient artifacts (like the pottery seen here) have been unearthed, increasing knowledge of the people who lived here before.

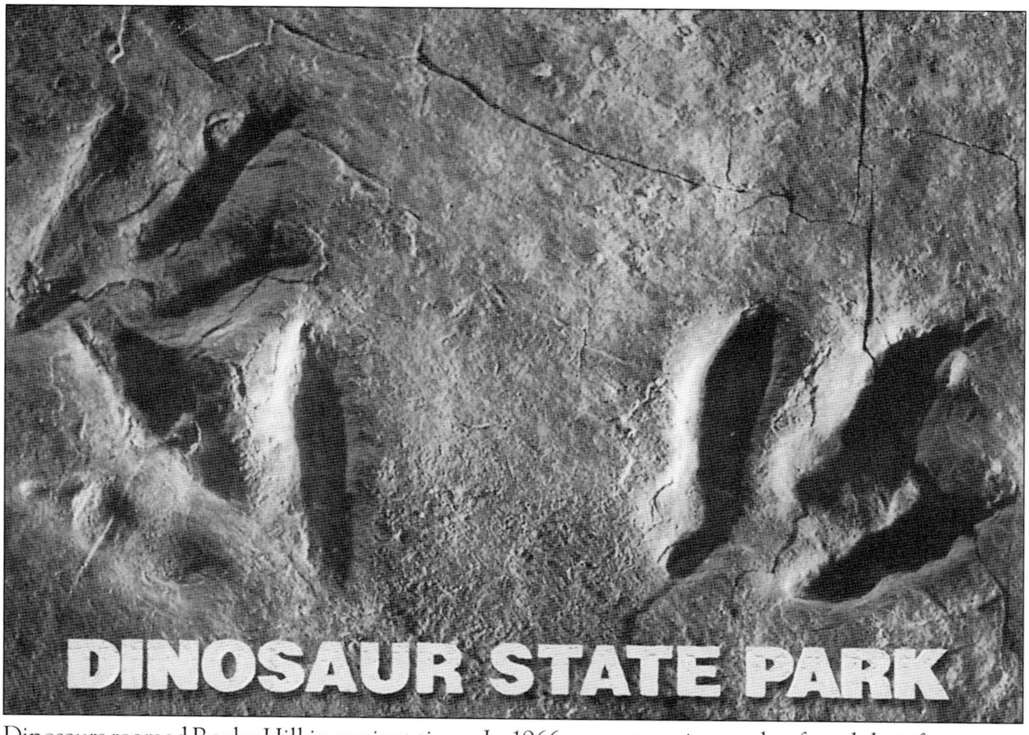

Dinosaurs roamed Rocky Hill in ancient times. In 1966, a construction worker found their footprints, and the result was Dinosaur State Park, with extensive facilities to describe the 250-million-year span of time and the creatures who lived here over some of its periods. (Courtesy of Dinosaur State Park.)

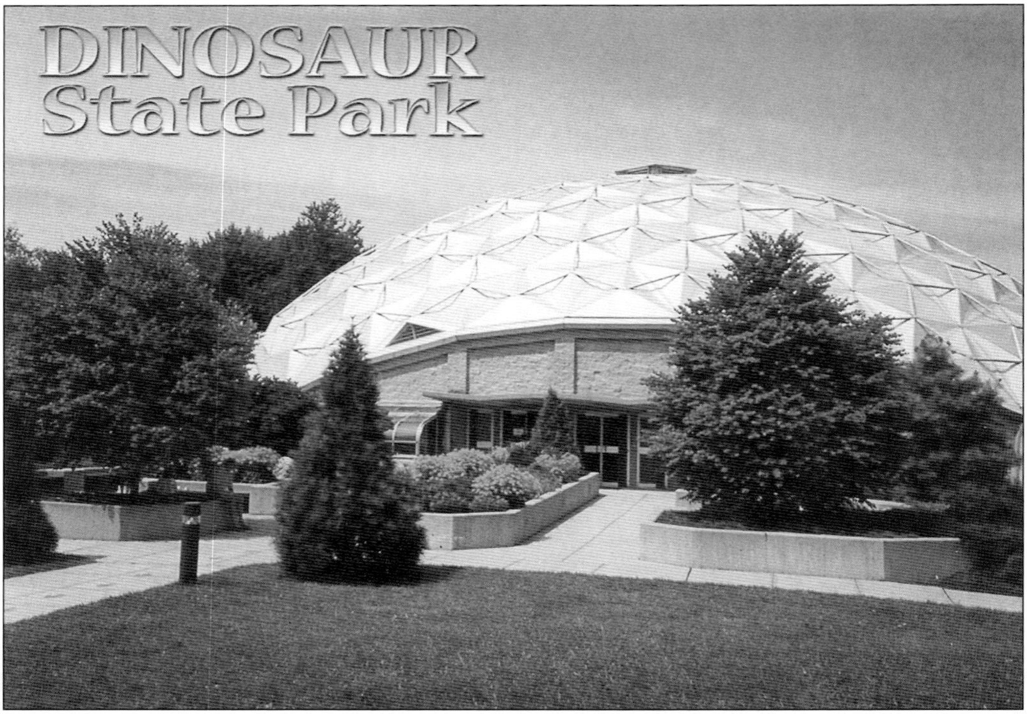

People come from all over the world to see the dinosaur artifacts housed in this dome and learn about their history. (Courtesy of Dinosaur State Park.)

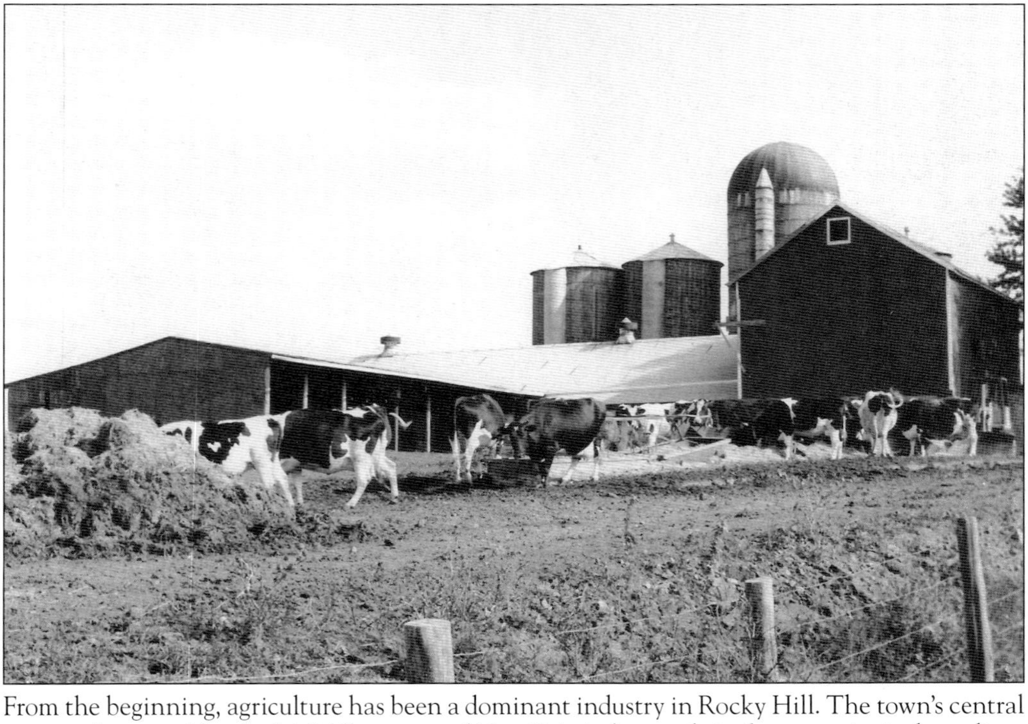

From the beginning, agriculture has been a dominant industry in Rocky Hill. The town's central position between Hartford, Middletown, and New Britain has made its farmers principal suppliers, particularly of dairy products, to these cities.

Two

Military Service

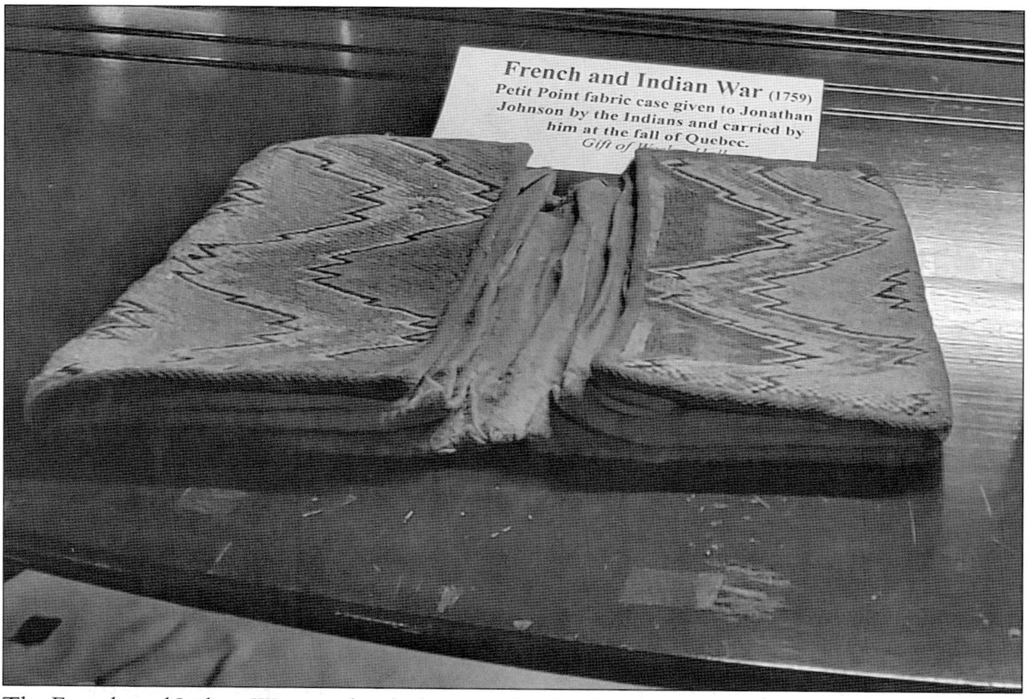

The French and Indian War was fought between England and France and their colonies from 1754 to 1763. Five veterans of the French and Indian War are buried in Rocky Hill's Center Cemetery. A petit-point fabric case in the Rocky Hill Historical Society's collection was given to Jonathan Johnson of Rocky Hill by Indians and carried by him at the fall of Quebec in 1759.

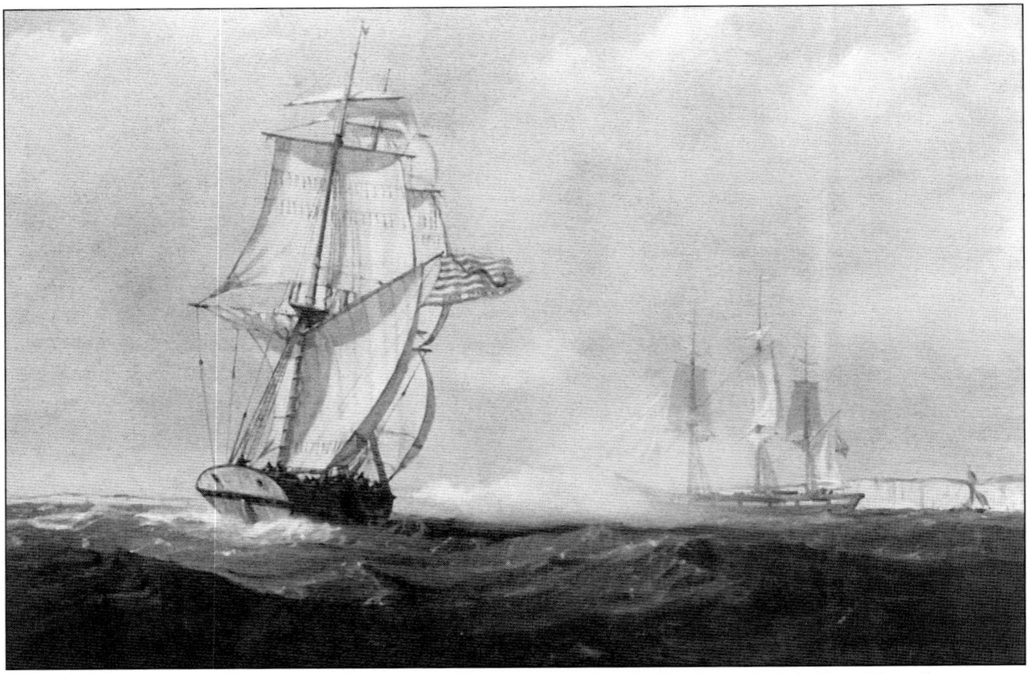

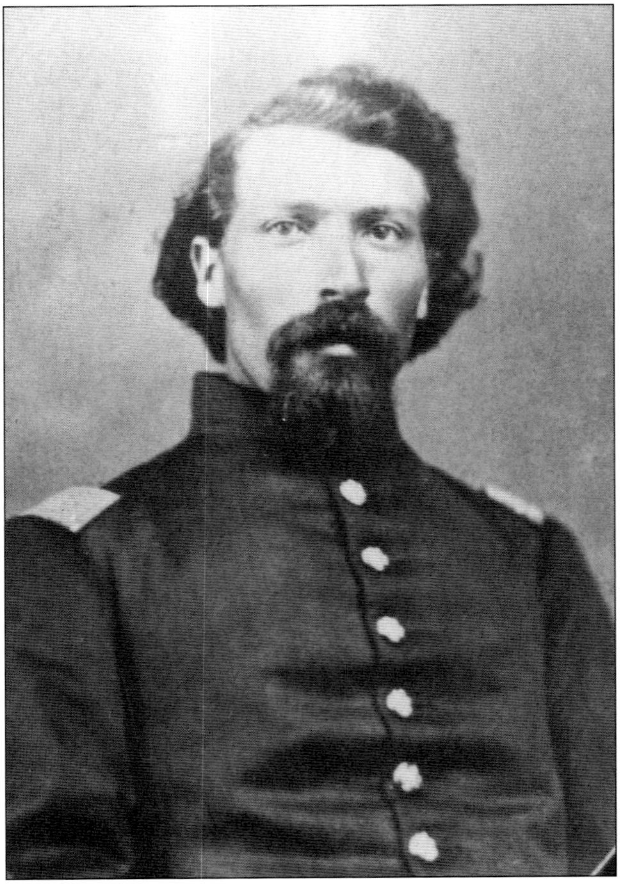

The *Minerva* (a brig like that in this drawing) was built in Rocky Hill. It was the first ship commissioned by the Connecticut Navy and was later a privateer. Benedict Arnold's attack on New London in 1781 was precipitated when the *Minerva* captured the British merchantman *Hannah* and took it to New London as a prize.

Rocky Hill committed 128 soldiers to the Civil War. The town's population was 1,102 in 1860, so all of its tightly interrelated families had at least one loved one in jeopardy. Rocky Hill soldiers fought at Antietam, Fredericksburg, and Plymouth, North Carolina. Capt. Jarvis Blinn (pictured) was killed at the Battle of Antietam in 1862. Several men captured at Plymouth died in Andersonville and other prison camps.

Many Rocky Hill men died or were captured during the Civil War. Roland LeVaughn was a first sergeant who was captured at Plymouth, North Carolina, in April 1864 and died at Charleston, South Carolina, that September. William O. LeVaughn was also a first sergeant captured at Plymouth. He died in the Andersonville prison camp. Donald LeVaughn, a private, was wounded at Antietam and returned home.

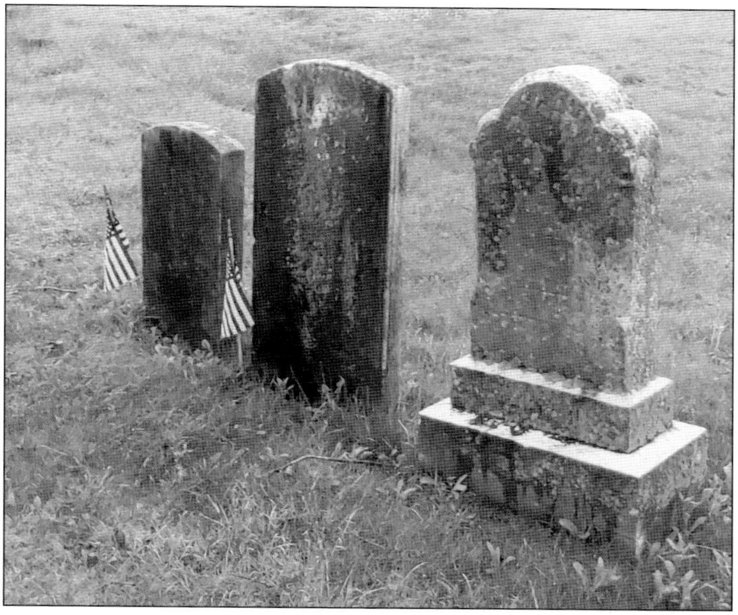

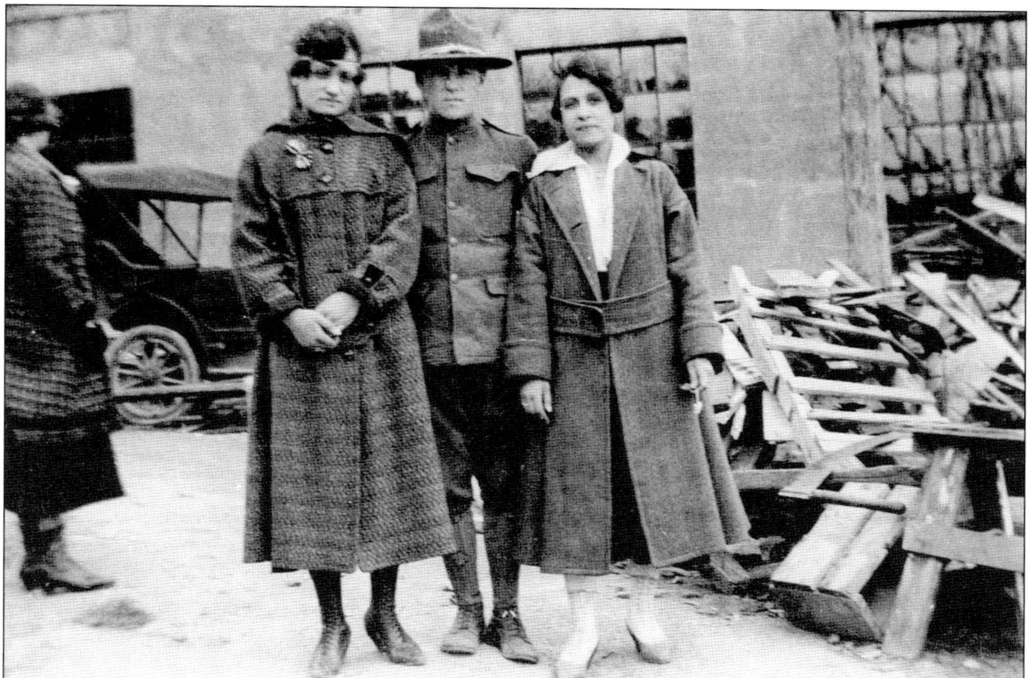

Ninety-five people from Rocky Hill, four women among them, enlisted in military service during World War I. The population at home pitched in to support sons and daughters at war and keep morale high. They faced shortages of essentials such as food and fuel as they provided agricultural and industrial goods for the war effort. (Courtesy of Mike Martino.)

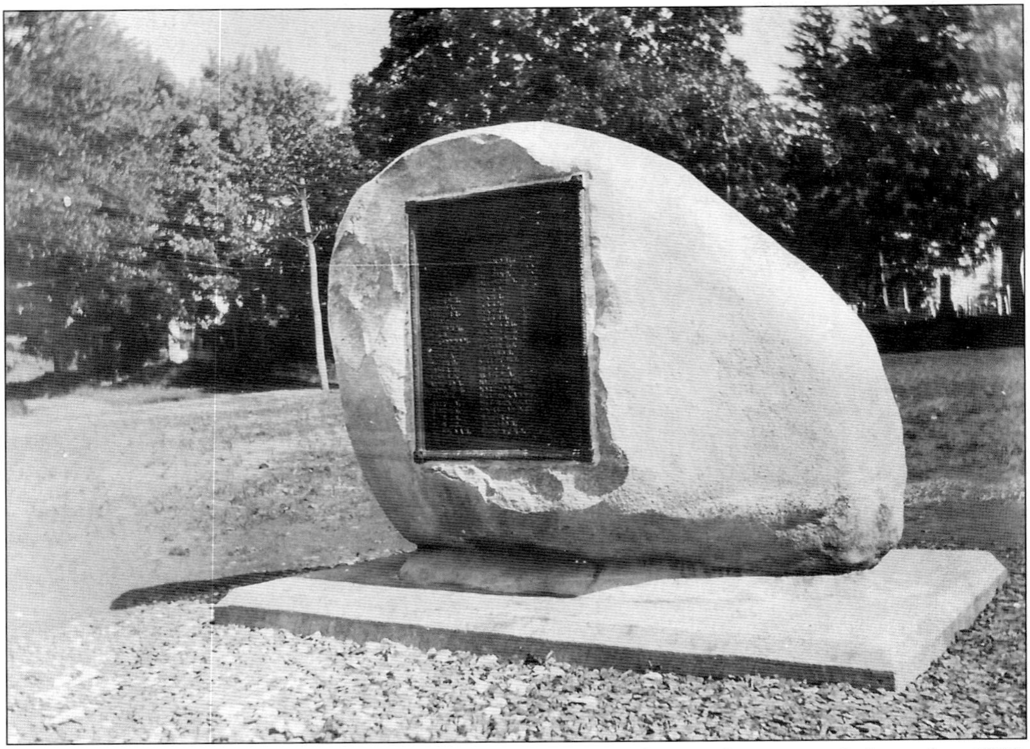

A stone memorial to Rocky Hill's World War I veterans on Center Green was dedicated in 1925. It is located in front of the Bulkeley flagpole, which was erected in 1917 to honor those serving in the war. The flagpole has been replaced twice, but a version of it still stands on Center Green.

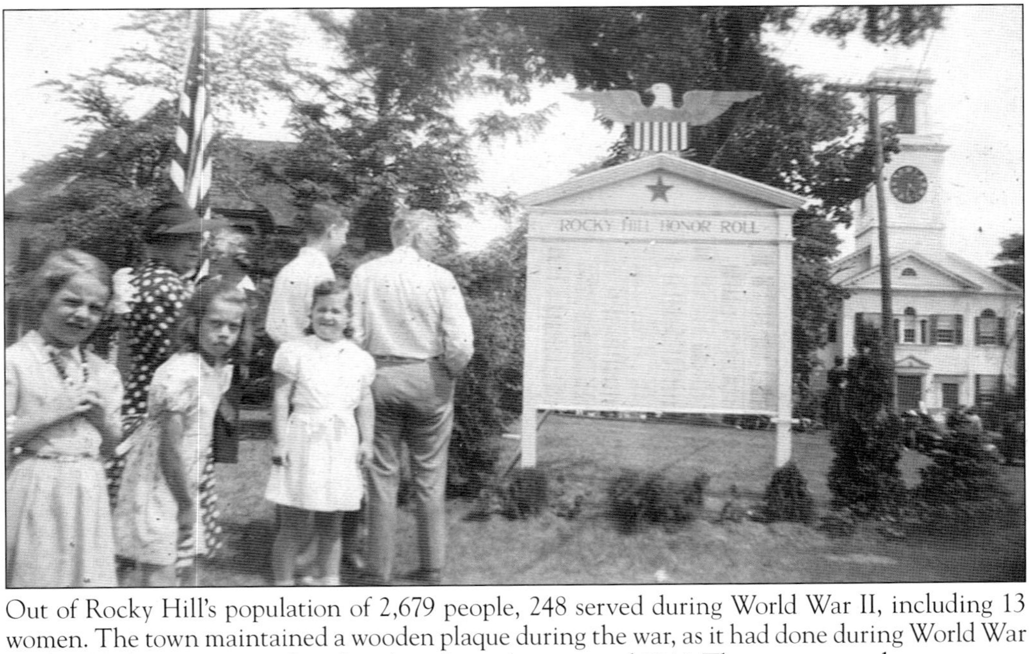

Out of Rocky Hill's population of 2,679 people, 248 served during World War II, including 13 women. The town maintained a wooden plaque during the war, as it had done during World War I, and added names as people enlisted, as shown here around 1944. The town erected a permanent monument on Center Green after the war. (Courtesy of Mike Martino.)

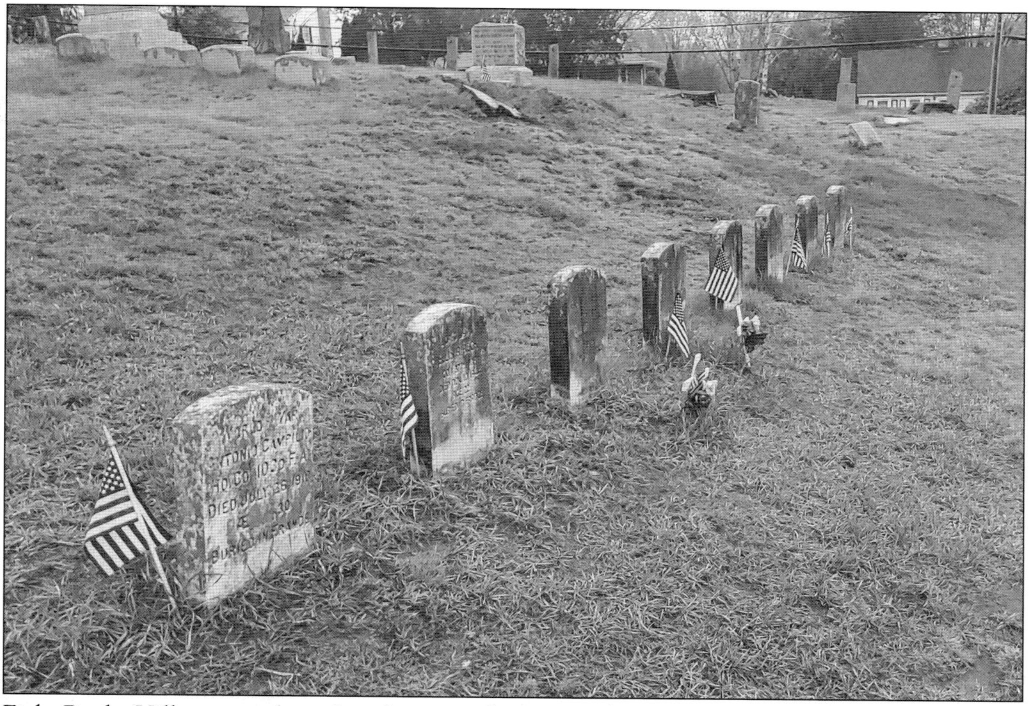

Eight Rocky Hill veterans buried on foreign soil are remembered with markers at Center Cemetery. Angelo Campilio was killed in France during World War I, and seven others—Ellis Beck, Frank and Horace Bennino, Armond Chapron, Richard Dexter, Albert Goss, and Henry Maxham—died during World War II.

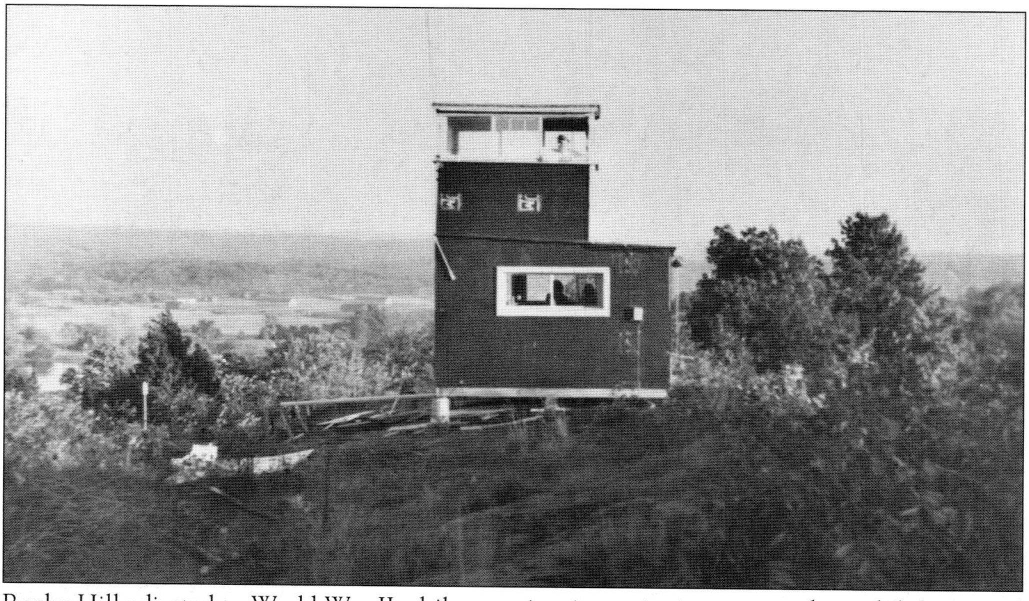

Rocky Hill adjusted to World War II while experiencing rationing, war work, civil defense, and concern for friends and loved ones at war. There were air raid wardens, scrap metal drives, and all the other activities associated with the war. Soldiers staffed a listening station off Matteson Avenue to detect enemy planes. These and the plane spotting tower on Quarry Hill pictured here protected Pratt and Whitney, Colt Firearms, and other defense industries.

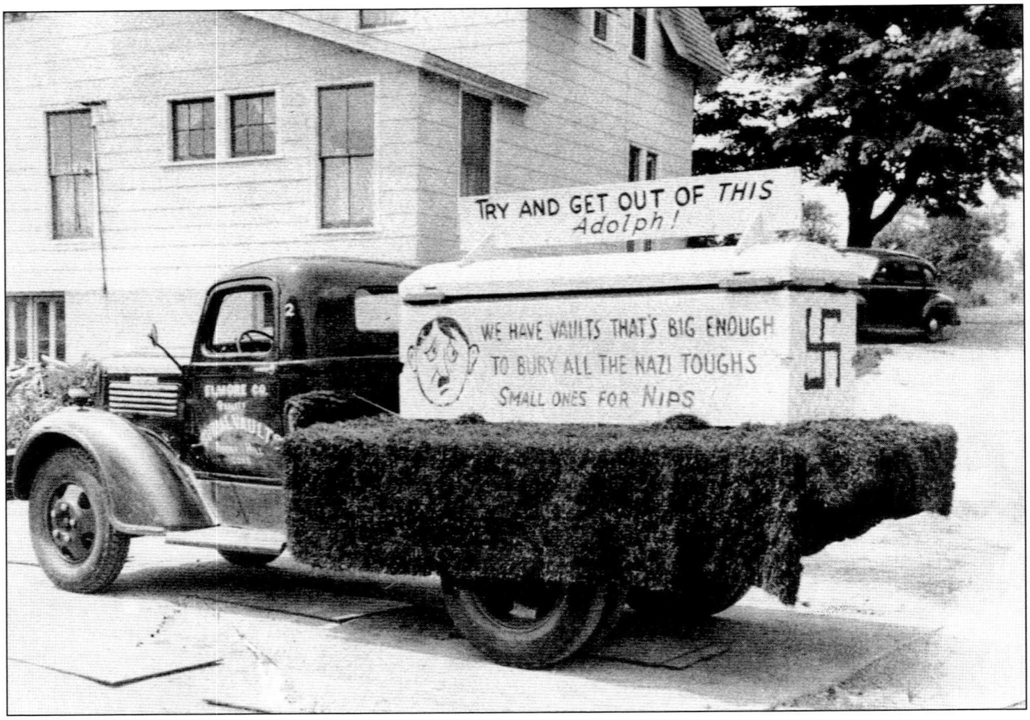

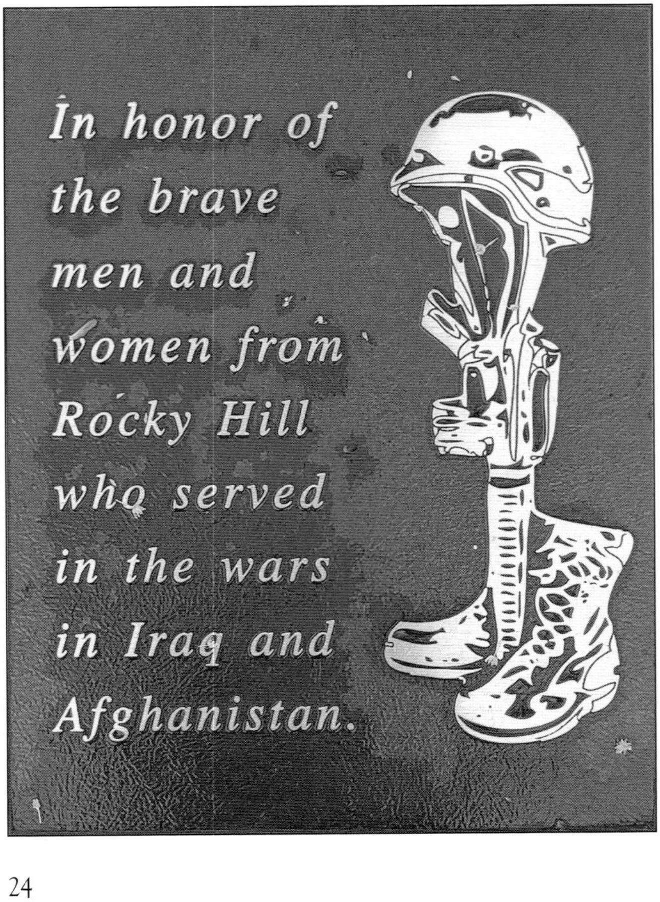

Support for the war was enthusiastic and visceral ("Nips," derived from Nippon, the Japanese name for Japan, was a widely used ethnic slur on Japanese during the war). The Elmore Monument Company crafted a symbolic burial vault for Adolph Hitler and other Axis leaders. (Courtesy of Mike Martino.)

In more recent times, people from Rocky Hill have fought in wars from Korea to the War on Terror. There are monuments to them, but the town's growing population and the increased number of veterans preclude listing them individually. The town tries to make their names known through other tributes.

Three

ROCKY HILL INSTITUTIONS

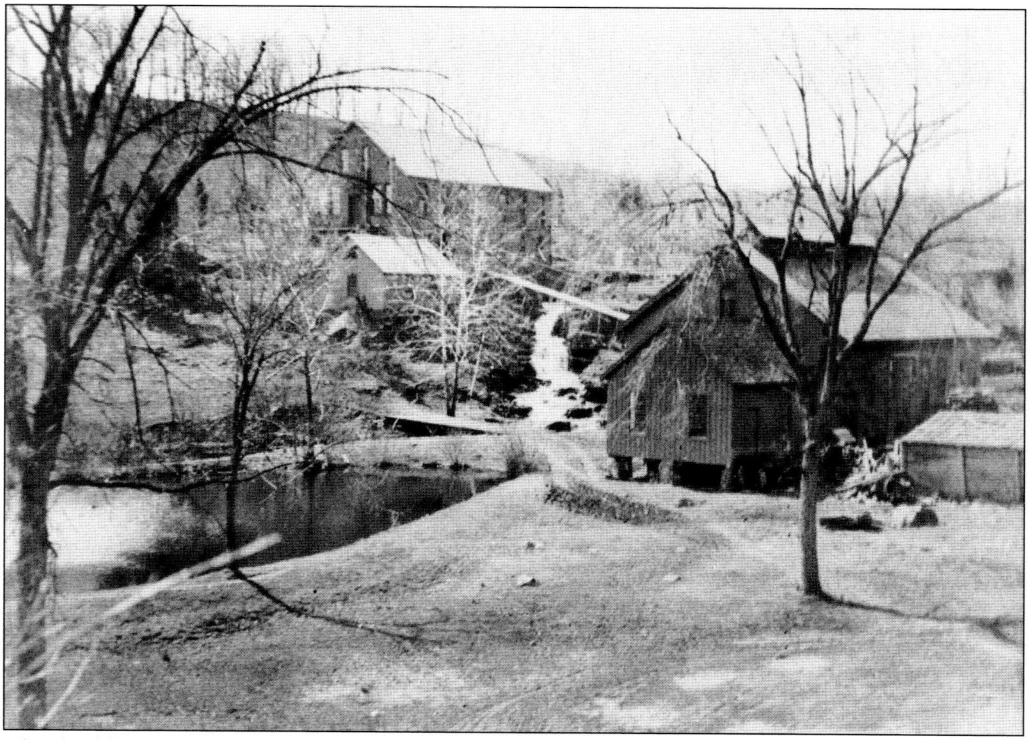

This building was used primarily for drop forging. Billings and Edwards Company opened at the turn of the 20th century at Dividend Brook in Rocky Hill. Charles Billings ultimately founded the Billings and Spencer Company of Hartford and Billings & Spencer Company Ltd. of Welland, Ontario, Canada.

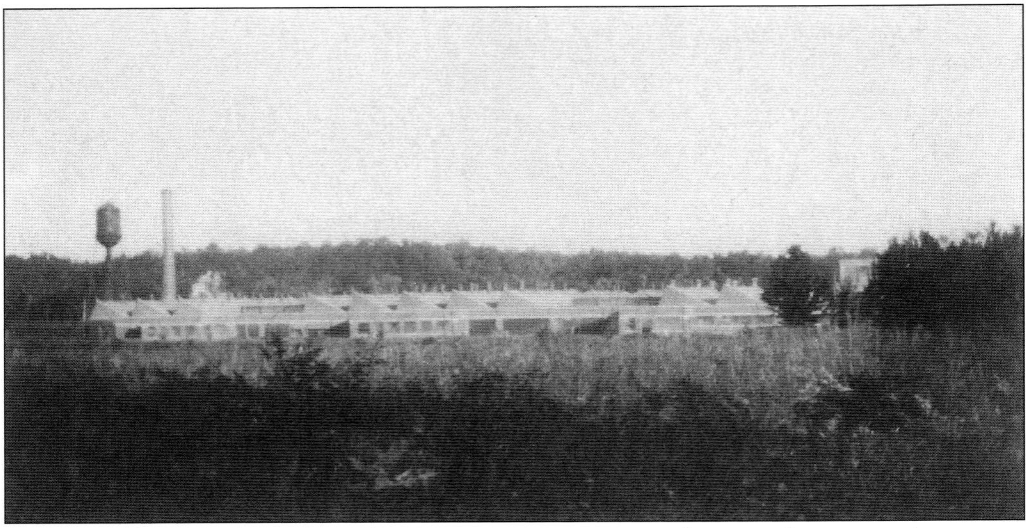

The 20th century brought the Belamose Corporation, a manufacturer of rayon, to the eastern end of Dividend Brook. This site became Belamose Industrial Park, home of several businesses, including branches of Pratt and Whitney and Colt Firearms. Early industry flourished in other parts of Rocky Hill, most notably along France Street on the west side of town. (Courtesy of Mike Martino.)

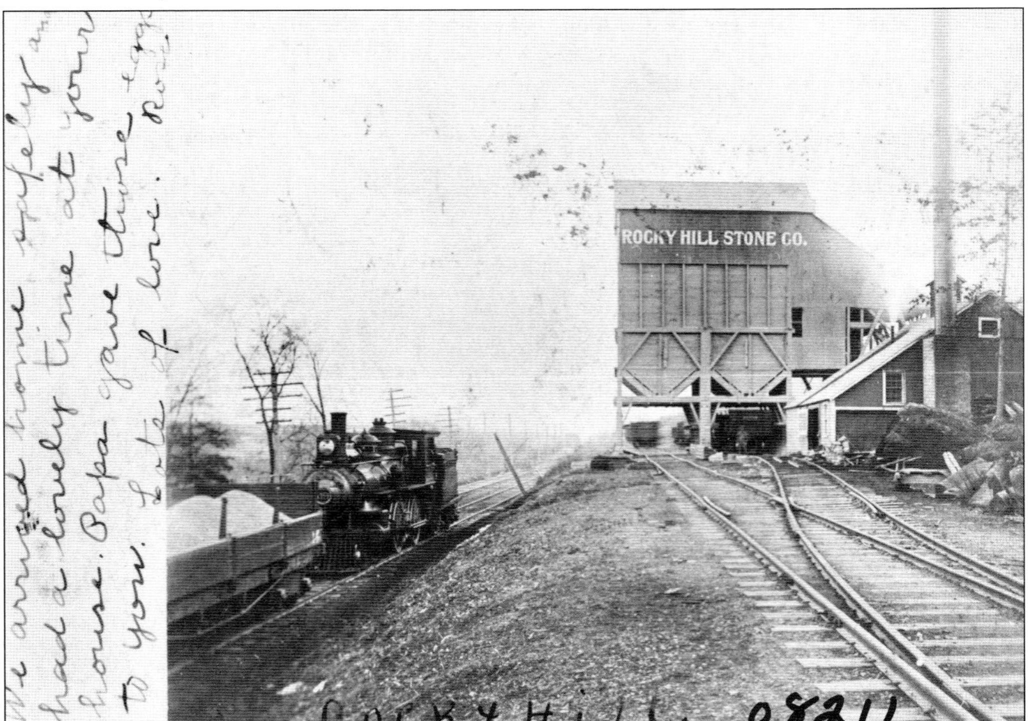

In 1898, there was one Italian American family in Rocky Hill. The quarry changed that. A crew of 15 Italians was hired to work on a railroad spur to the quarry, which had just opened. Italian miners, many from Carvara, Provincia di Pescara Abruzzo, came to work the quarry and stayed to become a major ethnic group and influence in Rocky Hill. (Courtesy of Archives & Special Collections, University of Connecticut Library.)

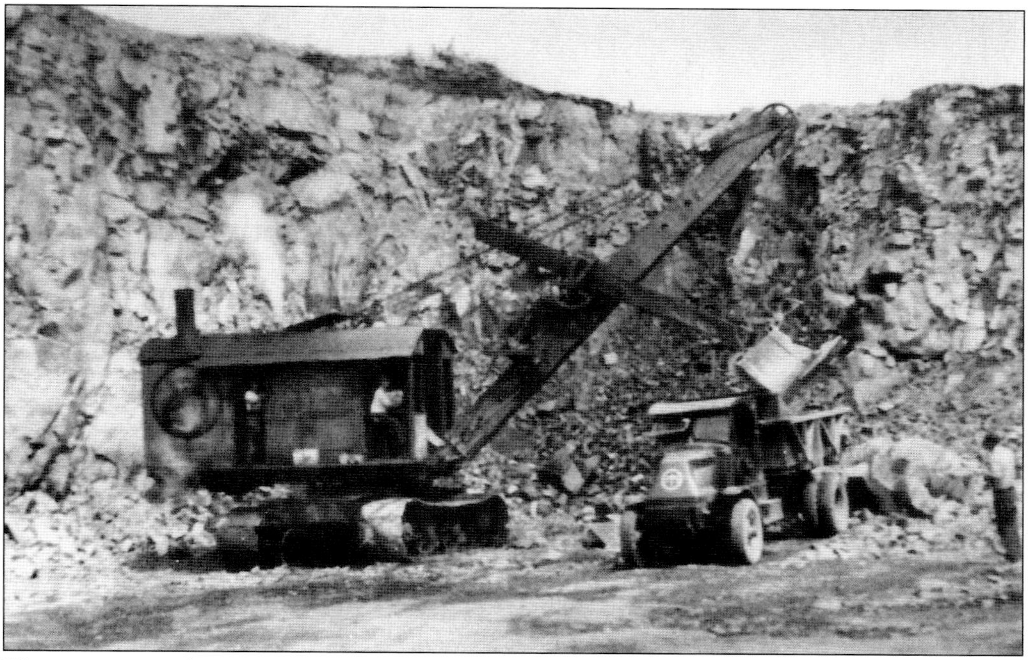

The quarry was a booming operation for many years. Oral histories from Dr. Constantine Zariphes and Ruth Warner Brooks describe the sounds of explosions in the quarry beginning early in the morning and the roars of huge, often hard-tired, trucks entering and exiting the quarry on Esther Road. The quarry closed in 1957, and the site is now a park.

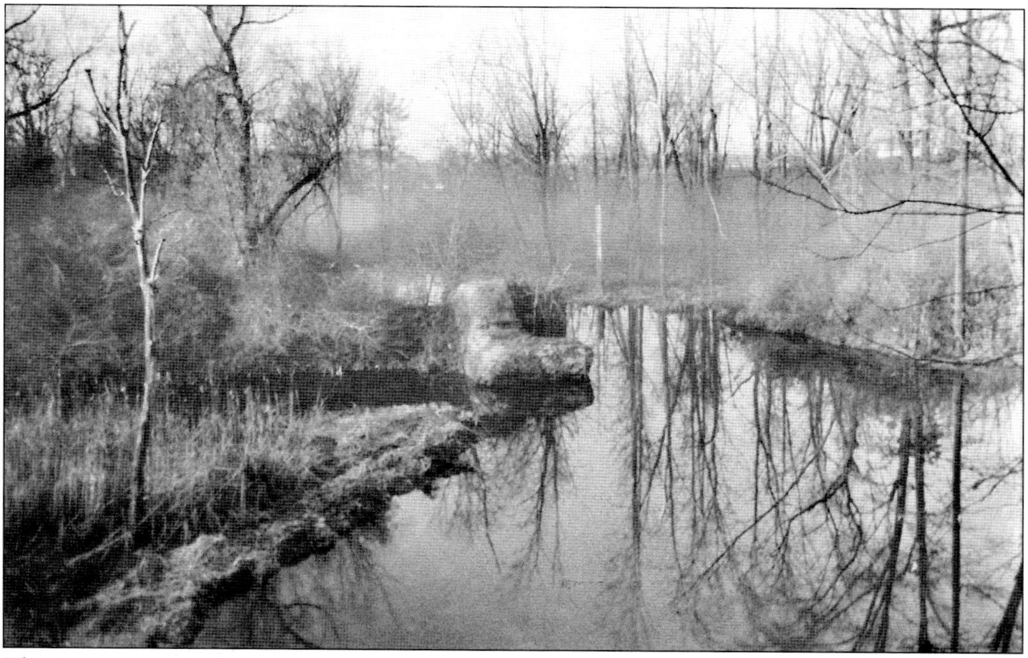

The Spring Brook Ice Company operated an extensive ice farm with a dam on Goffe Brook in Rocky Hill, which ran about one mile to modern Millwoods Park in Wethersfield. It supplied much of the ice to the greater Hartford area before the widespread use of refrigeration in the 1930s.

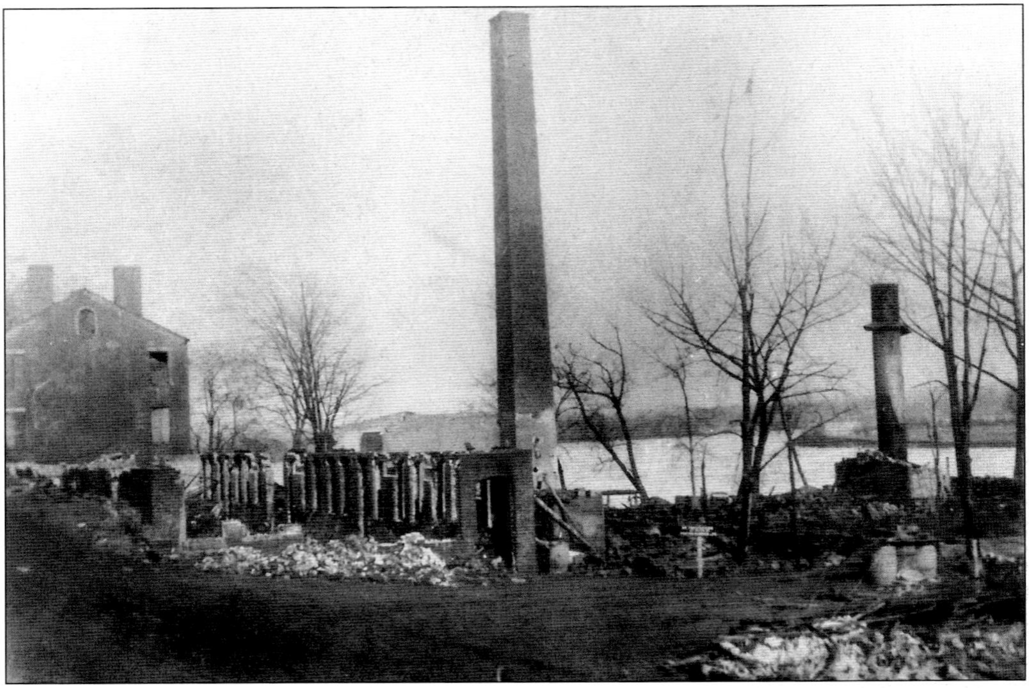

A foundry operated at the end of Glastonbury Avenue for many years. A dock on the northern riverbank simplified delivering the coal required for its operation. Although the foundry burned down twice, the second time in 1918 (pictured), it was rebuilt both times. (Courtesy of Mike Martino.)

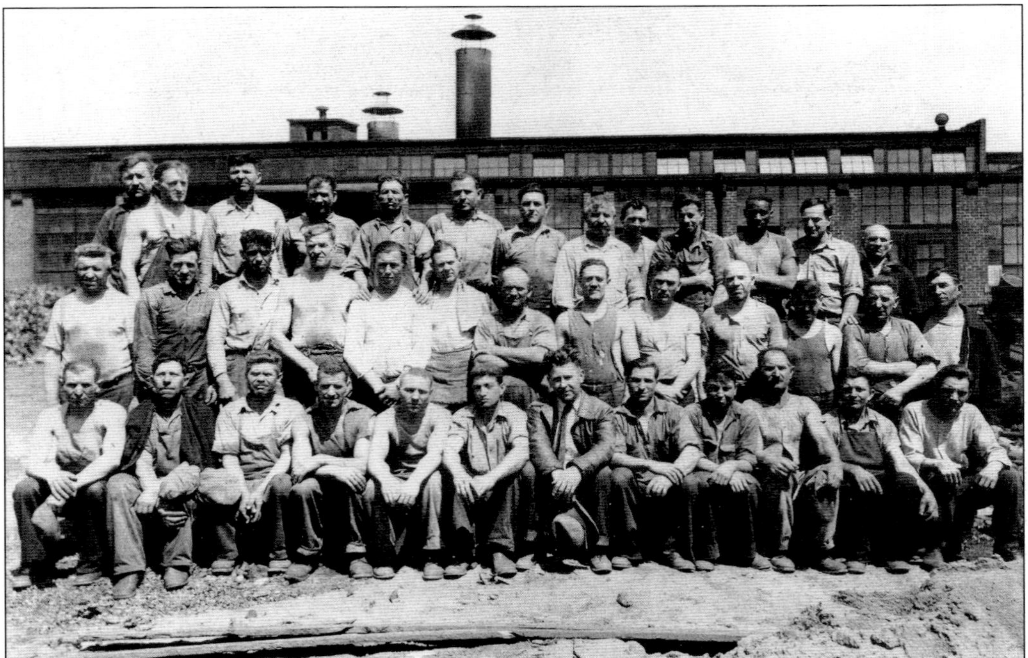

The foundry was in almost continuous operation from 1919 until 1983. These men worked there in 1935. The foundry experienced labor issues in the 1970s. These and pollution issues caused its closure in 1983. (Courtesy of Mike Martino.)

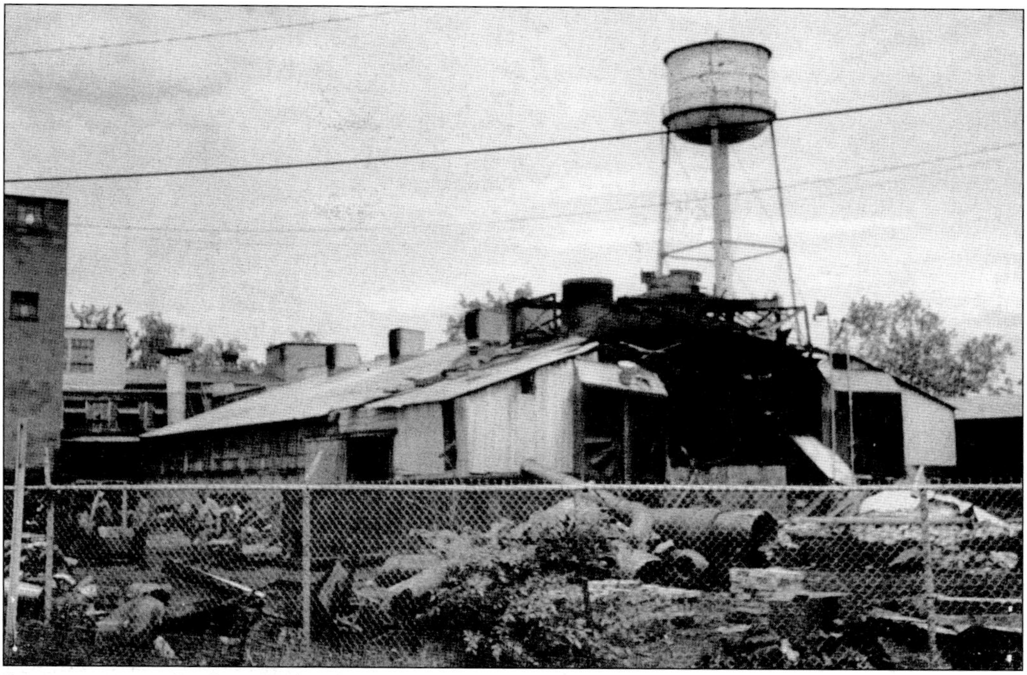

In recent years, the foundry has become an eyesore on the riverfront. There are plans for the site to be redeveloped as a multipurpose commercial and residential complex. (Courtesy of Mike Martino.)

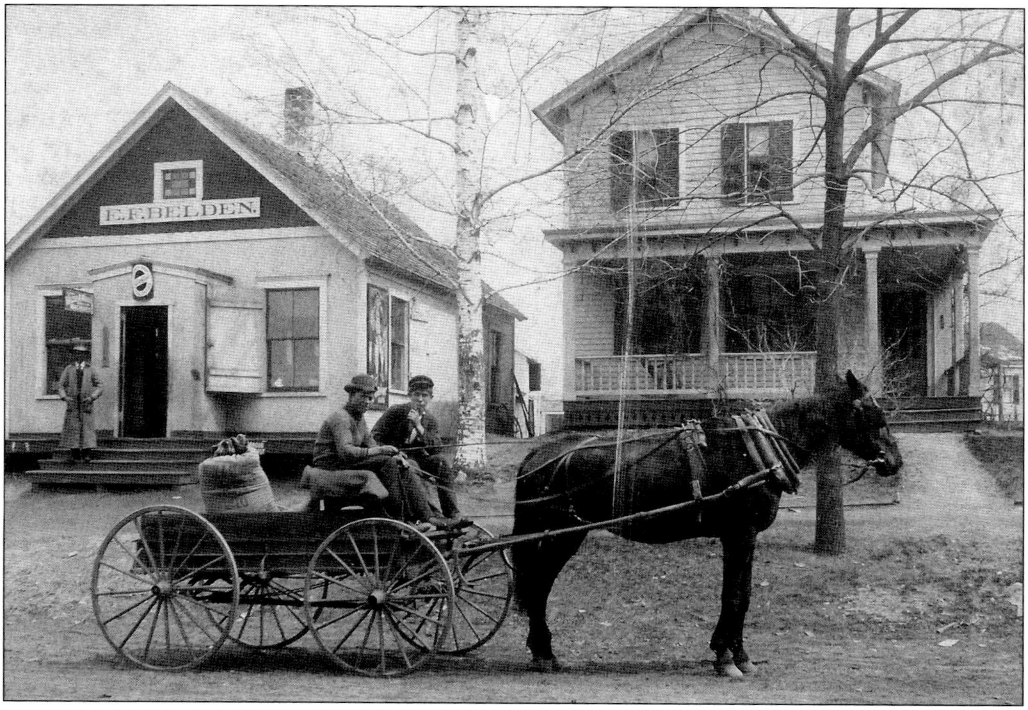

Many small shops have existed in Rocky Hill, such as general stores and blacksmith shops. Many Rocky Hill people engaged in several endeavors. Elwood F. Belden, for example, had a series of general stores, a farm, a gristmill, and a fleet of fishing boats. This store, shown in 1902, was across Old Main Street from the later store, which burned down in 1921. (Courtesy of Mike Martino.)

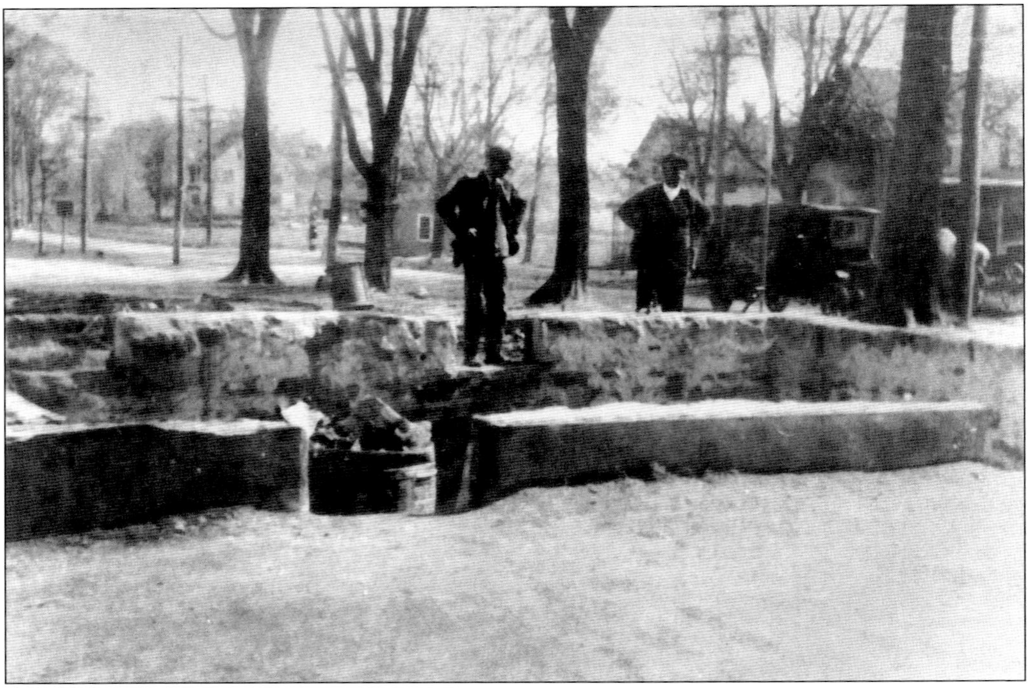

Sometime before 1921, Elwood F. Belden moved his store across Old Main Street. In that year, a fire started in the store when someone filled a kerosene tank with gasoline. It ignited, destroying several buildings on Old Main Street. (Courtesy of Mike Martino.)

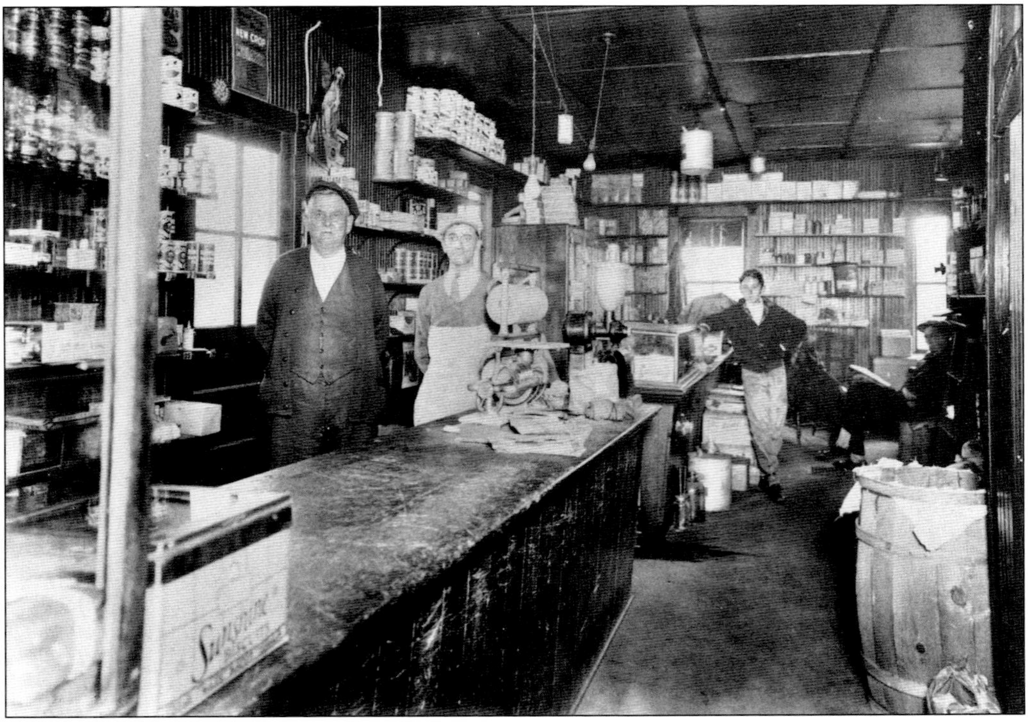

Elwood F. Belden (left) moved his store to Glastonbury Avenue after the great fire of 1921. (Courtesy of Mike Martino.)

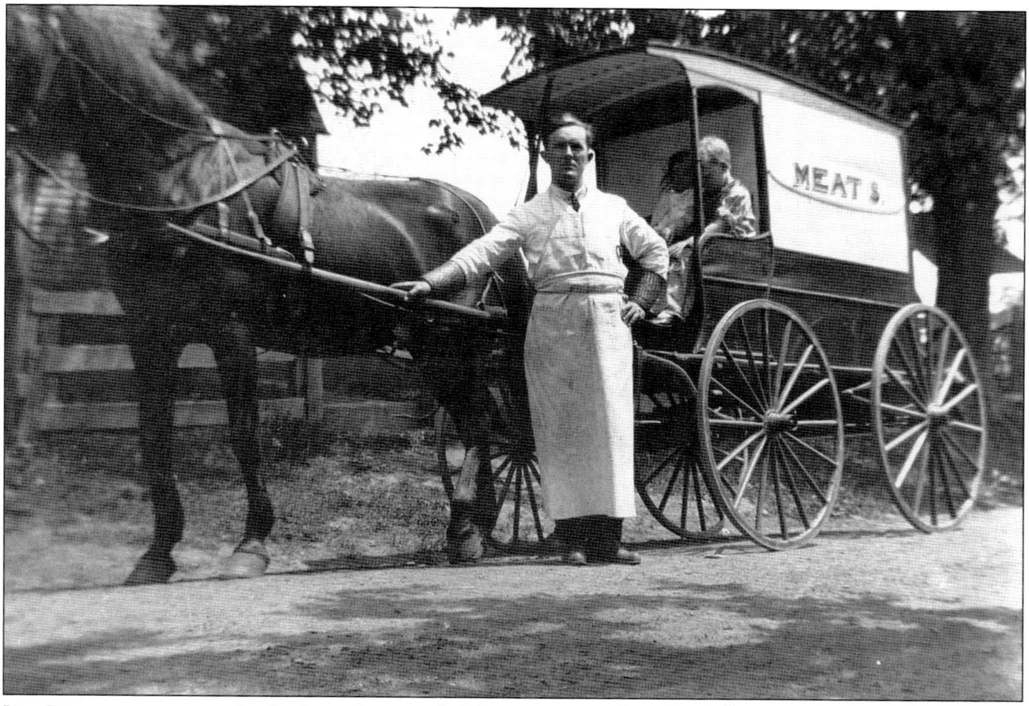

Jim Donovan was typical of vendors and delivery men who plied their wares in Rocky Hill at the turn of the 20th century. He delivered meat to Rocky Hill stores, restaurants, and homes. (Courtesy of Mike Martino.)

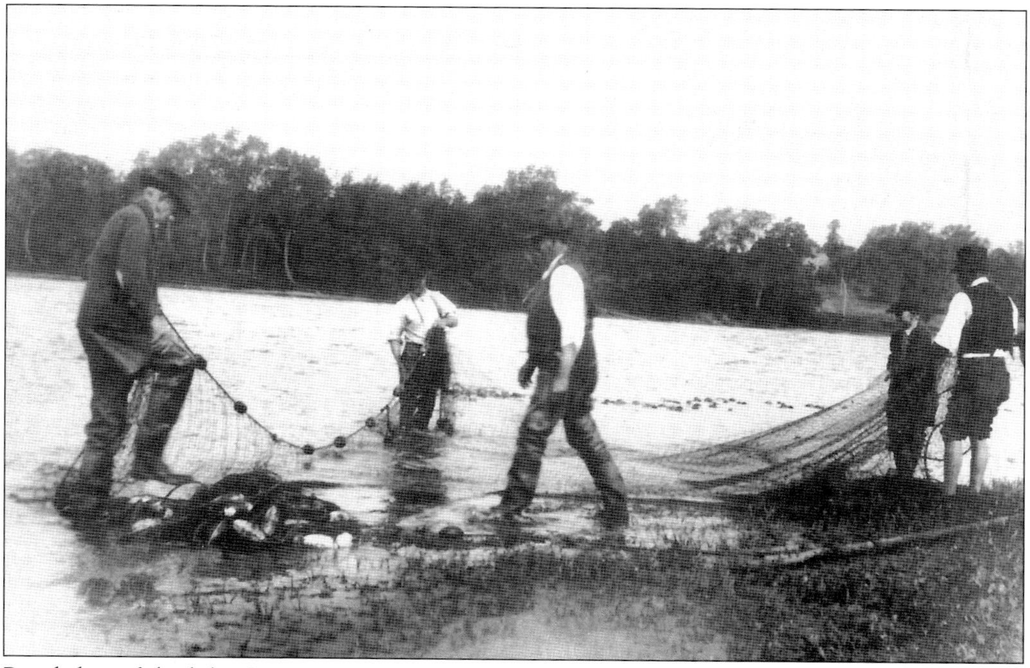

People have fished the Connecticut River throughout history. Indigenous hunter-gatherers, sailors, farmers, ferrymen, and shopkeepers all fished. It was a common way for Rocky Hill residents to supplement their food supply and income.

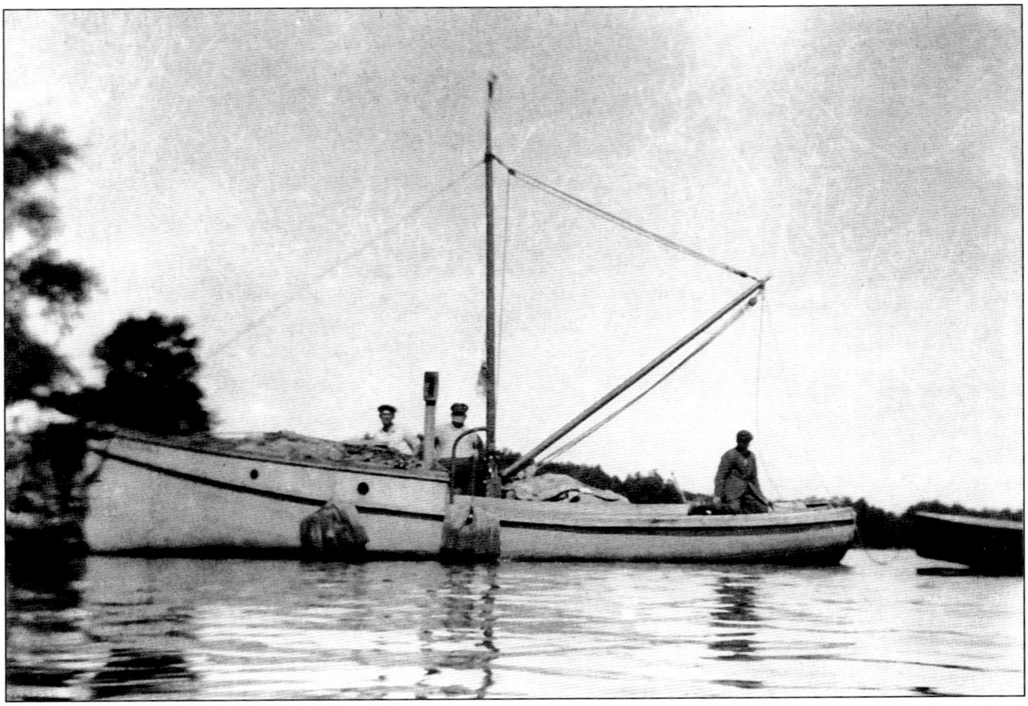

The Hale family, shown in the late 1920s or early 1930s, were prominent rivermen. Hales fished the river for many years. Several also captained Connecticut River ferries.

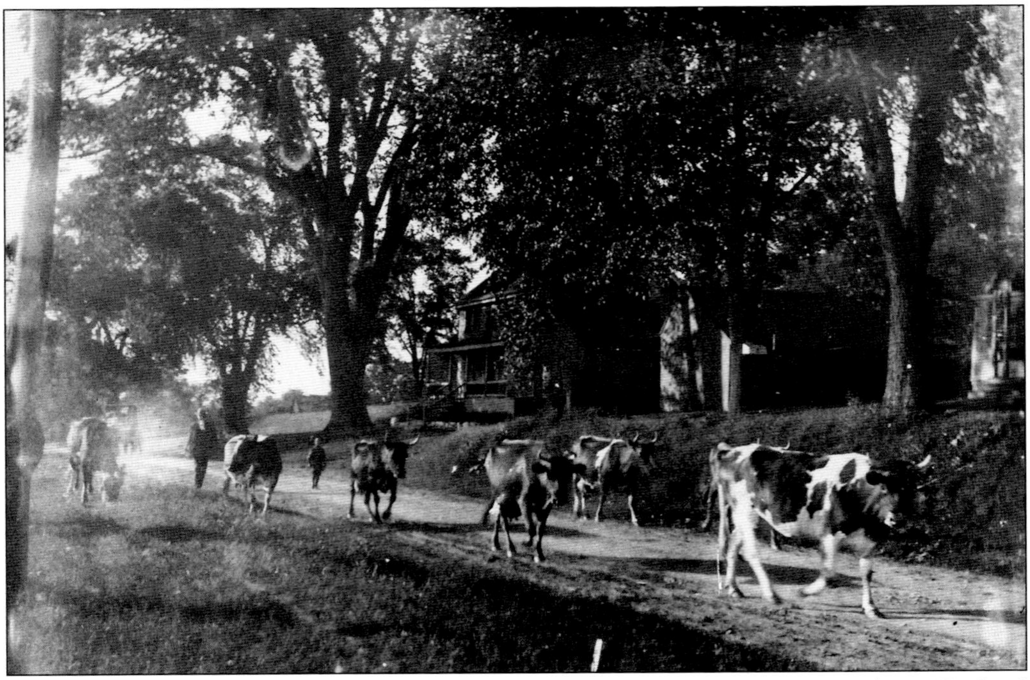

Had it not been for its position as a river port, Rocky Hill might have been a typical New England rural agricultural community. Ships' cargos that left Rocky Hill included many agricultural goods. This created a market that allowed Rocky Hill farms to prosper. The Broadview Farm cows in this c. 1870s photograph are walking on Old Main Street just north of Parsonage Street.

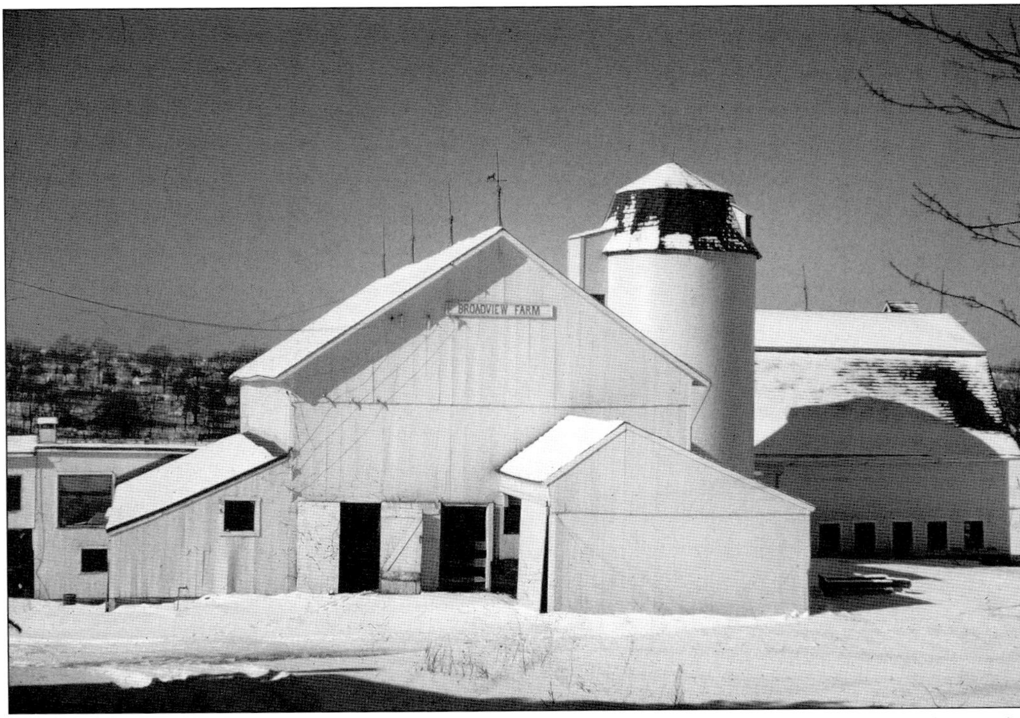

This was the barn of Broadview Farm on Old Main Street not long before it was burned to make way for development in 1965. Today, the Greenfield Village apartment complex and some private residences are located on the site. Broadview Farm had been in the Robbins family since the 1760s.

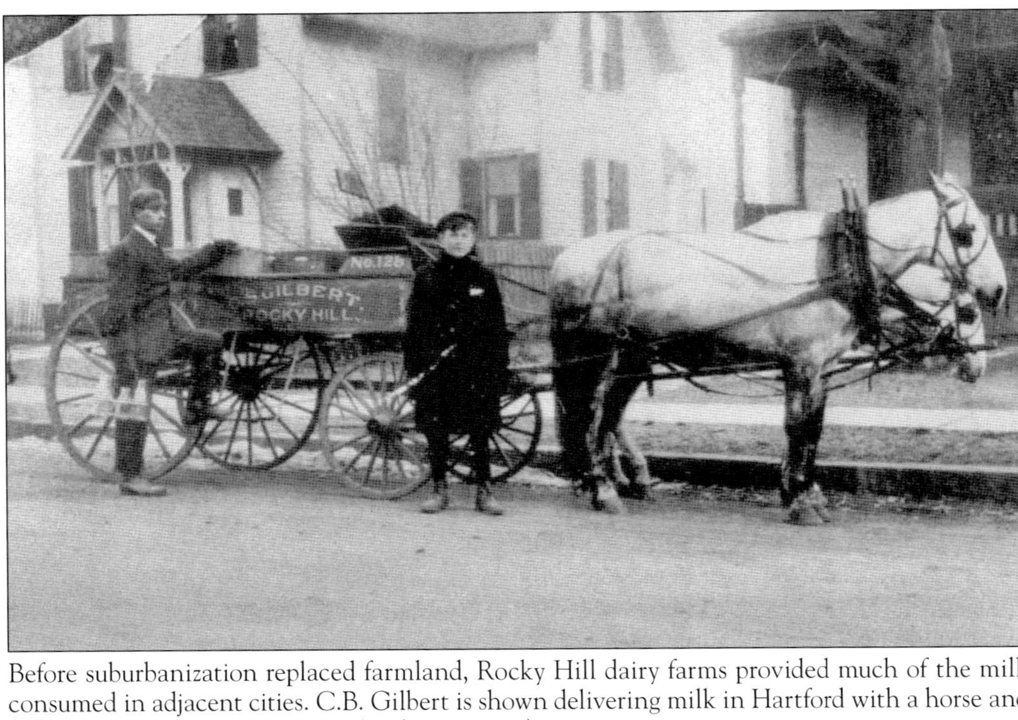

Before suburbanization replaced farmland, Rocky Hill dairy farms provided much of the milk consumed in adjacent cities. C.B. Gilbert is shown delivering milk in Hartford with a horse and wagon in the 1890s. (Courtesy of Mike Martino.)

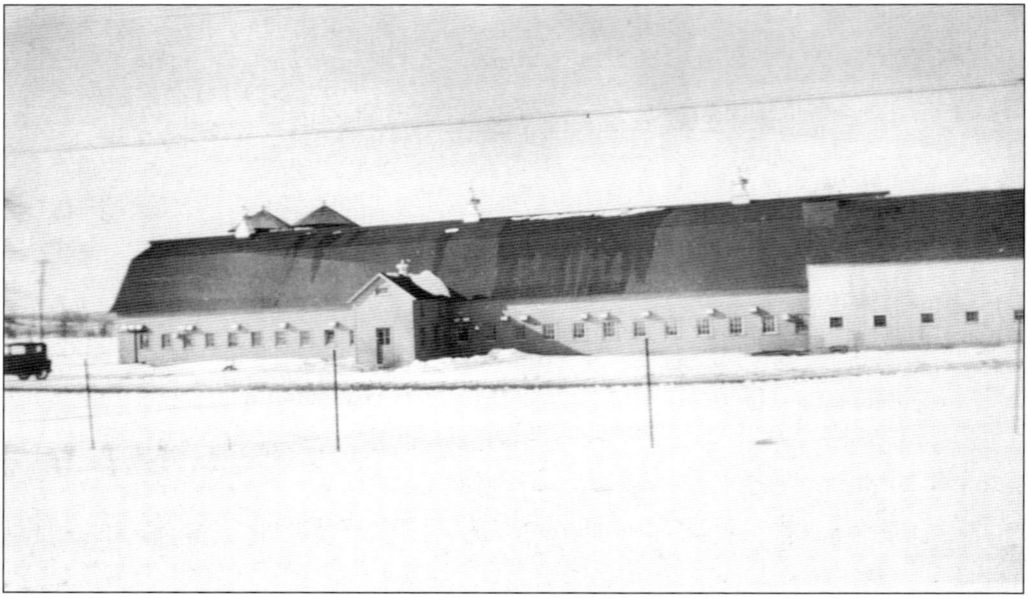

The Sunnycrest Farm cow barn and silos on Parsonage Street, shown here, replaced a similar barn that burned to the ground in July 1939. This barn also burned to the ground on Saturday, December 16, 1944, and was again replaced. (Courtesy of Mike Martino.)

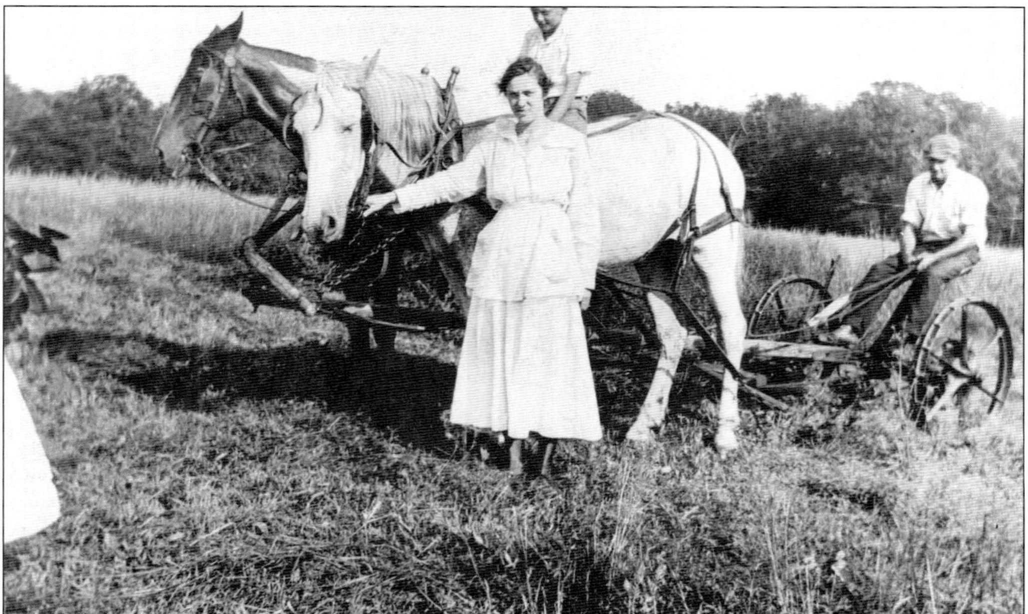

There were several large farms in Rocky Hill, among them Broadview Farm, Sunnycrest Farm, and the Gilbert farm. Cora and Carl Neumann (pictured) owned a farm now replaced by Interstate 91 and the Big Y supermarket. (Courtesy of Mike Martino.)

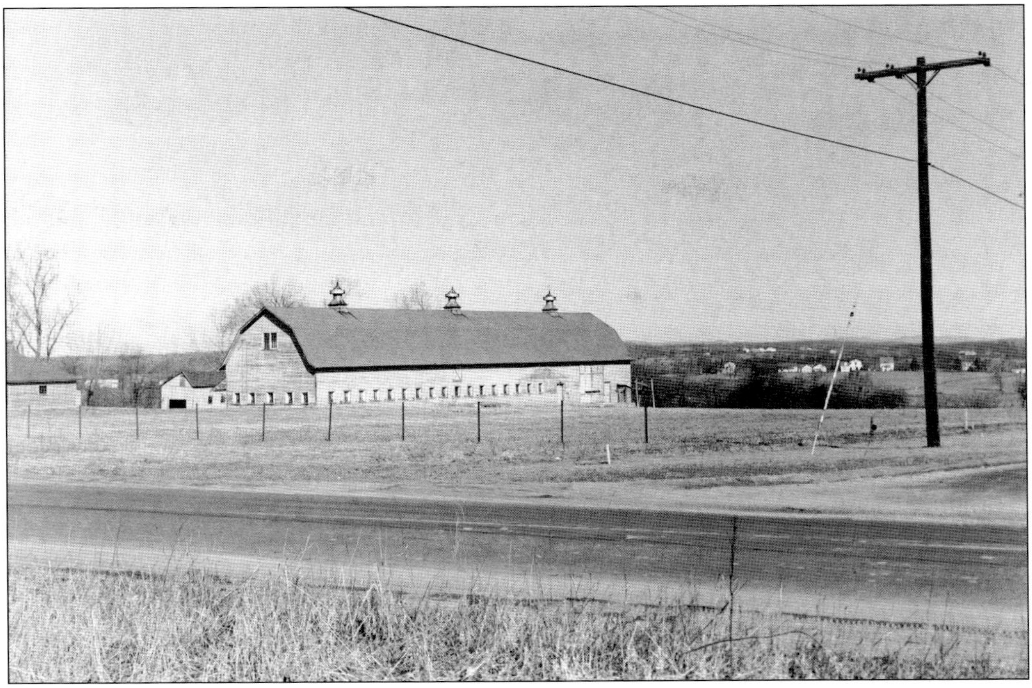

How the landscape has changed. The Anulewicz farm, shown here, was across Elm Street from the Neumann farm. Like the Neumann farm, it was burned down in 1963 to make way for Interstate 91. The site is now occupied by the large Elms Apartments complex at 965 Elm Street. (Courtesy of Mike Martino.)

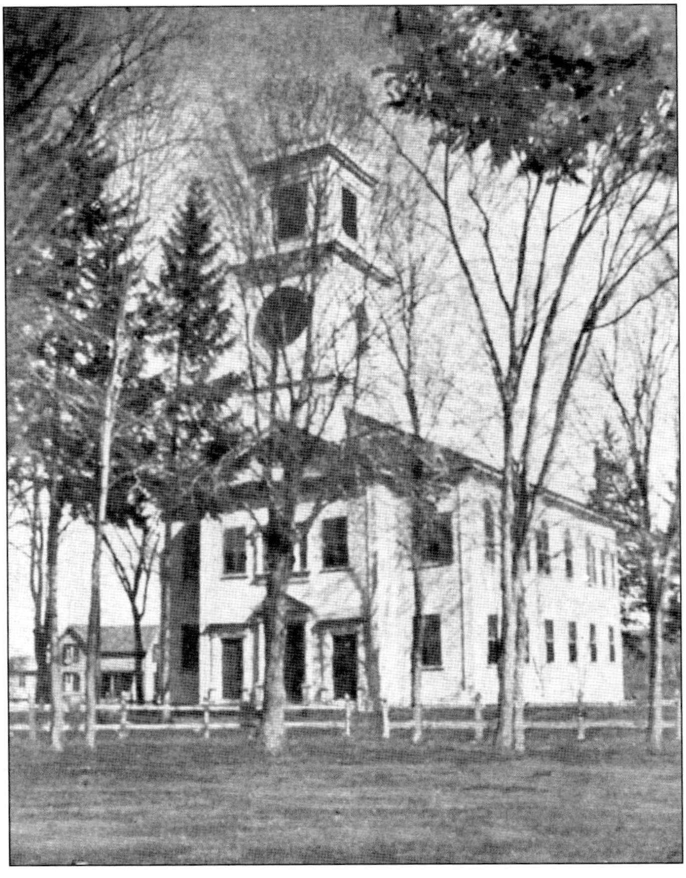

The Rocky Hill Congregational Church was dedicated in 1727. The current church opened in 1808. The Congregational Church was Connecticut's official state church until 1818, when separation of church and state was established. The Rocky Hill Congregational Church is still a pillar of the community today.

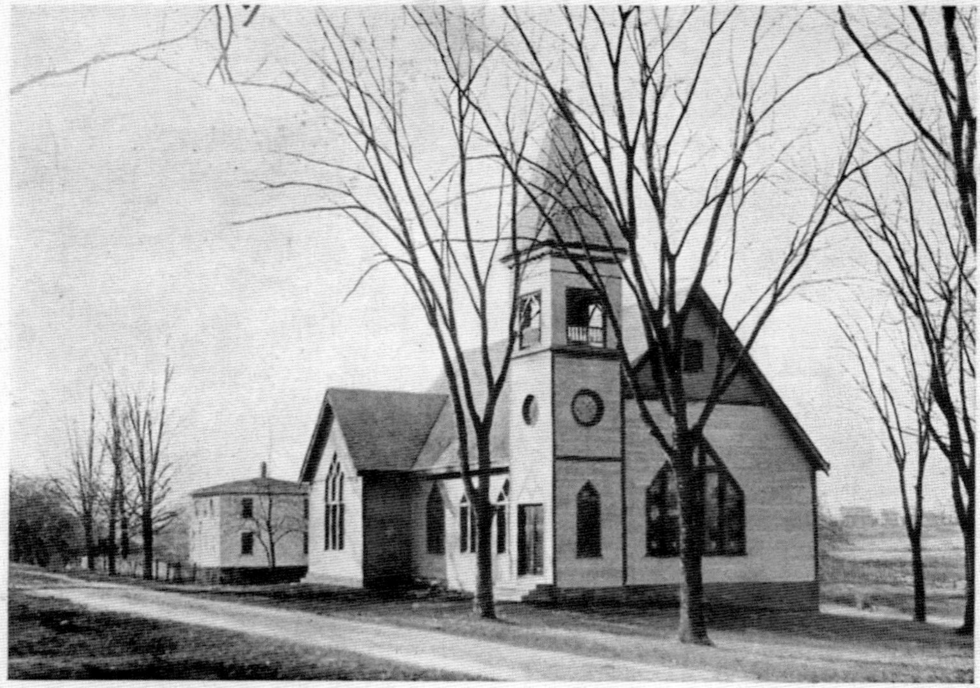

METHODIST EPISCOPAL CHURCH, ROCKY HILL, CONN.

The Methodist church began in 1830 in the Sail Loft House at 276 Meadow Road. Venues changed frequently. About 1840, William Bradford's store was moved from the riverfront to the corner of Old Main and Church Streets to become the first Methodist church at this location. It was replaced by a second church in 1859. That church burned down in 1894, and the present church was dedicated in 1895.

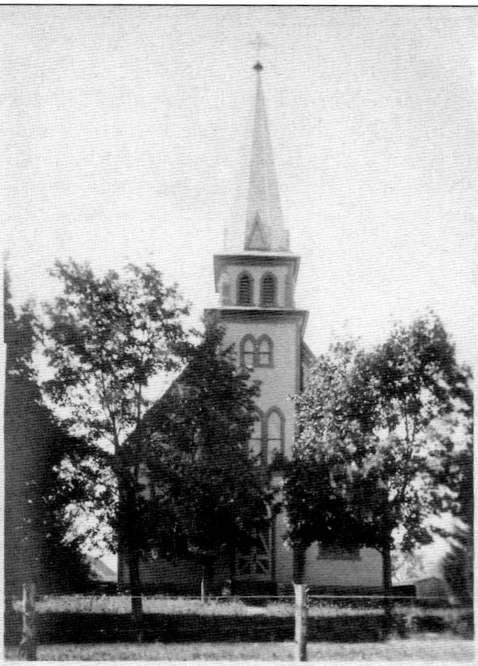

Catholic Church. Rocky Hill, Conn.

St. James Catholic Church on Chapin Street was built around 1880. By 1960, the present St. James Church on Elm Street had been built and dedicated. St. Elizabeth Seton Church, on Brook Street, opened in 1984. The two churches were consolidated in 2017. The new church holds services at both locations. It is named St. Josephine Bakhita after a Sudanese saint of the late 19th century. (Courtesy of Mike Martino.)

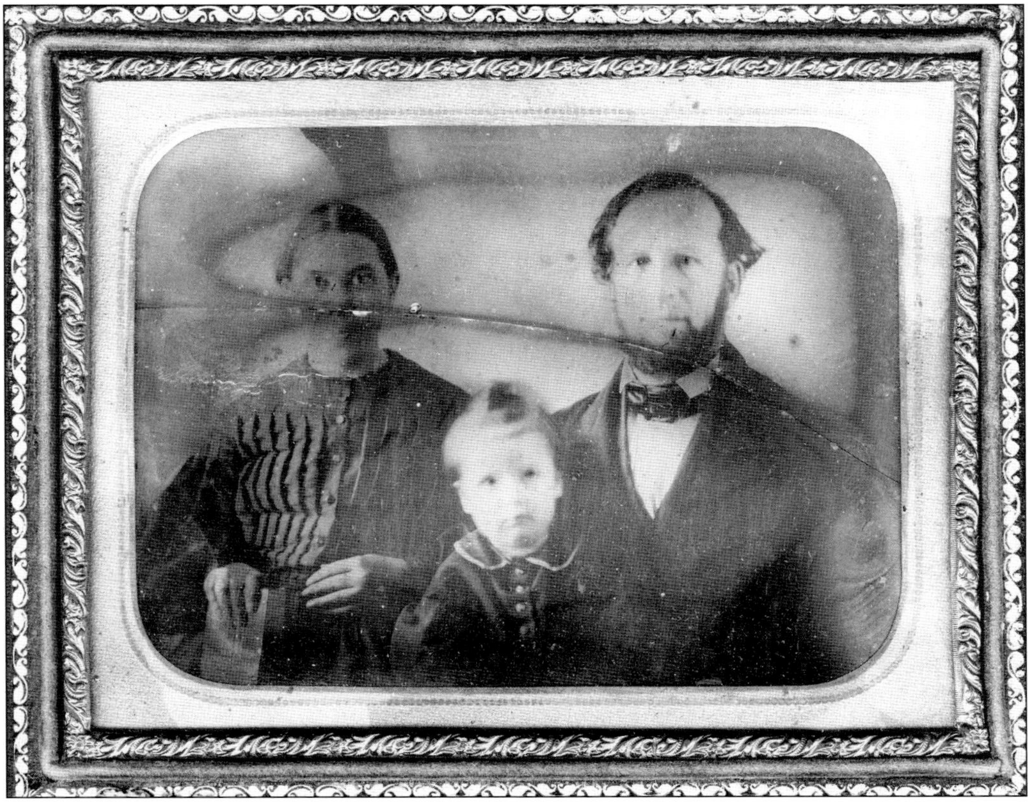

In the 1840s, Ellen White, a founding mother of the Seventh-day Adventists, and her husband, James, were staying with Albert Belden at his farm on France Street when Ellen had a vision. She sensed that God wanted her husband to cease his labors for Belden and write about his faith. A tract entitled *Present Truth* became the foundation for much subsequent Seventh-day Adventist belief and literature.

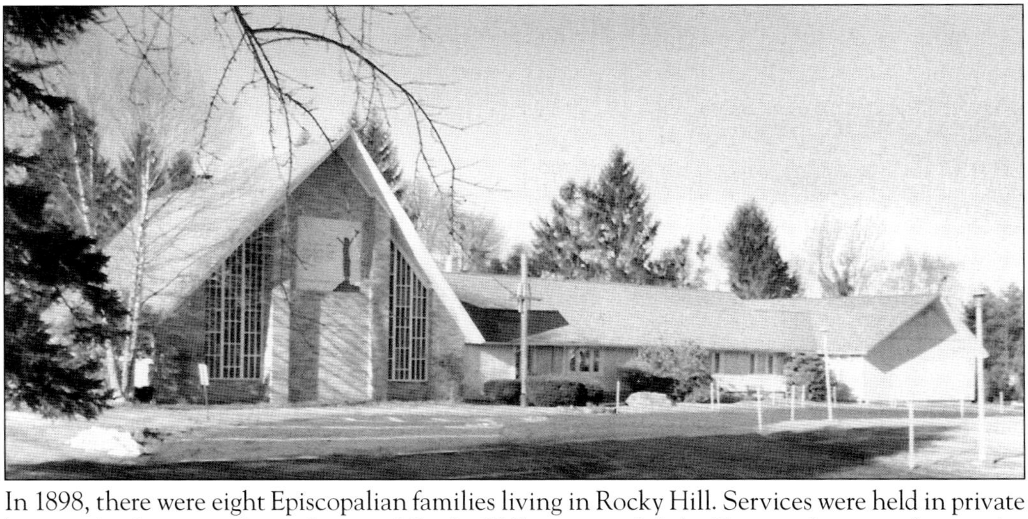

In 1898, there were eight Episcopalian families living in Rocky Hill. Services were held in private homes. As the general population of Rocky Hill grew, so did the Episcopalian population. An Episcopal mission began holding services at the Myrtle H. Stevens School in February 1961. Services at the newly constructed St. Andrew's Episcopal Church began in December 1962.

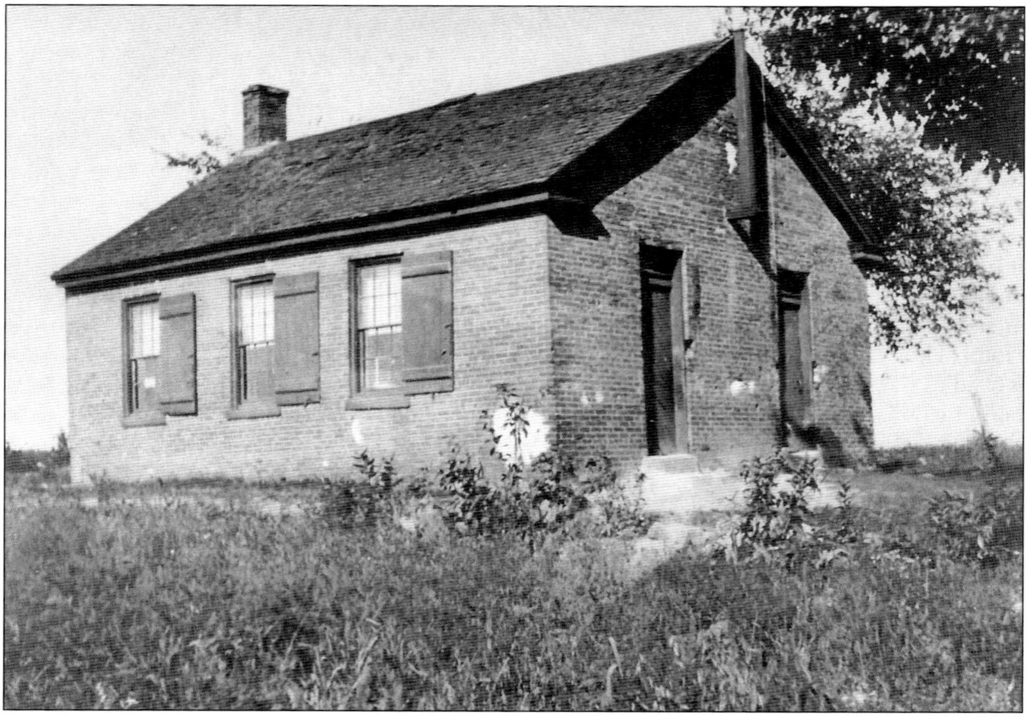

Prior to 1927, there were three classic one-room brick grammar schoolhouses and another school at Academy Hall. In 1927, the South School was replaced by a larger school. It became Oran A. Moser School in 1949. North School is now a private residence. West School (pictured around 1900) has been replaced several times. West School was the precursor of the modern West Hill School.

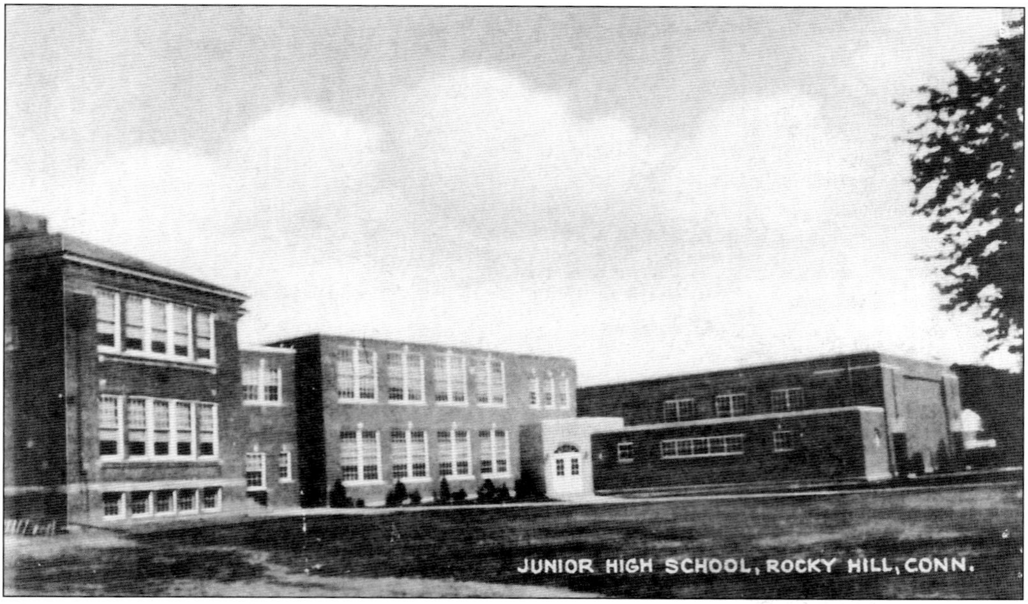

The junior high school, which took the name Center School from the older school at Academy Hall, was built in 1916. Part of this building has since been incorporated into town hall. A high school was built in 1958 and was replaced by a more modern one in 1980. Two other modern schools, Myrtle H. Stevens School and Albert D. Griswold Middle School, have also been built.

Rev. Calvin Chapin became the first librarian in 1794, keeping books in his home. The library was subsequently relocated to a store on the ferry landing. It has operated out of people's homes and at the Valley Hotel. The library moved to this building on Church Street in 1899. The town began running the library in 1950, and it moved to its current building in 1966. (Courtesy of Mike Martino.)

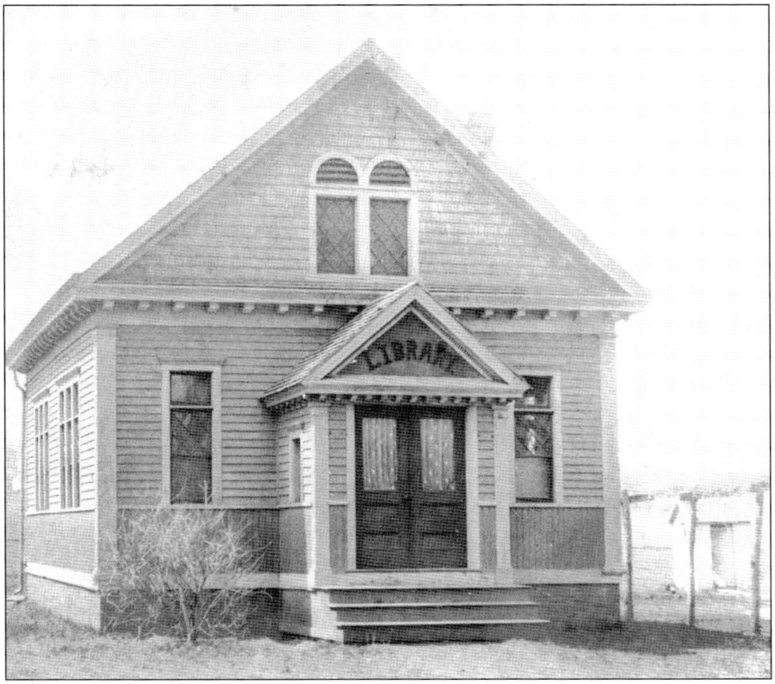

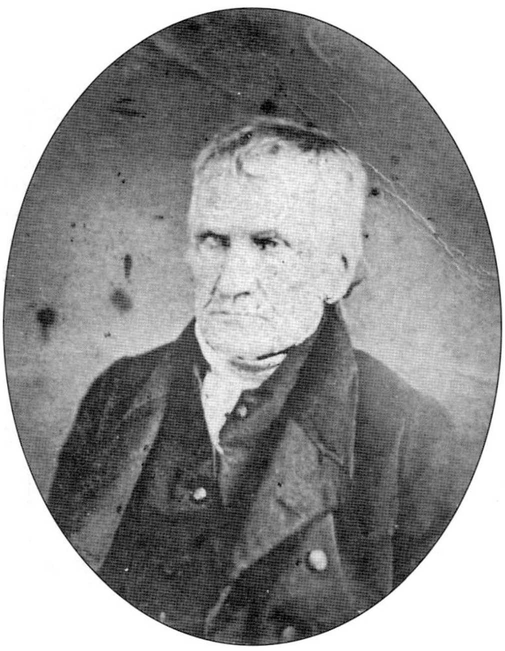

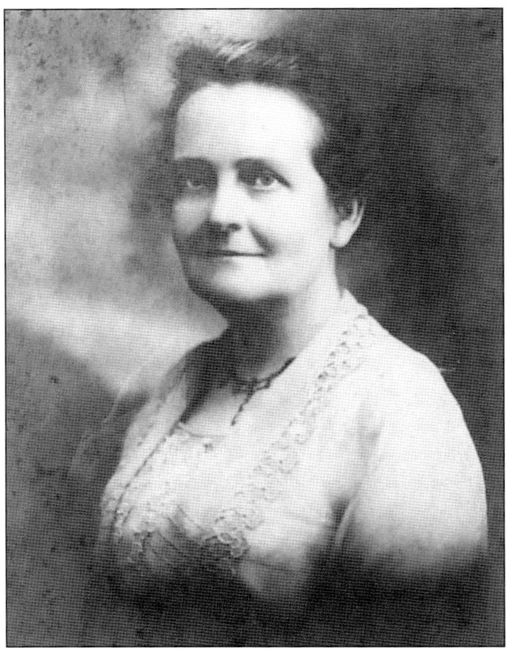

In 1950, the library was named after Cora J. Belden (right) who had been active in its support. Cora and her husband, Elwood, were active in town affairs, and she replaced him as tax collector after his death. Reverend Chapin is on the left.

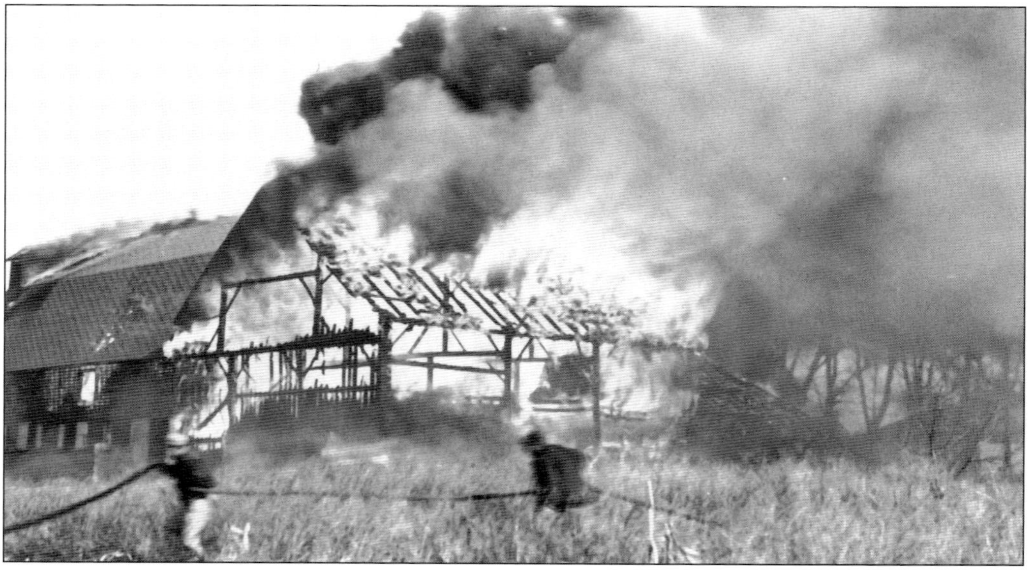

From the town's early days until 1927, fire protection was provided by ad hoc groups of townspeople who responded to alarms issued from the bells of the Congregational church to form bucket brigades. Disastrous fires, like the one at Elm Hill Farm in 1952 pictured here, have been a common part of Rocky Hill life. (Courtesy of Mike Martino.)

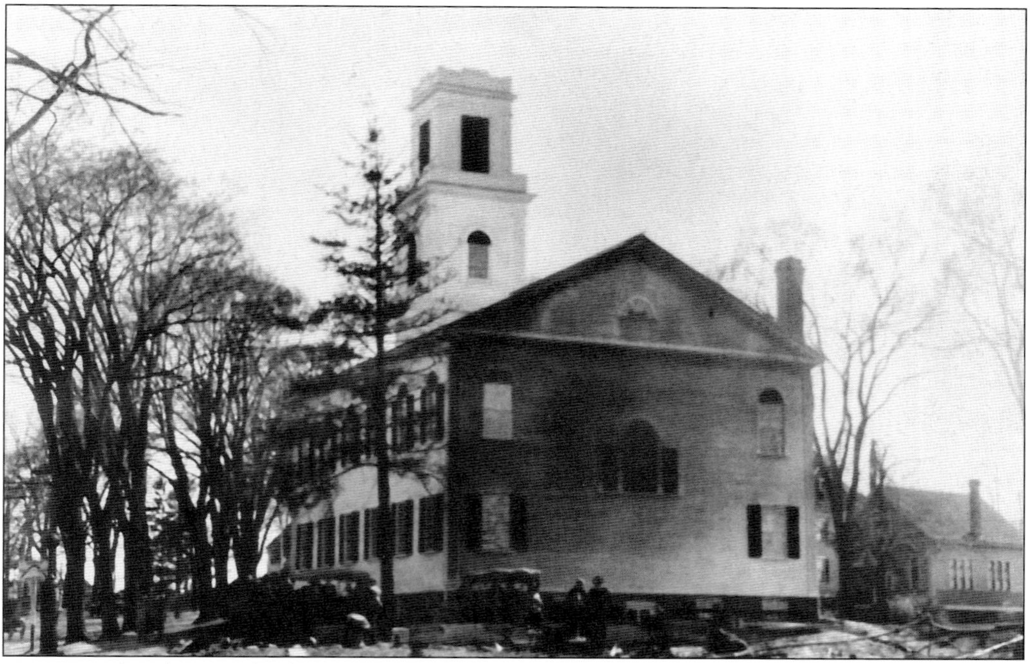

In 1921, a fire destroyed a large part of the center of town, including the Grange Hall, Belden's store and outbuildings, and a barbershop. Academy Hall and the Congregational church (pictured) were damaged but saved by a bucket brigade and, subsequently, apparatus from Wethersfield and Hartford. The need for a fire department became clear. The Rocky Hill Fire Department was established in 1927. (Courtesy of Mike Martino.)

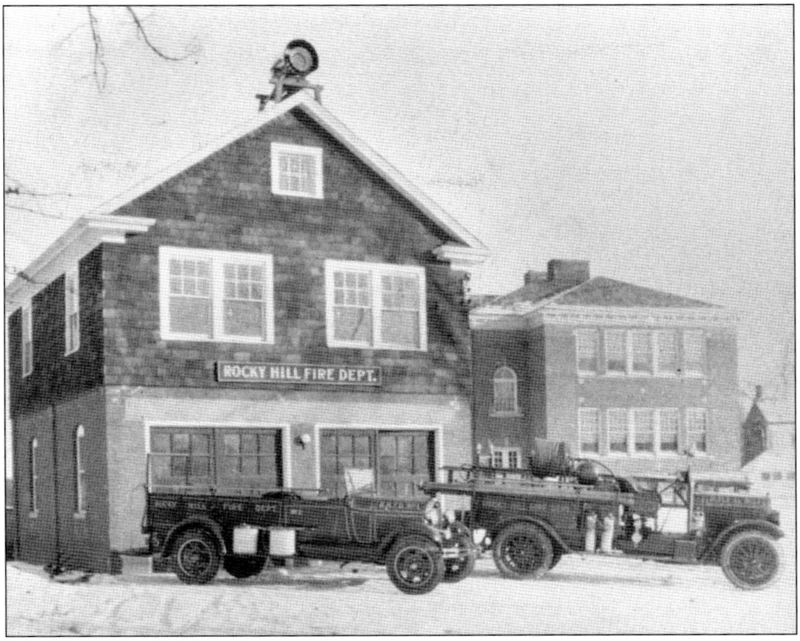

The 1921 fire resulted in the formation of the volunteer fire department. A 1927 REO fire engine and a 1929 Ford Model A hose wagon are shown parked in front of the original Company 1 firehouse on Church Street. Center School, which was then the junior high school, is in the background. (Courtesy of Mike Martino.)

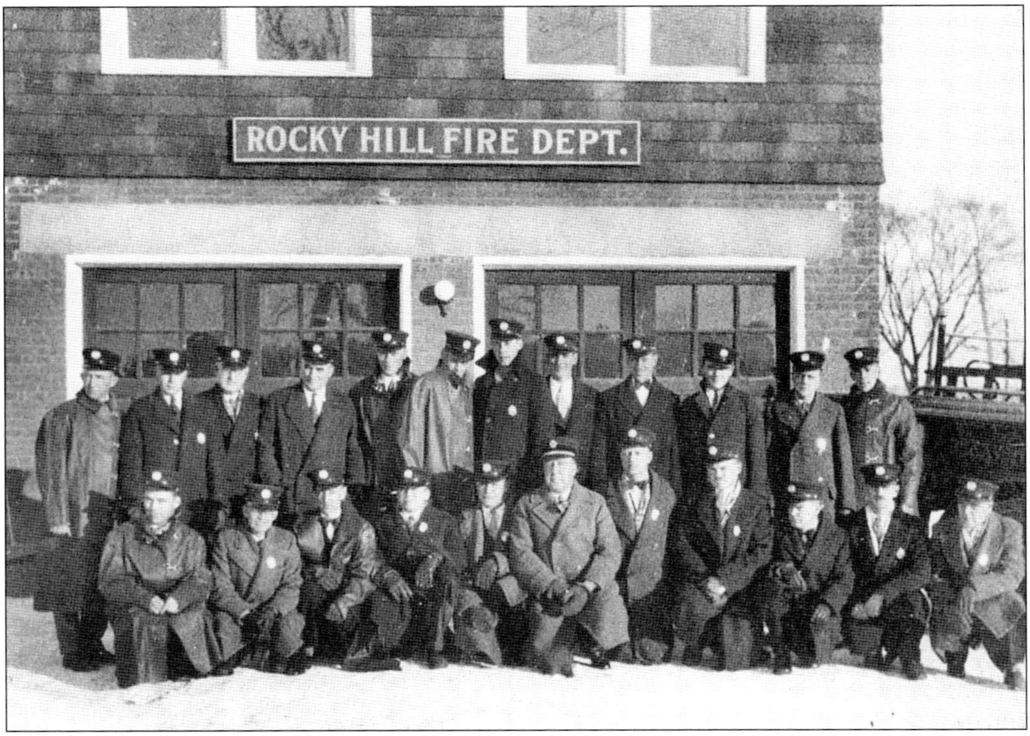

This was the first volunteer fire department. From left to right are (first row) Benjamin Elmore, Louis Button, Charles Reduker, Lee Sherwood, Assistant Chief Gerald Huntoon, Chief Starr Elmore, Phillip Sherwood, Assistant Chief Raymond Gallup, Alexander Kean, Lester Webster, and Herbert Spencer; (second row) Frank Smith, Horace Hills, Edmund Courtney, Frank W. Churchill, John Geohan, William Wallin, Richard Morgan, Charles Pawlich, Joseph Reduker, Cleveland Ladd, Walter Belden, and Charles Spencer. (Courtesy of Mike Martino.)

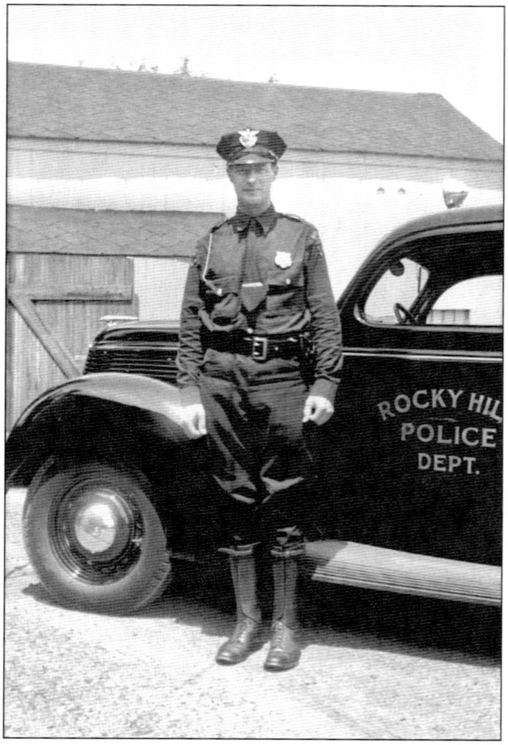

Until 1937, law enforcement was done by state police and town constables. That year, the board of police commissioners was formed, and the town hired a full-time police officer, Elmer J. Edwards. It also bought a black 1938 Ford Standard Tudor. As the town grew, the police department grew with it. Staff and equipment have been upgraded to keep pace with technology and population growth. (Courtesy of Mike Martino.)

In 1954, Rocky Hill regular and supernumerary police officers were, from left to right, Chief Elmer Edwards, Stanley H. Burz, Alfred Quintiliano, George L. Adams Jr., Robert Karpe, Hulett Hunt, Edward J. Anulewicz, Myron J. Klewicki, Alfred K. Spellman, and Robert W. Russ. (Courtesy of Mike Martino.)

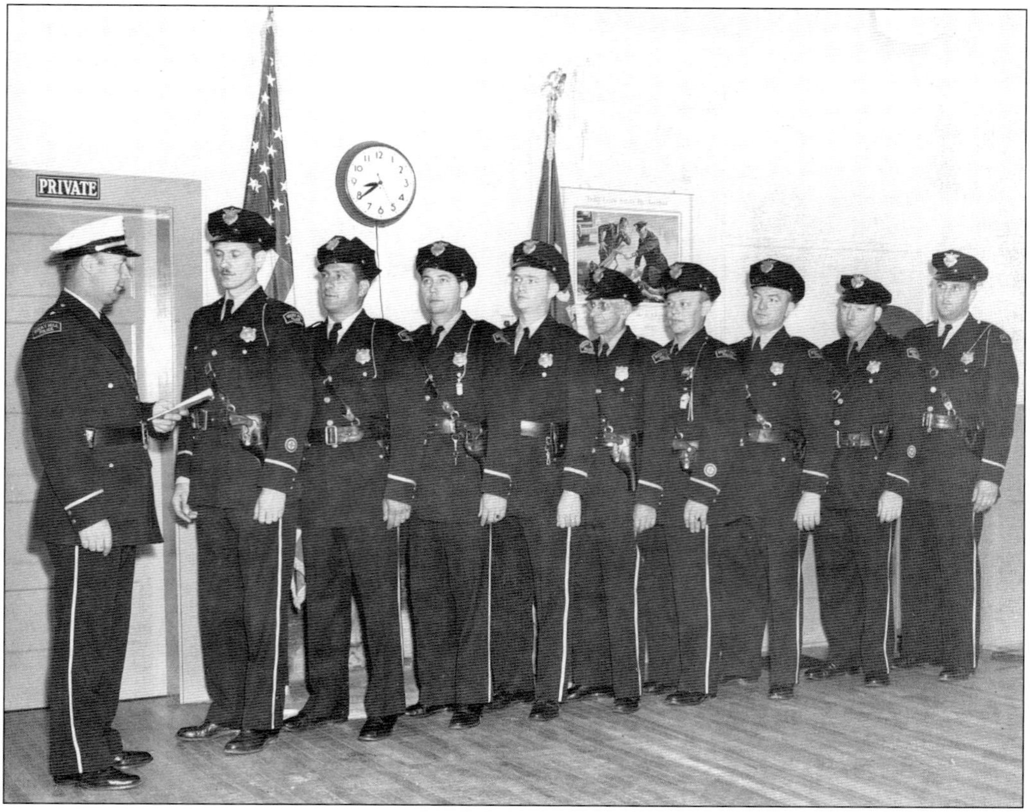

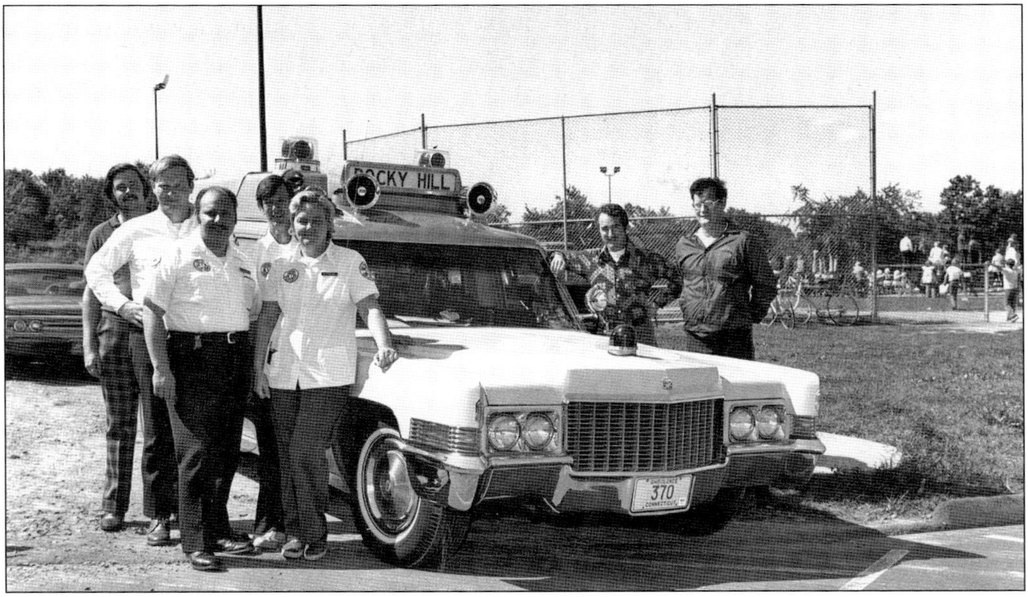

Members of the Rocky Hill Volunteer Ambulance Association pose at Elm Ridge Park after completing one year of service to the town in 1974 with their first ambulance, a 1970 Cadillac. From left to right are Bill Pierson, Ed Peruta, Matty Stillman, Ralph Houlihan, Dee Houlihan, Elliott Mag, and Gene Clemens. (Courtesy of Mike Martino.)

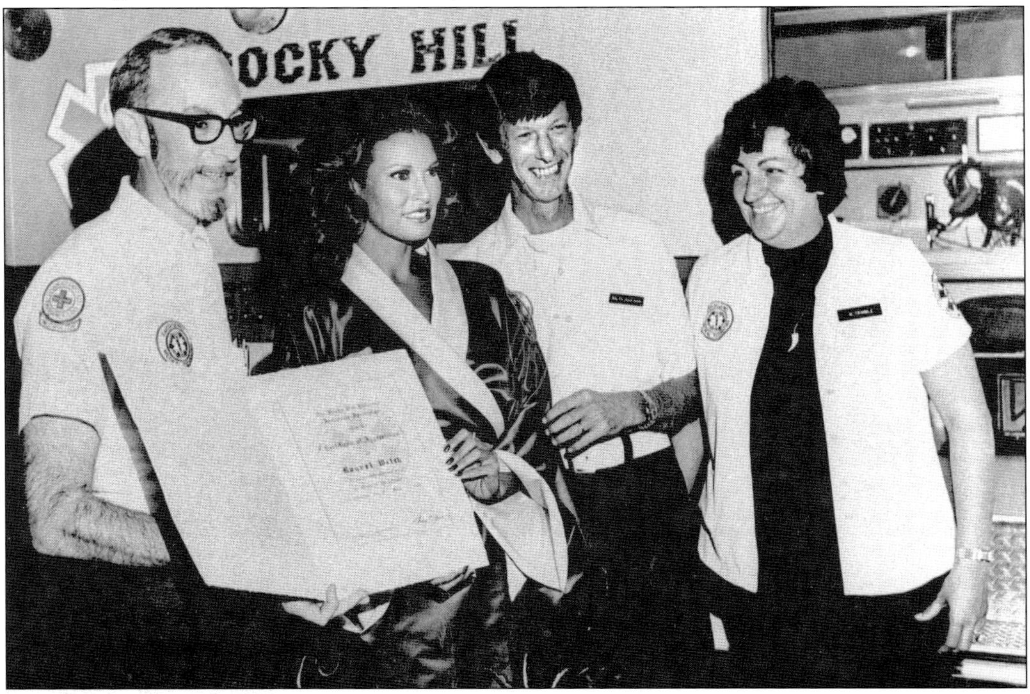

Film star Raquel Welch took time out from her performance at the Oakdale Theater in 1976 to pose with members of the Rocky Hill Volunteer Ambulance Association after autographing their new ambulance. This was part of a promotion for the ambulance-themed film *Mother, Jugs and Speed*. From left to right are Tom Gross, Raquel Welch, Ralph Houlihan, and Marilyn Trumbull. (Courtesy of Mike Martino.)

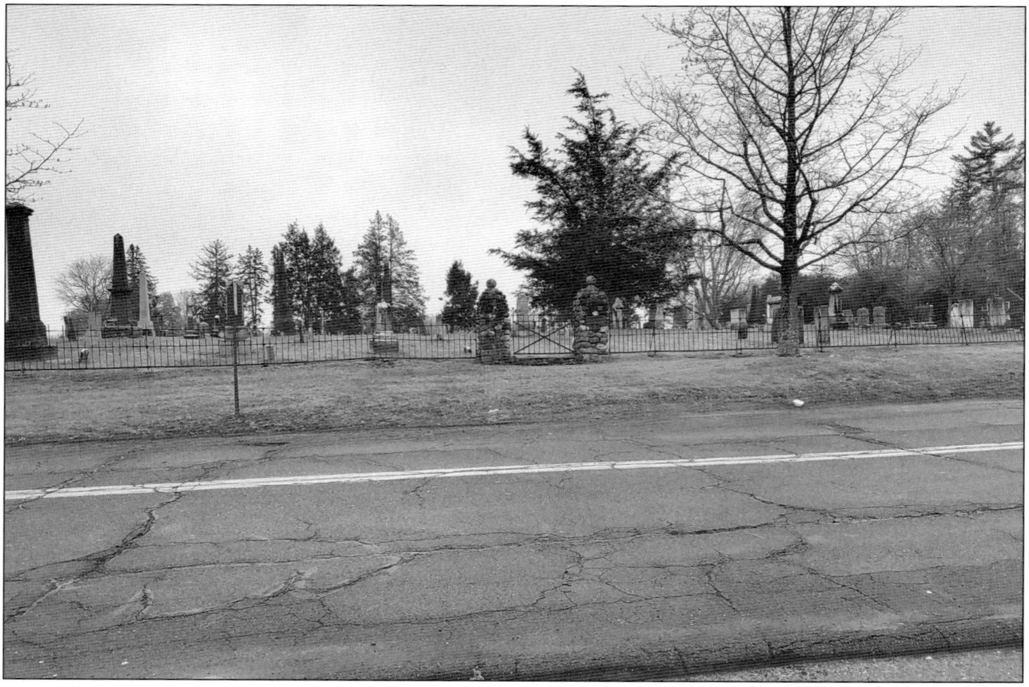

Center Cemetery was established on January 19, 1730/31, shortly after Rocky Hill was authorized as a separate Wethersfield parish. Although Rose Hill Cemetery has eclipsed it as a burying ground, it is still an active cemetery as well as being an invaluable historical resource.

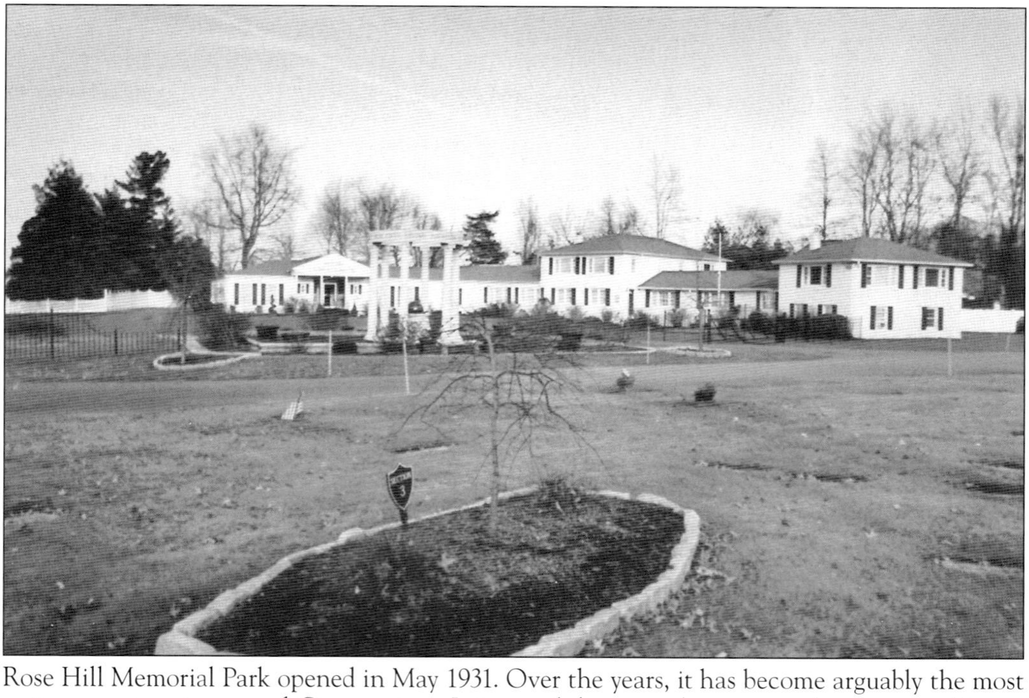

Rose Hill Memorial Park opened in May 1931. Over the years, it has become arguably the most active cemetery in central Connecticut. It is a park because there are no headstones. Graves are marked by flat bronze markers. In 1946, a nonsectarian mortuary and funeral home opened, which simplified matters for the bereaved at a time of loss and sadness.

Four

Transportation and Suburbanization

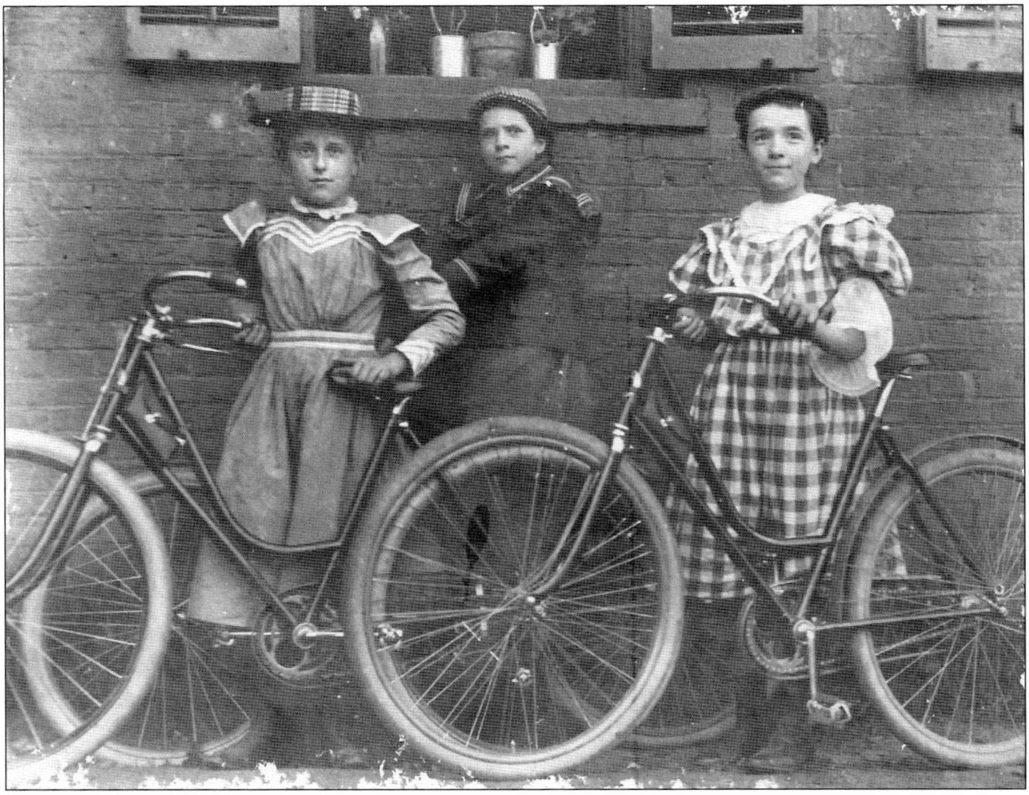

Through most of its history, people got around Rocky Hill on foot, on horseback, or in animal-drawn carts. By the end of the 19th century, children as well as adults got around town on bicycles. From left to right, Anne Robbins, Mabel Churchill Sherwood, and Livy Griswold Stoddard pose in front of the old Center School (Academy Hall) around 1900.

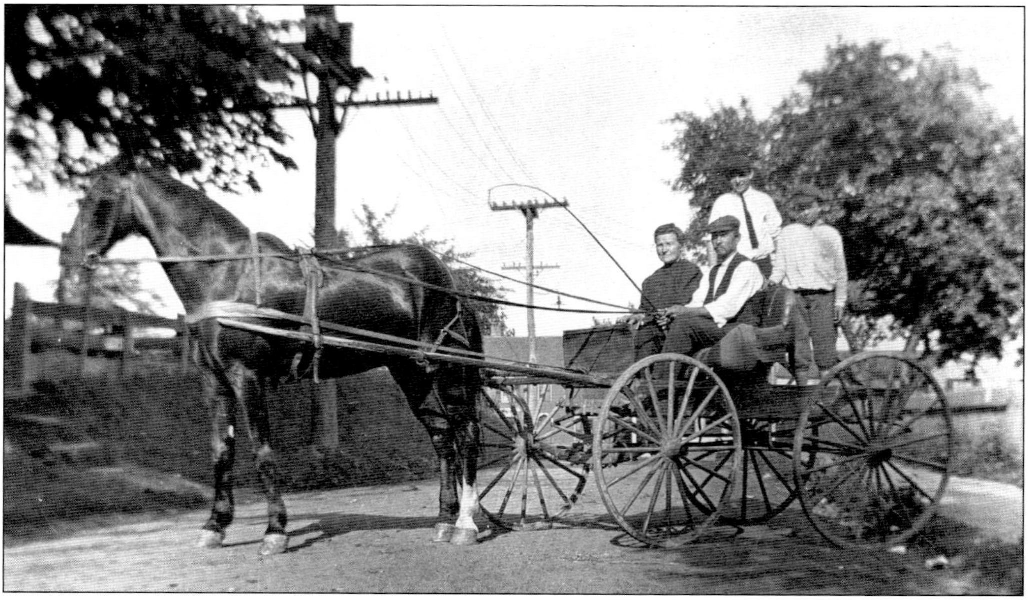

This family seems to have gotten around Rocky Hill in a trim horse-drawn cart. The photograph was taken at the eastern end of Glastonbury Avenue (then Ferry Road) around 1910. (Courtesy of Mike Martino.)

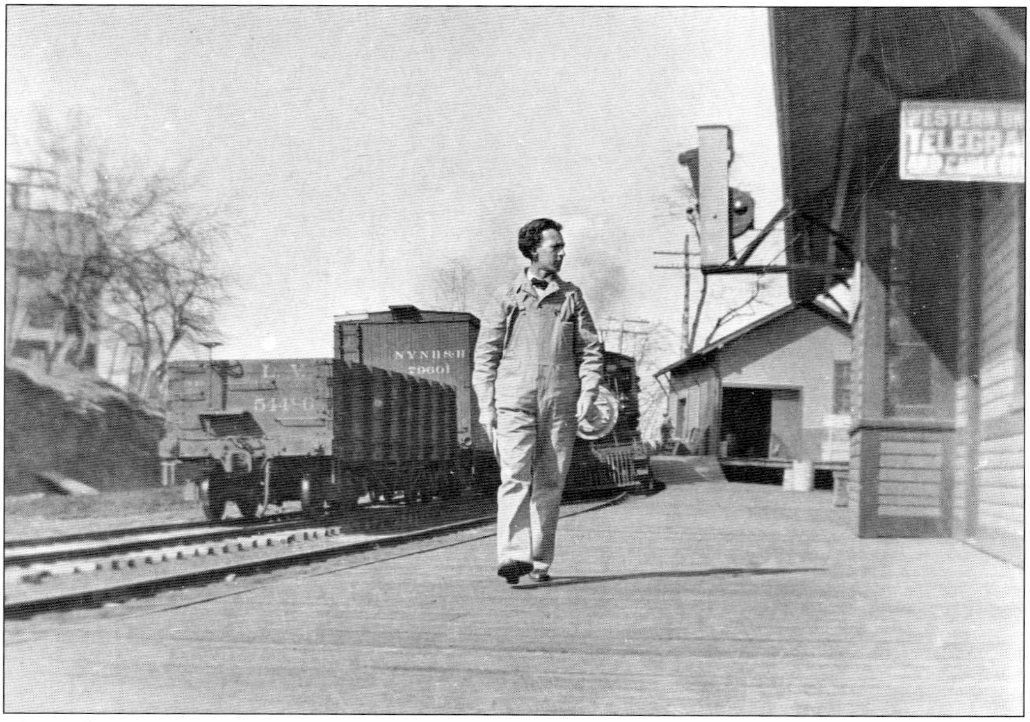

The Valley Railroad arrived in Rocky Hill in 1871, stimulating commerce and enabling commuting to nearby cities. Unlike boats, railroads operated except in the most extreme weather. Trains took advantage of the nearby Rocky Hill–Glastonbury Ferry to pick up and unload cargo crossing the river. The railroad operated in Rocky Hill until 1975. Charles Yeager, longtime railroad agent, is shown walking the station platform. (Courtesy of Mike Martino.)

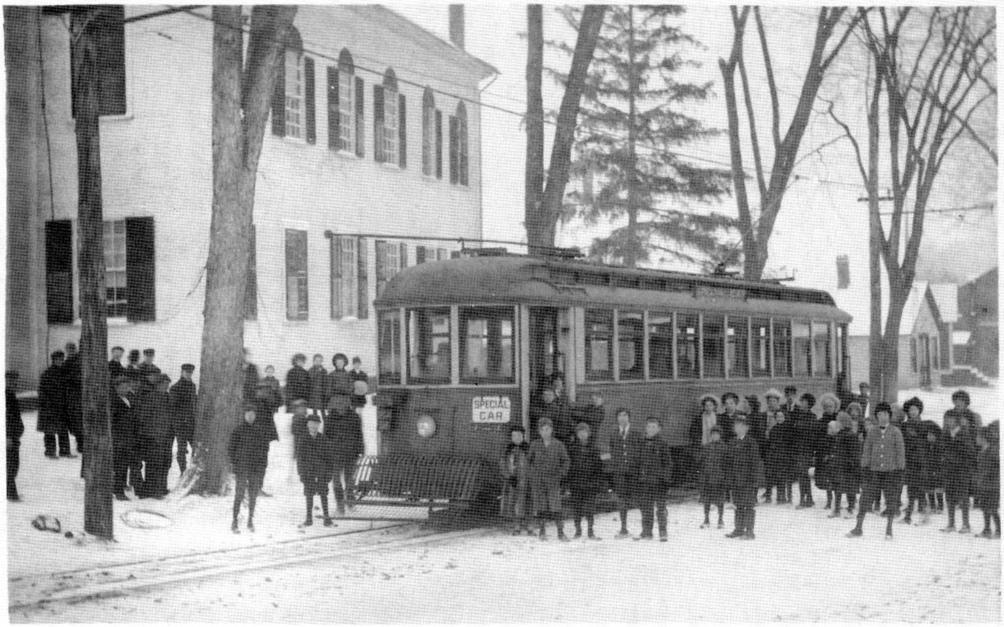

Although the arrival of the railroad enabled some level of commuting between the cities of Hartford and Middletown, train arrivals and departures happened once or twice a day. The trolley, which began running between these locations in 1909, ran on a regular schedule and made commuting much more convenient.

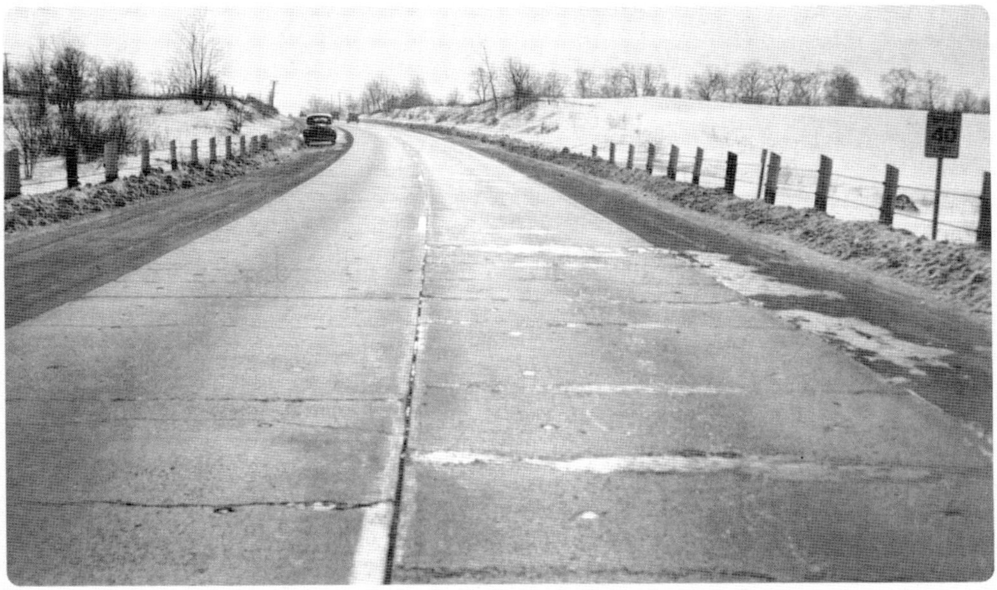

Looking south on the Silas Deane Highway near what is now the Waterchase Dr. intersection. Jan. 1946.

The Silas Deane Highway, shown here just south of modern-day Interstate 91, was finished in 1930, enabling automobile commuting to Hartford. Ralph Hick remembered his father, Harry, commuting in a carpool that originated in Higganum. The population of Rocky Hill jumped from 1,633 to 2,021 when the Silas Deane was completed. (Courtesy of Mike Martino.)

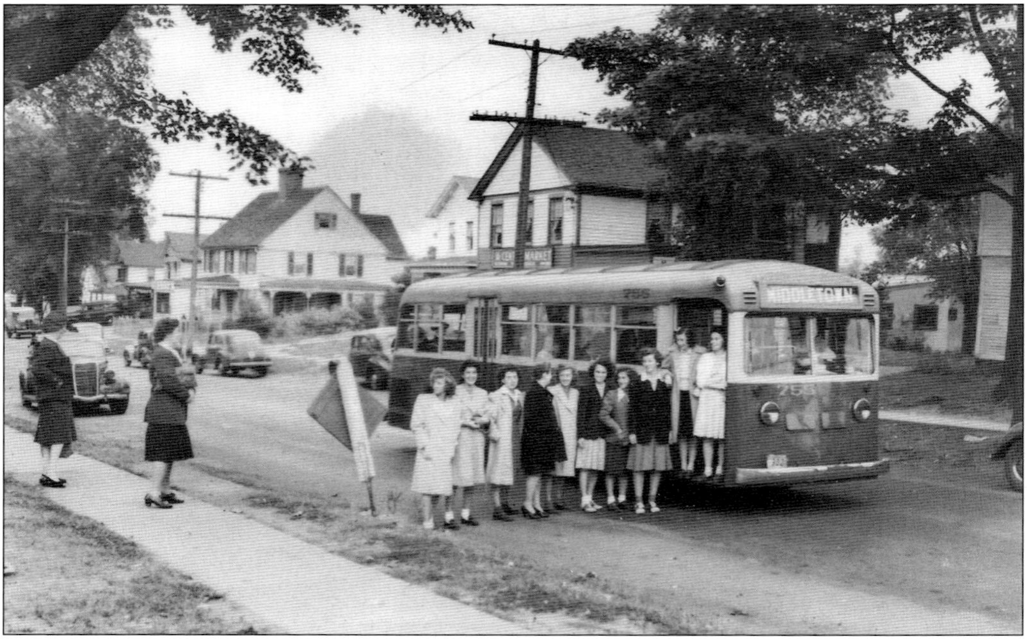

The trolley was retired and replaced by commuter buses in the early 1930s. Here, people board a bus to Middletown near the Rocky Hill Congregational Church at the corner of Old Main Street and Glastonbury Avenue in 1943.

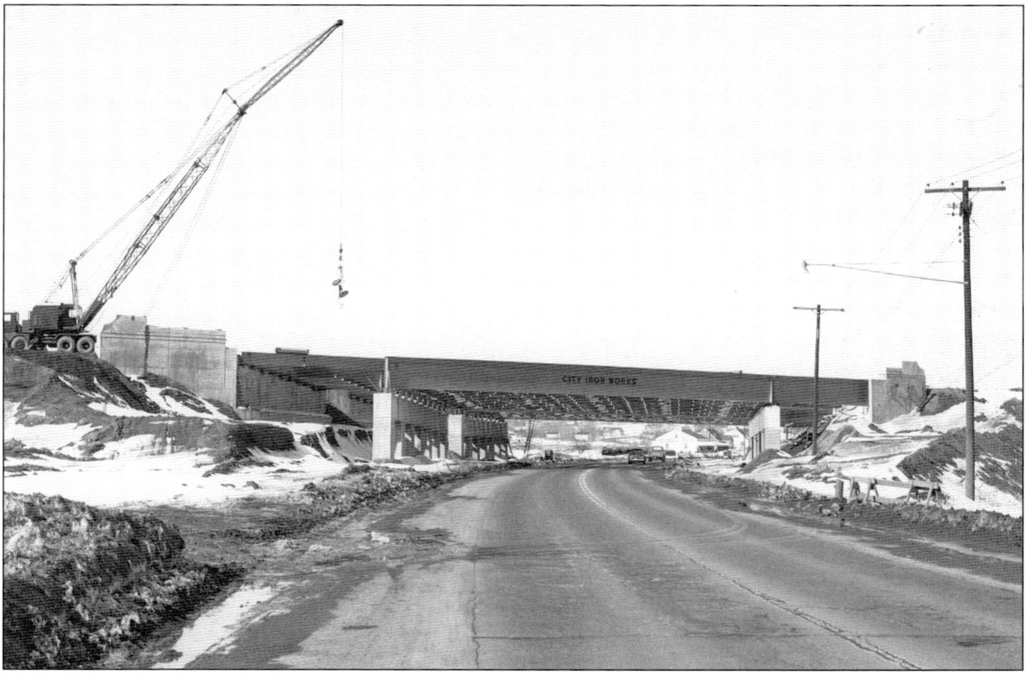

Interstate 91 was completed in Rocky Hill in 1965. This photograph was taken looking north on the Silas Deane near the Wethersfield town line. Interstate 91 fundamentally changed the town in that it made it practical for people to leave crowded cities and buy homes in the suburbs. From 1960 to 2019, the population has increased from 7,404 to approximately 20,000. (Courtesy of Mike Martino.)

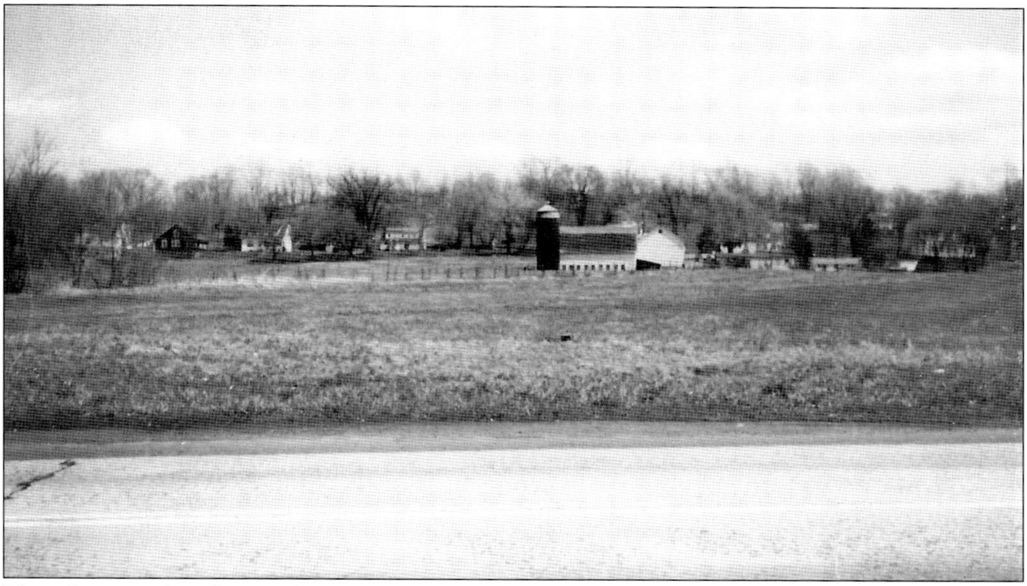

This photograph, taken in the 1960s, looks east at Broadview Farm from the Silas Deane Highway south of Parsonage Street. The area is greatly changed and densely populated today. (Courtesy of Mike Martino.)

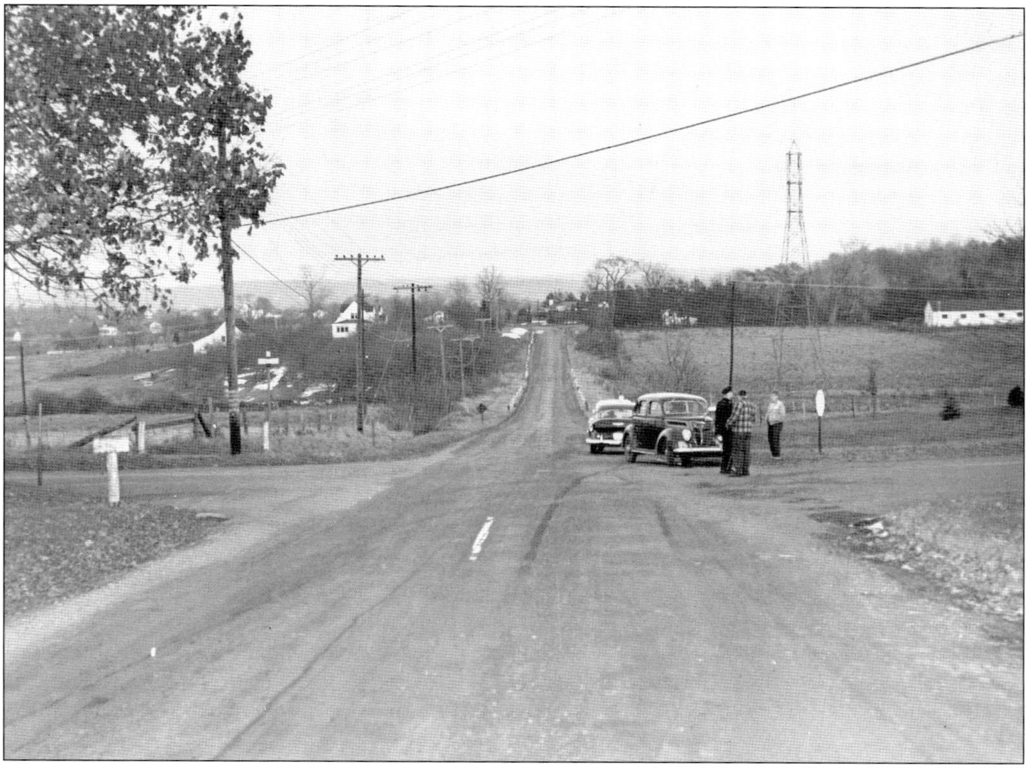

Looking east at the intersection of Elm Street and Gilbert Avenue, one once saw a country road and farmland containing few structures. The house on the left is 629 Elm Street. Today, houses line both sides of the road, this is a very busy intersection, and Elm Street is part of Connecticut Route 160. (Courtesy of Mike Martino.)

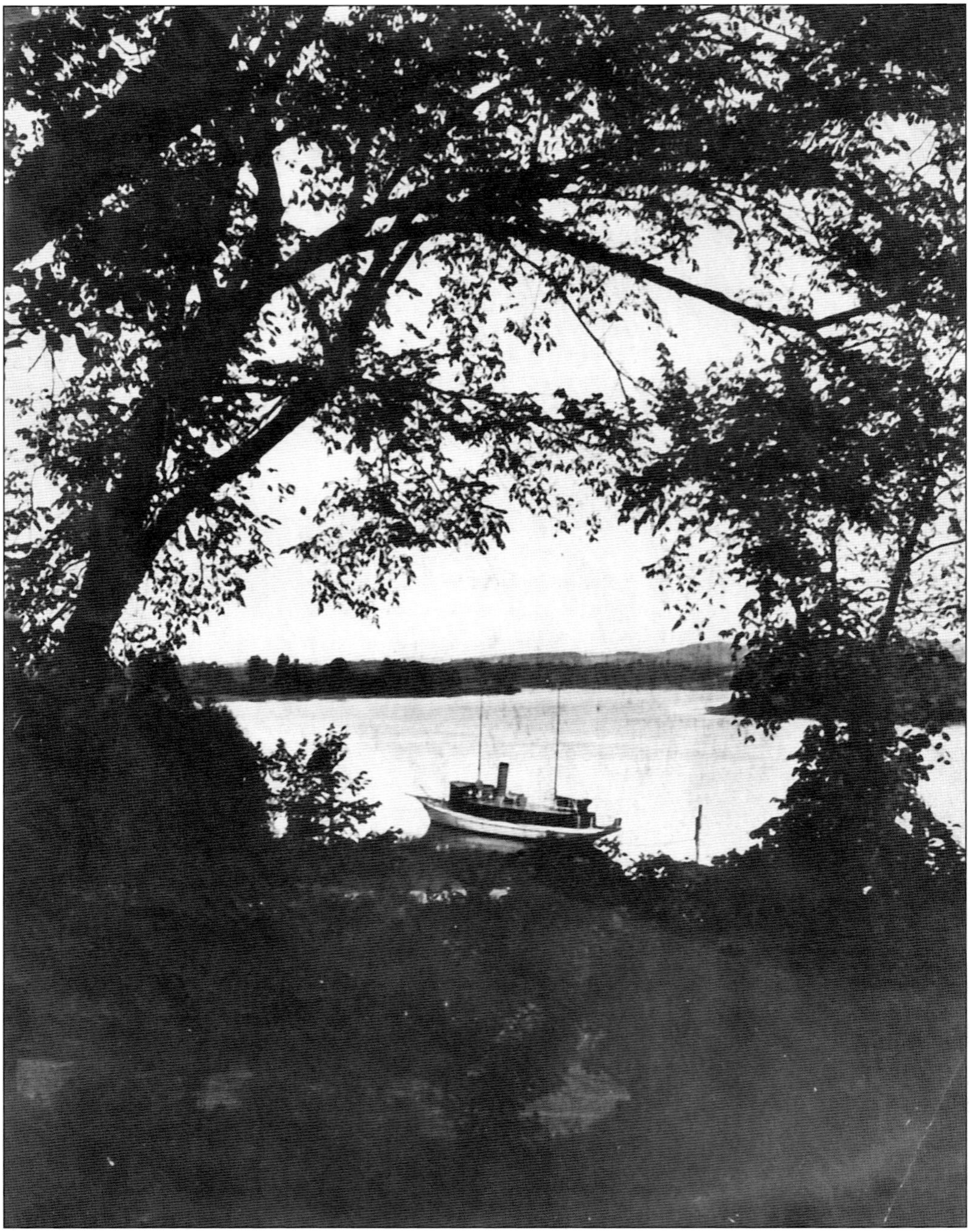

The Connecticut River has been a transportation avenue throughout Rocky Hill's history, from the era when Rocky Hill ships sailed to foreign ports to the industrial age, when materials for foundries, highway construction, and river improvements were delivered via the river. Recreational use of the river continues to this day. Pictured here is the excursion boat *Agnes*, operated by John Ellis in the early 20th century.

Five

Neighborhoods, Buildings, Shops, and People

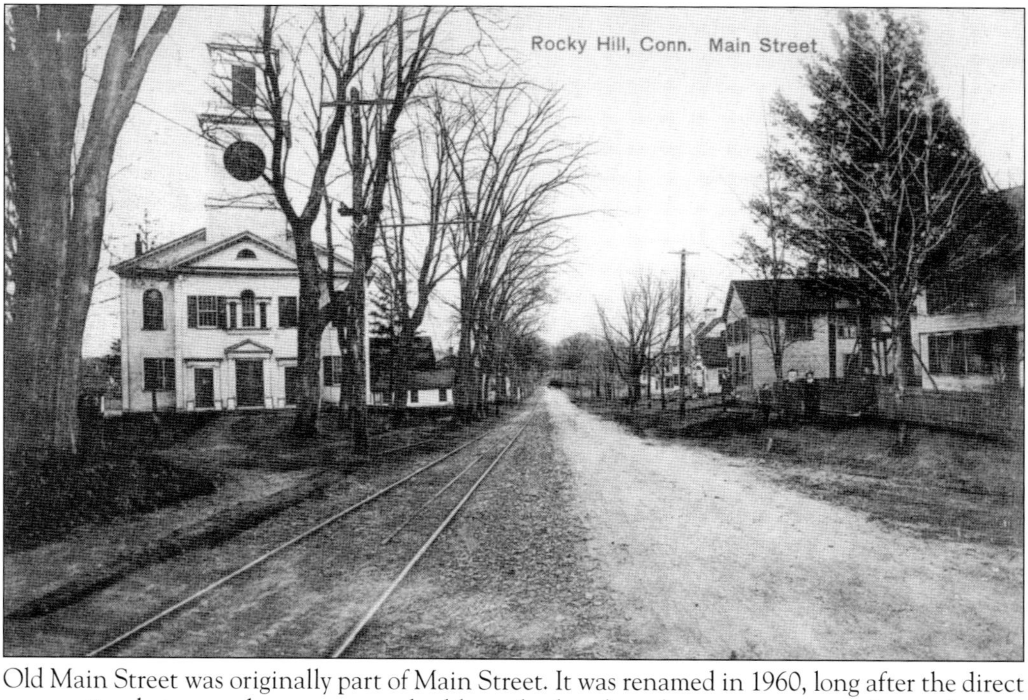

Old Main Street was originally part of Main Street. It was renamed in 1960, long after the direct connection between the two streets had been broken by subsequent construction and street reconfigurations. The trolley, completed in 1909, ran out from Hartford, down present-day Old Main Street to Main Street, and continued down what is Route 99 today to Middletown and beyond. (Courtesy of Gail Shay.)

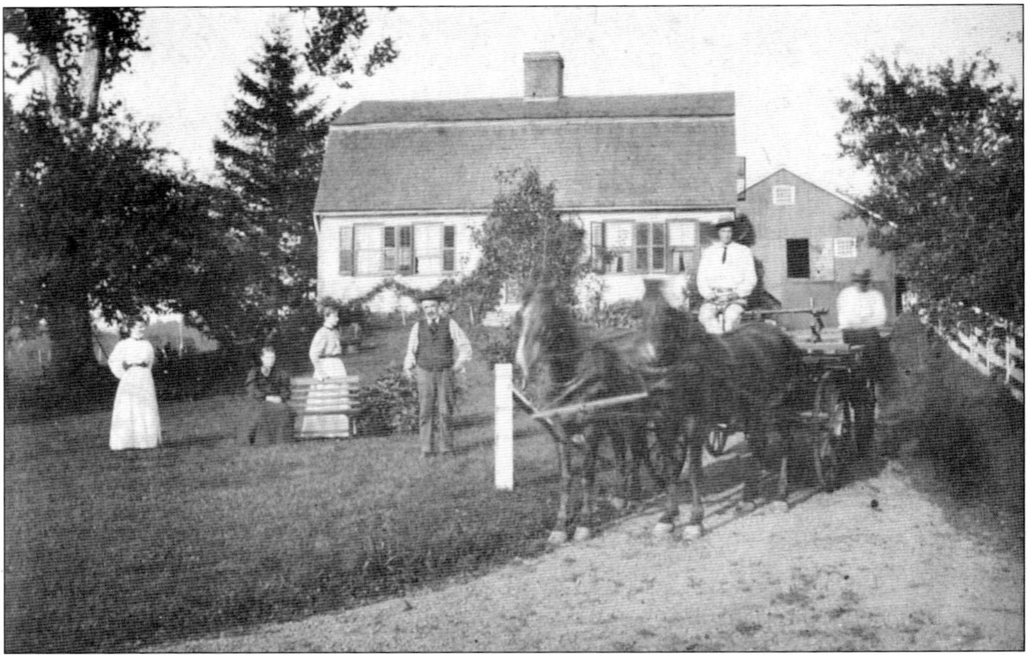

The Phillip Goffe House is the oldest existing house in Rocky Hill. William Goffe and Edward Whalley, the supposed executioners of King Charles I, may have stayed here prior to seeking refuge in West Haven. William Goffe seems to have been a relative of Phillip Goffe. Members of the Whelen family (pictured) bought the house and farm from the Goffe family in 1864. They sold the house about 1935. (Courtesy of Mike Martino.)

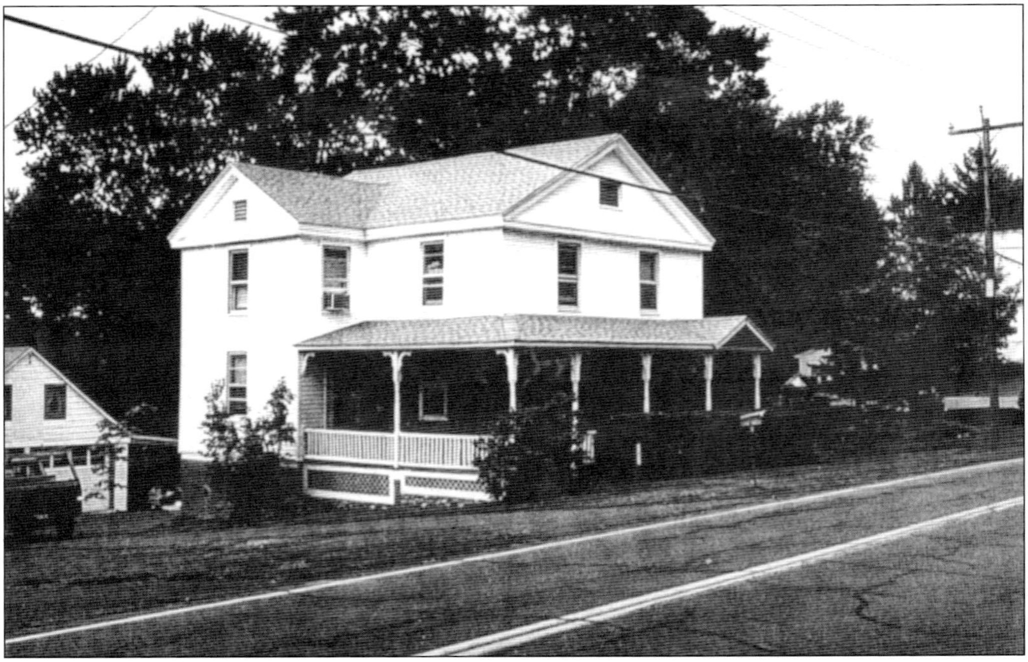

The house at 347 Old Main Street was built in 1756 as the North District School, one of four brick Rocky Hill one-room schoolhouses. It was rebuilt in 1845. It was converted to a residence around 1920, and the new owner, William D. Robbins, had a second floor added to the brick first floor.

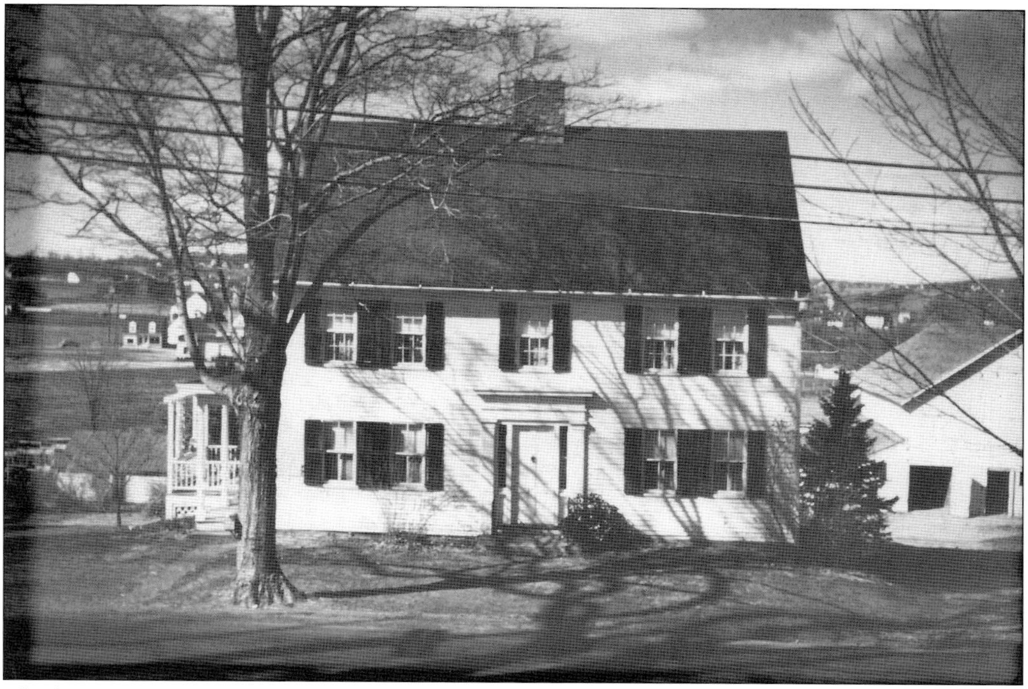

The house at 401 Old Main Street was built in 1790 for Elijah Robbins. He was the grandnephew of squire John Robbins, builder and owner of the Duke of Cumberland Inn at 262 Old Main Street. The Robbins family has occupied this house continuously since it was built. It served as the farmhouse for Broadview Farm until the land was sold for development in the 1960s.

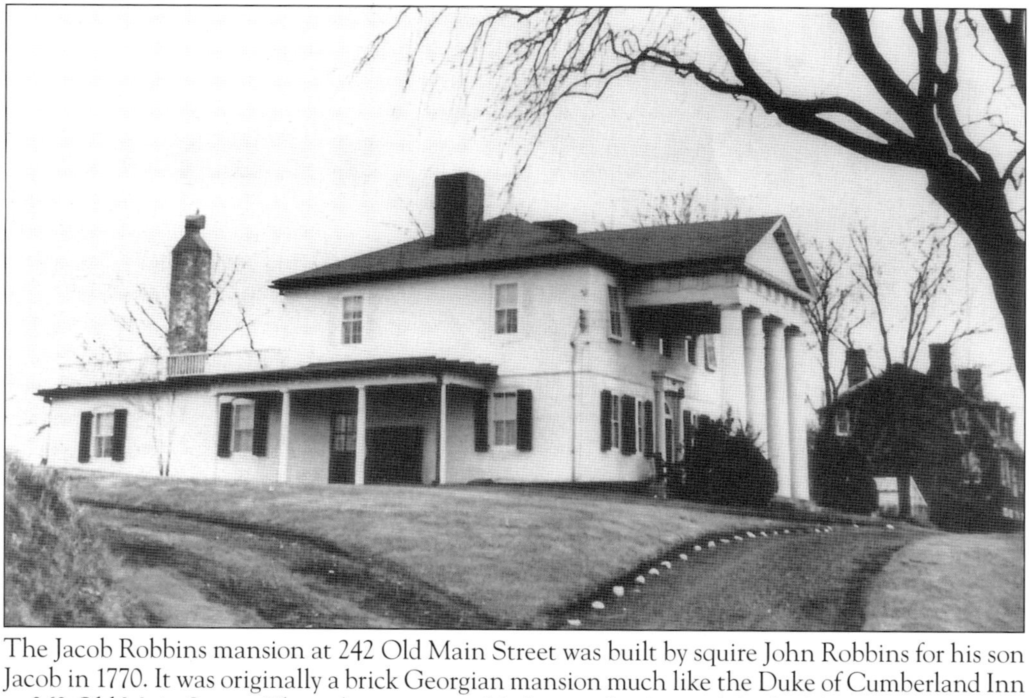

The Jacob Robbins mansion at 242 Old Main Street was built by squire John Robbins for his son Jacob in 1770. It was originally a brick Georgian mansion much like the Duke of Cumberland Inn at 262 Old Main Street. The columns were added around 1920, and the building was apparently painted white at that time.

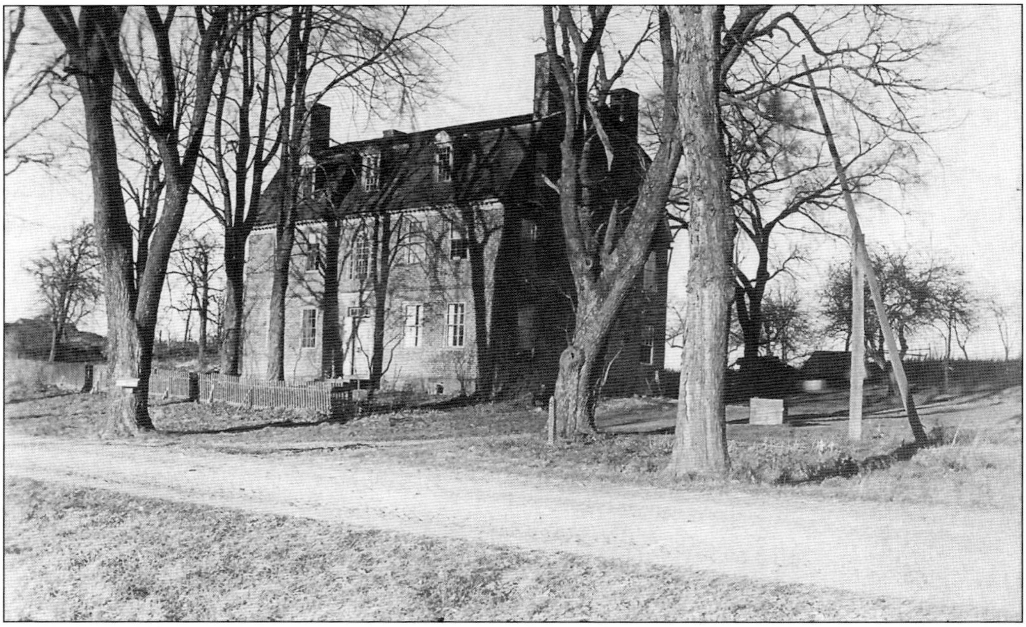

John Robbins acquired 2,000 acres, including the land on which the building at 262 Old Main Street stands, from several landowners between 1762 and 1765. The house was built in 1767. Robbins was a sea captain, prosperous farmer, member of the Connecticut General Assembly, and slave holder. Slaves made the bricks for the building from local clay.

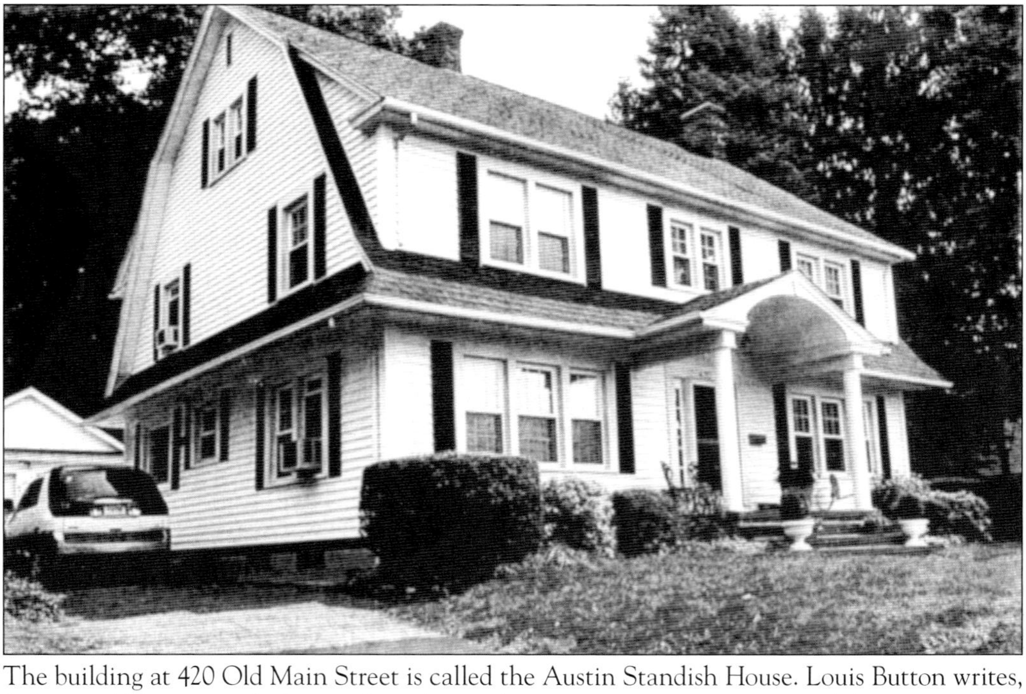

The building at 420 Old Main Street is called the Austin Standish House. Louis Button writes, "prior to 1898 . . . it was badly run down having been used as a store at one time." It was remodeled by George Chandler, chairman of the Connecticut Commission on Publicity, during World War I. Wethersfield historian Jared Standish says Chandler "thoughtlessly modernized" the house about 1898. (Courtesy of the Connecticut State Library.)

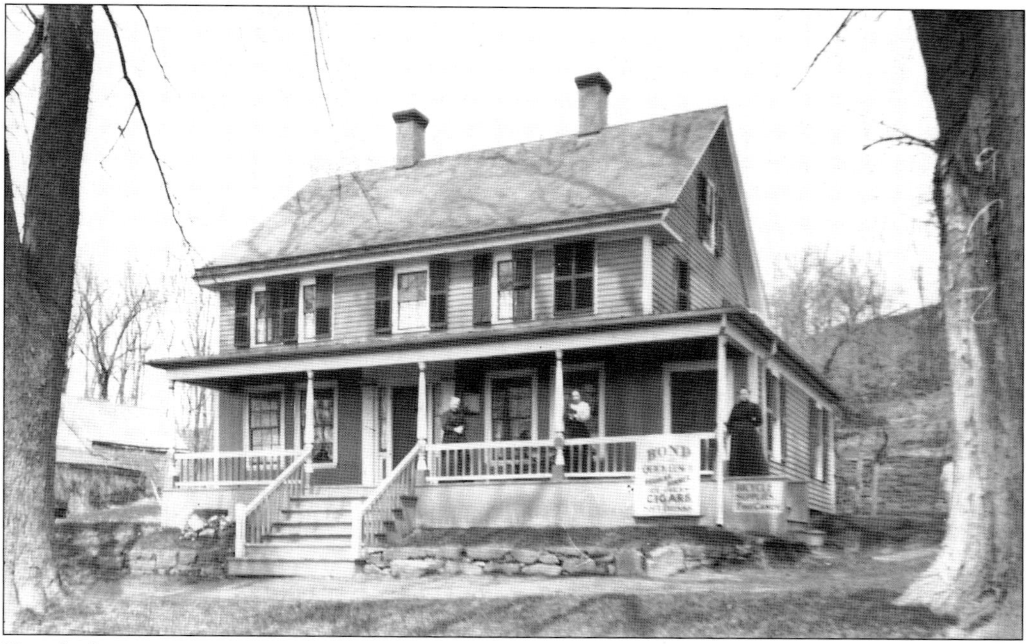

Hartford was a major city in the Gilded Age, the home of luminaries like Samuel Colt, Mark Twain, and J.P. Morgan. Dinners with shad from the Connecticut River and the atmosphere of the local inns and taverns attracted people like these to Rocky Hill. The DeRyer Hotel, noted for such shad dinners, was located at the northern foot of the high road off Old Main Street. It burned down in 1916.

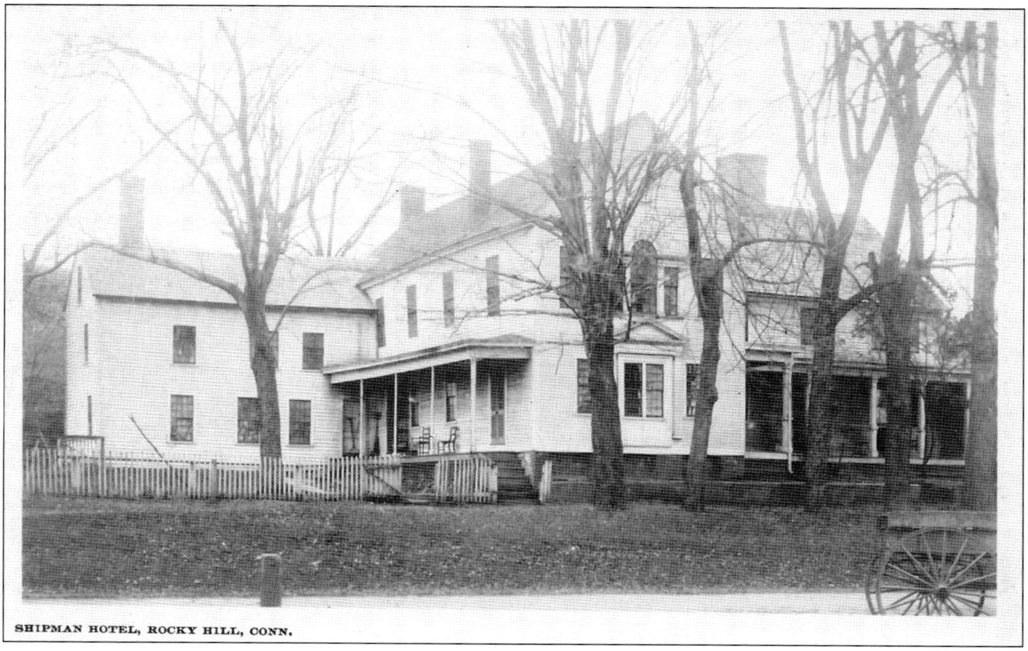

For many years, the Shipman Tavern was located about where 582, 588, and 594 Old Main Street are today. Built in 1770 and also known for shad dinners, at various times it had rooms to let, a dance hall with a spring-loaded dance floor, a bowling alley, and a tavern-restaurant. It was disassembled in 1931 and moved to Far Hills, New Jersey, where it burned in 1936.

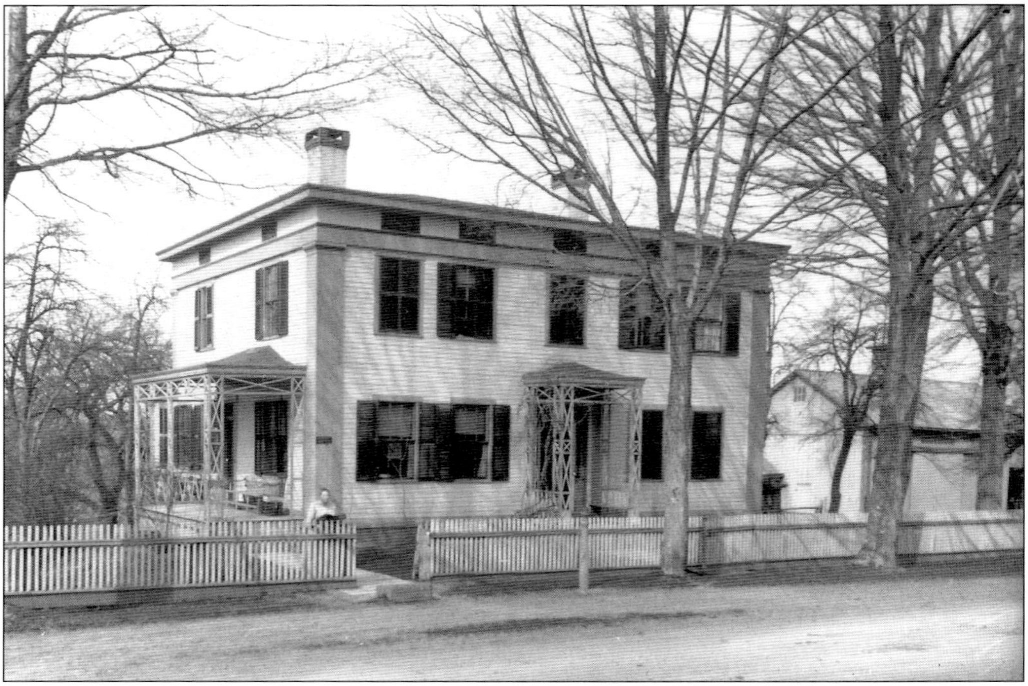

The building at 557 Old Main Street was constructed in 1850. It was owned by William Neff, who ran a wagon shop near the ferry landing. Dr. Frank L. Burr lived here and practiced medicine starting in the 1880s. He was also a town clerk and notary public.

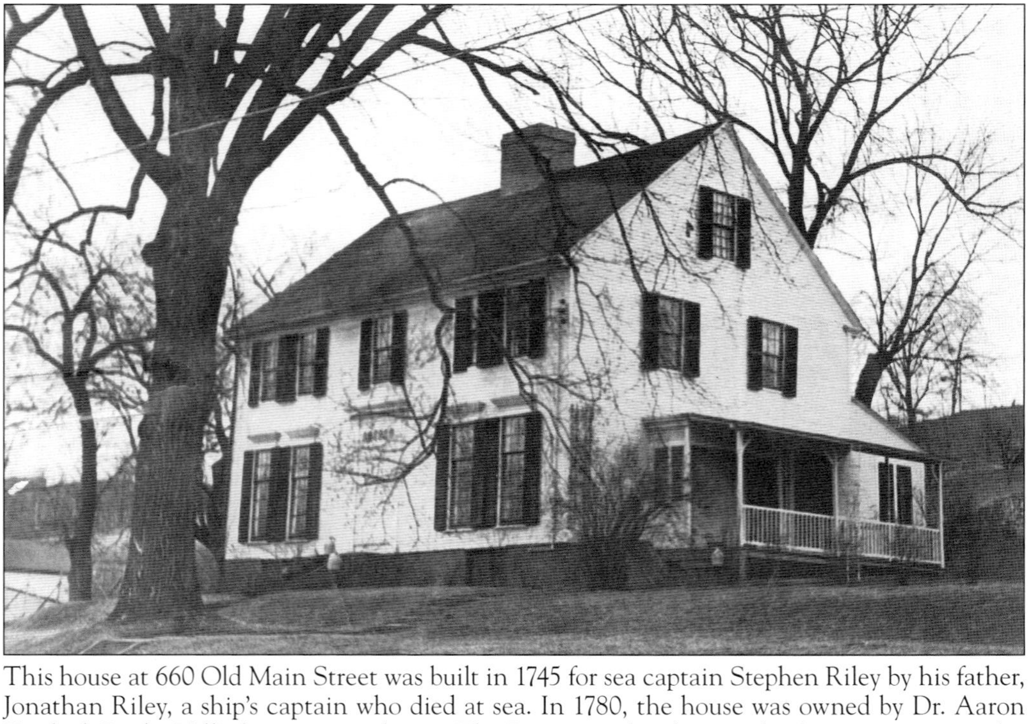

This house at 660 Old Main Street was built in 1745 for sea captain Stephen Riley by his father, Jonathan Riley, a ship's captain who died at sea. In 1780, the house was owned by Dr. Aaron Hosford, Rocky Hill's first country doctor. The Beaumont family owned it for many years, and it was at one time the Beaumont Academy girls' school. (Courtesy of the Connecticut State Library.)

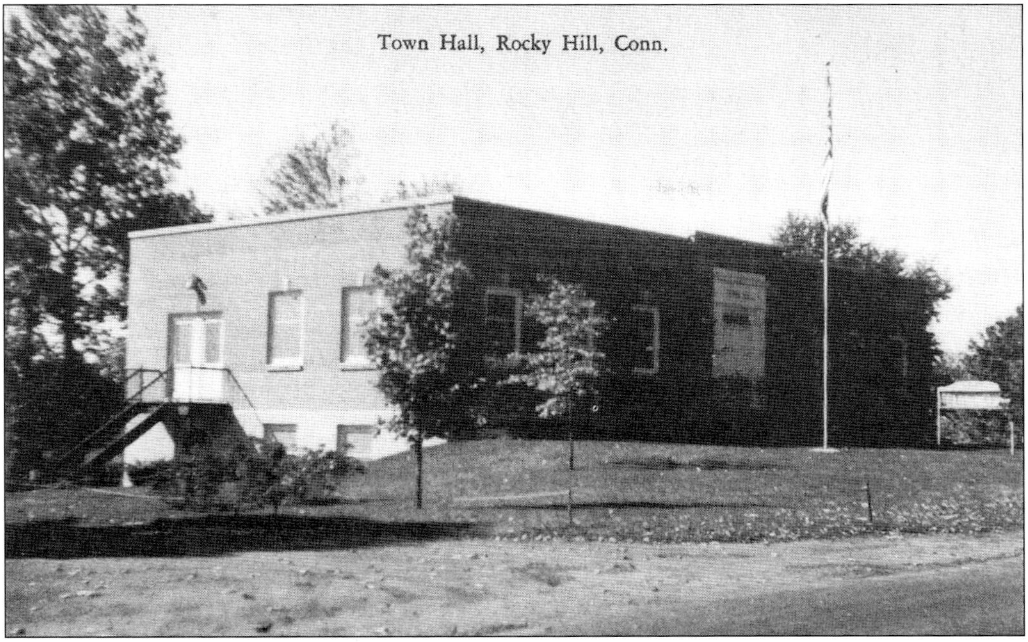

At various times in Rocky Hill's history, the town hall had been located in private homes, in rooms at the old Cora J. Belden Library, at Academy Hall, and at other temporary locations. The old Rocky Hill Town Hall, intended to be a permanent location for town government, opened in 1954. (Courtesy of Mike Martino.)

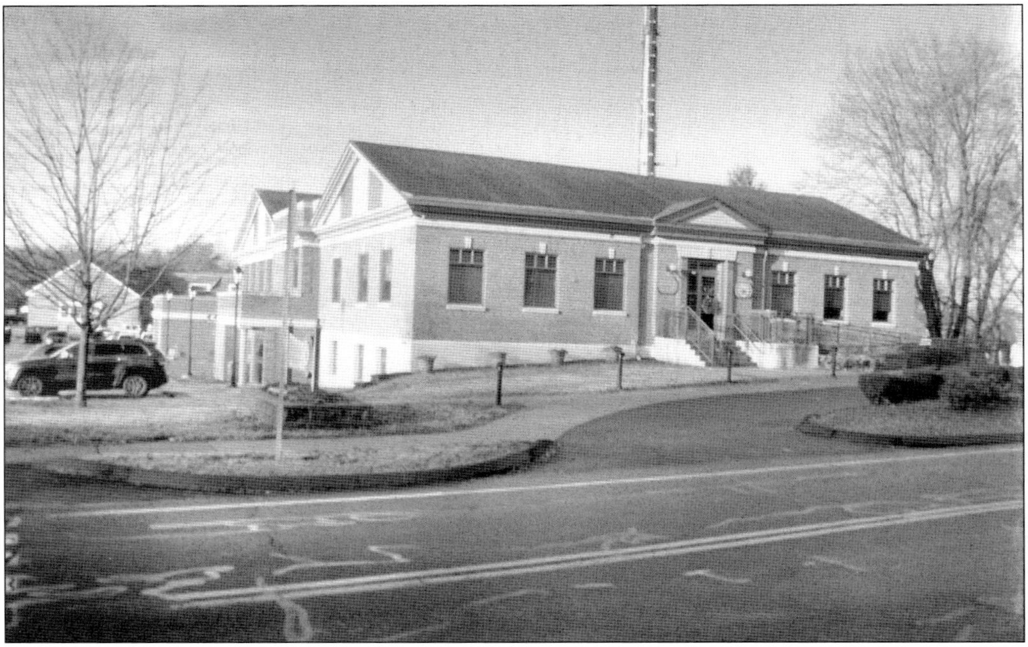

When the new town hall opened in 2002 to accommodate a population that had grown dramatically, the 1954 town hall was repurposed for police operations and youth and human services.

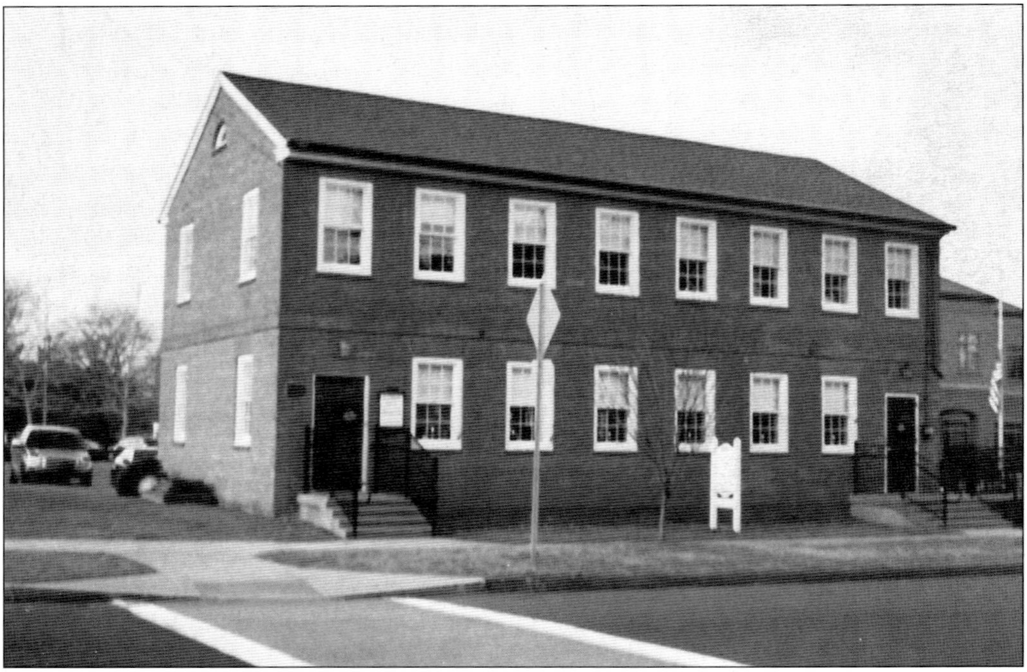

Academy Hall was built in 1803, during Rocky Hill's period as a maritime hub. It has been a maritime academy, a public school, and a venue for many private and public organizations. It has been the home of the Rocky Hill Historical Society and Museum since 1963. On October 7, 1977, it was listed in the National Register of Historical Places.

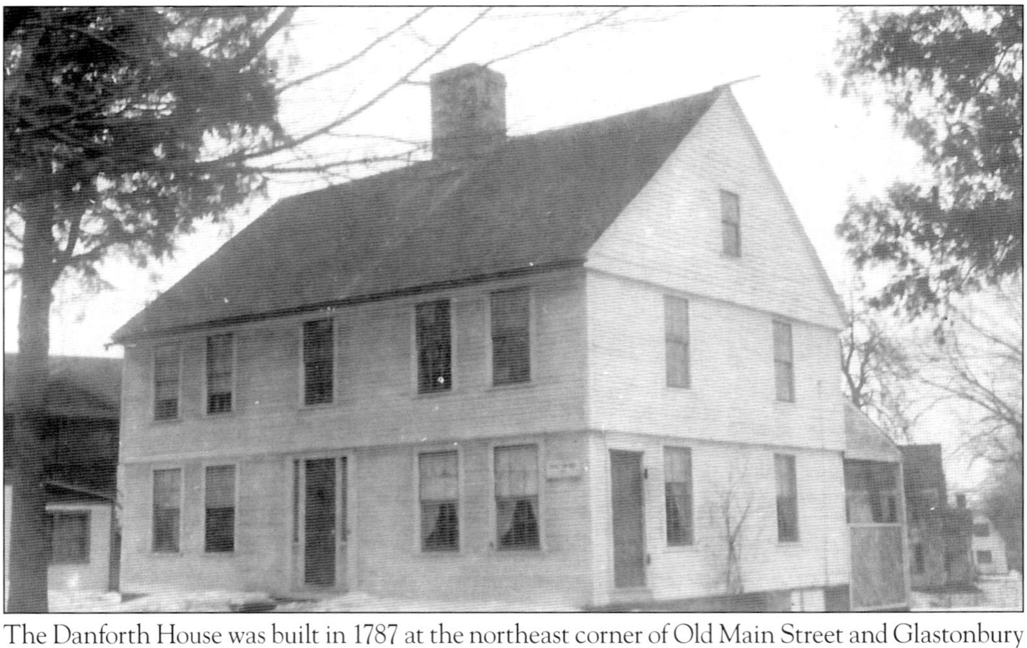

The Danforth House was built in 1787 at the northeast corner of Old Main Street and Glastonbury Avenue. Thomas Danforth, Thomas Danforth Jr., and Thomas Danforth III were renowned tinsmiths. They sponsored Yankee peddlers and trained Rocky Hill–born Ashibel Griswold, the famous Meriden silversmith. The Danforths had shops in Philadelphia; Augusta, Georgia; and near the ferry landing in Rocky Hill. Danforth Pewter still does business in Middlebury, Vermont.

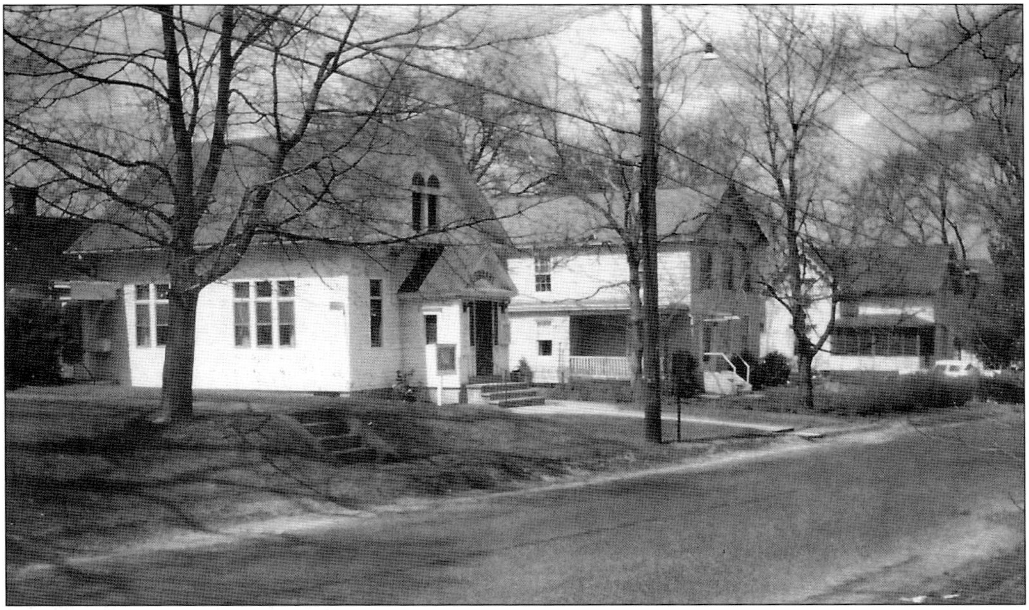

Before the Silas Deane Highway was built in 1930, Church Street connected directly to Main Street on one end and the present Old Main Street on the other. It was part of the Hartford–Saybrook Turnpike. This photograph was taken near the south end of Church Street in 1961. Today, the south end is closed off, and a small park has been installed there.

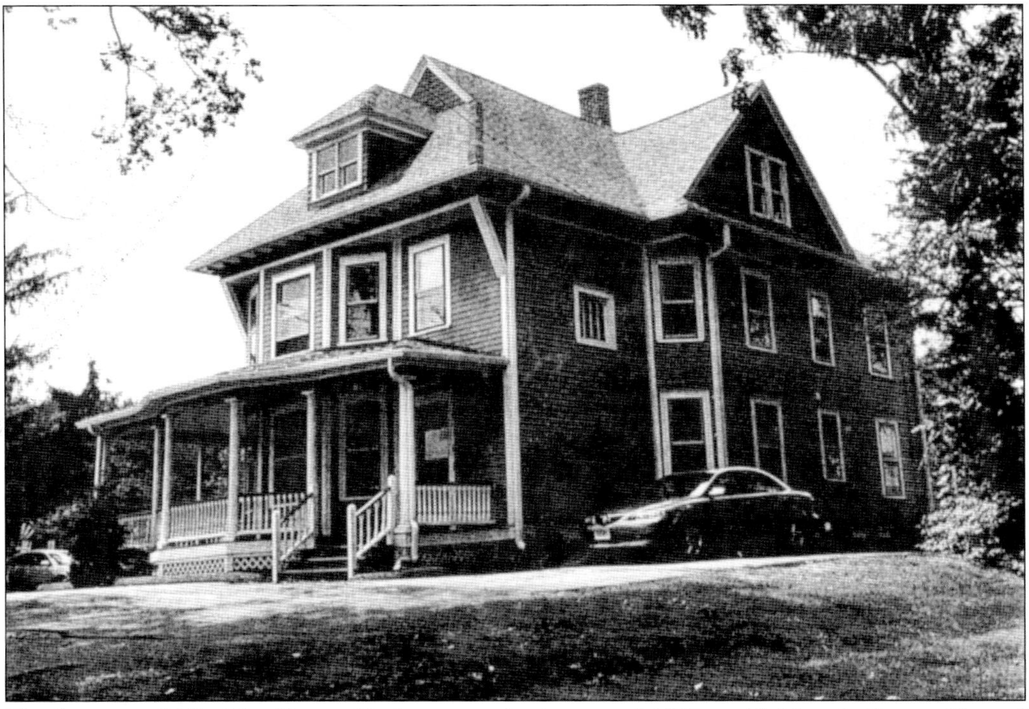

The house at 2347 Silas Deane Highway was built around 1900 as 60 Church Street. Elwood F. Belden, a Rocky Hill businessman and political leader, and his wife, Cora J. Belden (after whom the town library is named), bought the house when it was new. (Courtesy of Rocky Hill Assessor's Office.)

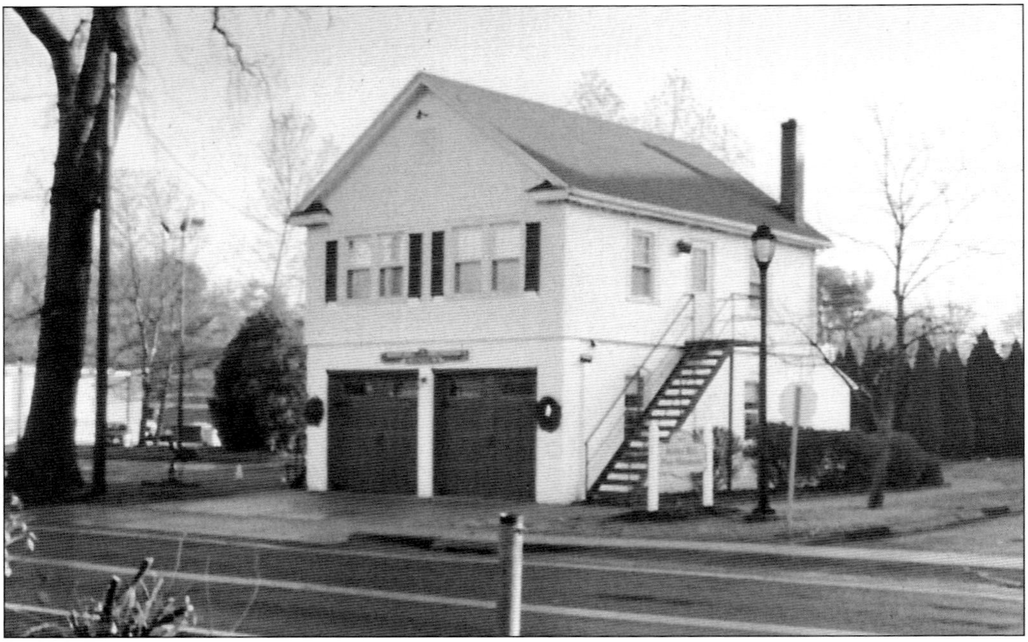

The original firehouse at 35 Church Street opened in 1927. As the town grew, more stations opened. Station 2 opened on New Britain Avenue in 1946. In 1961, a new main station opened on Old Main Street, replacing the original firehouse. Station 3 opened on Main Street in 2002. The original fire station was dedicated as a museum in 2010. (Courtesy of Rocky Hill Volunteer Fire Department.)

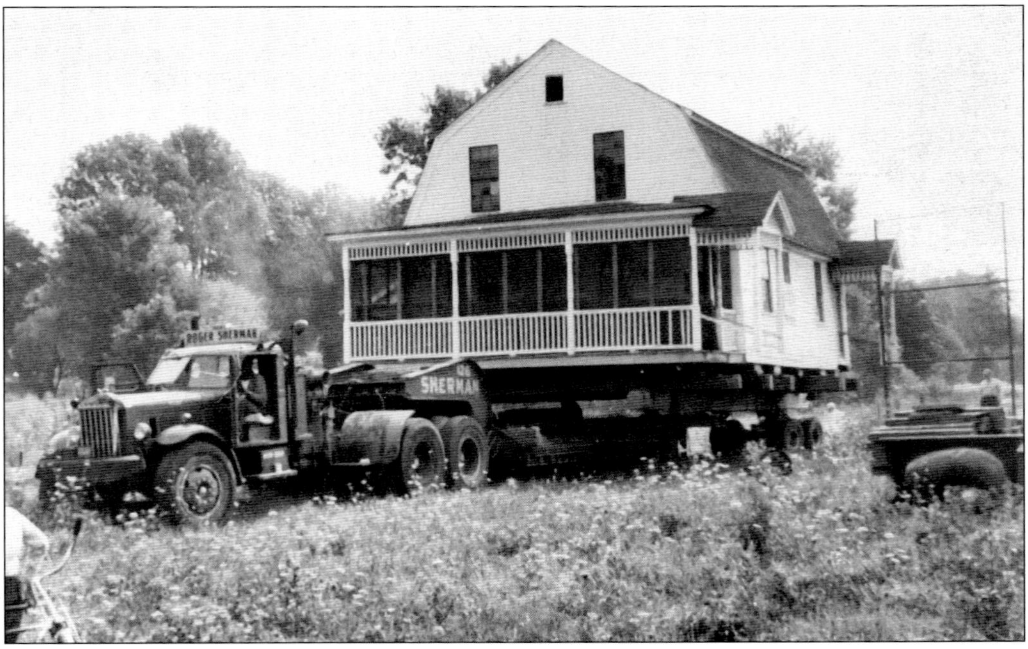

The house at 11 Church Street was built in 1790. Wait Warner, its original owner, died in 1804. It was owned by another Wait Warner in 1869. It was not unusual for buildings to be moved in Rocky Hill. This house was located on Old Main Street. It was moved to make way for construction of the new town hall in 1954. (Courtesy of Martin Smith.)

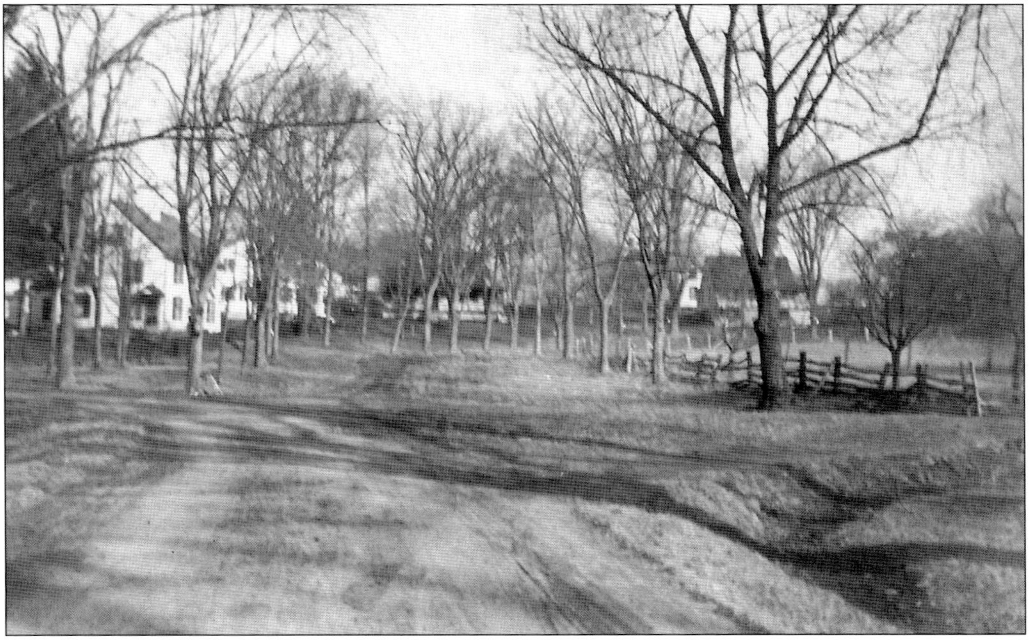

This photograph of the north end of Riverview Road was taken between the late 1880s and the early 1900s. Riverview Road has been known at various times as Fairview Street, Prospect Street, and Hill Road. Many homes on this road were built by people in maritime trades and by Congregational church ministers.

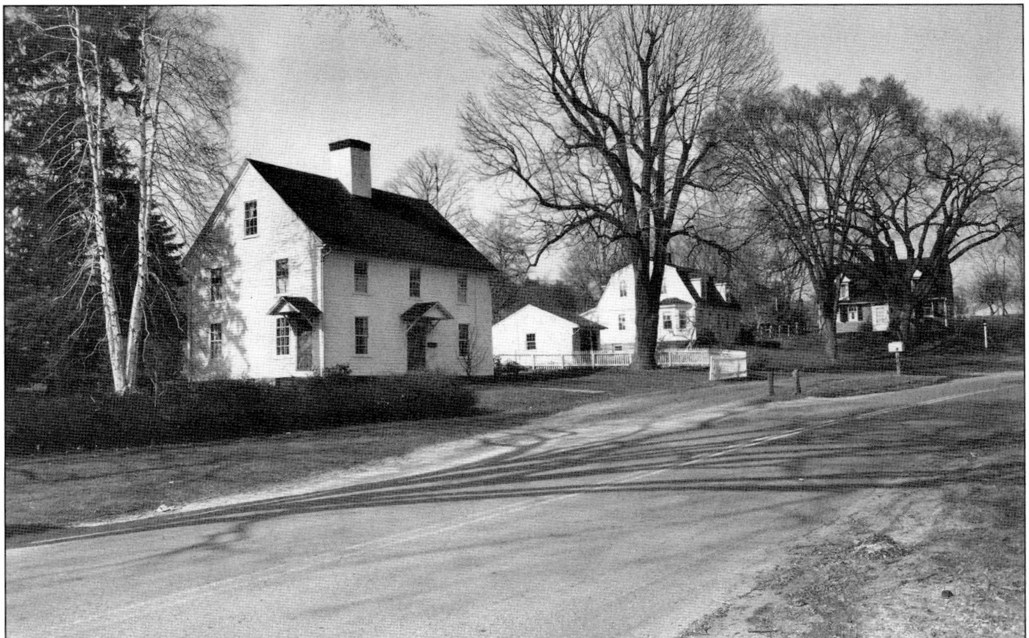

The house at 3 Riverview Road was built in 1710 by sea captain David Riley. This area is known as Riley's Corner, because many of the houses belonged to Riley family members, many of whom were sea captains. This was the home of physician and historian Dr. Rufus W. Griswold in the late 19th century. Dr. Griswold and his son Roger were noted sources of Rocky Hill's history.

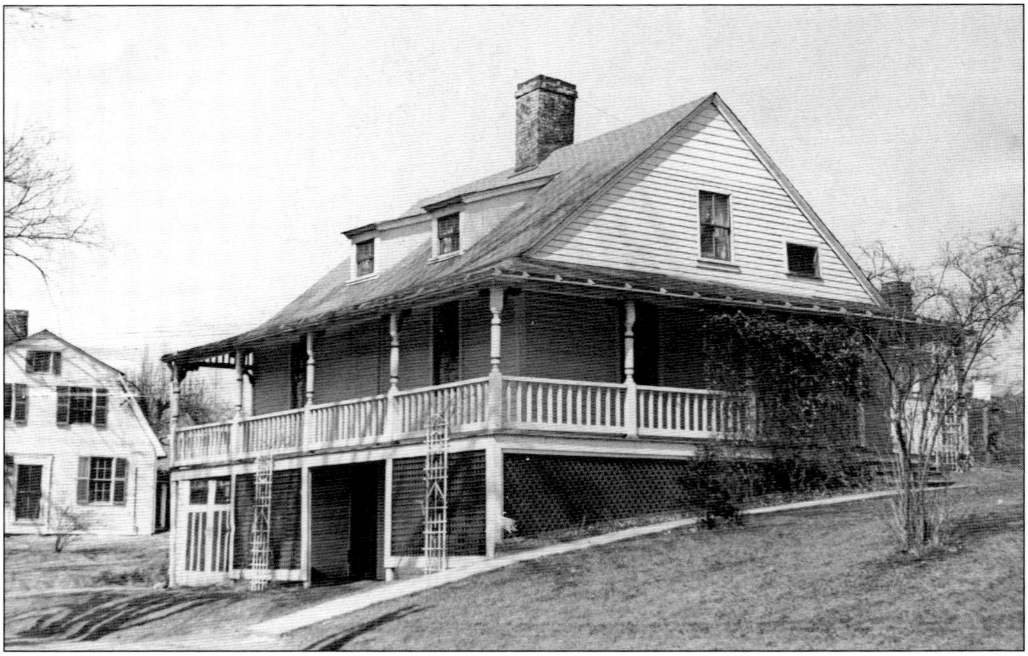

The house at 13 Riverview Road was built in 1795. It was owned by Henry Robinson, who owned much property on the northeast corner of Riverview Road in the mid-19th century. The Sherwood family owned it from the late 19th to the mid-20th century. The porches and dormer were added in the 19th century. The current owners restored the house to its original simple Colonial condition.

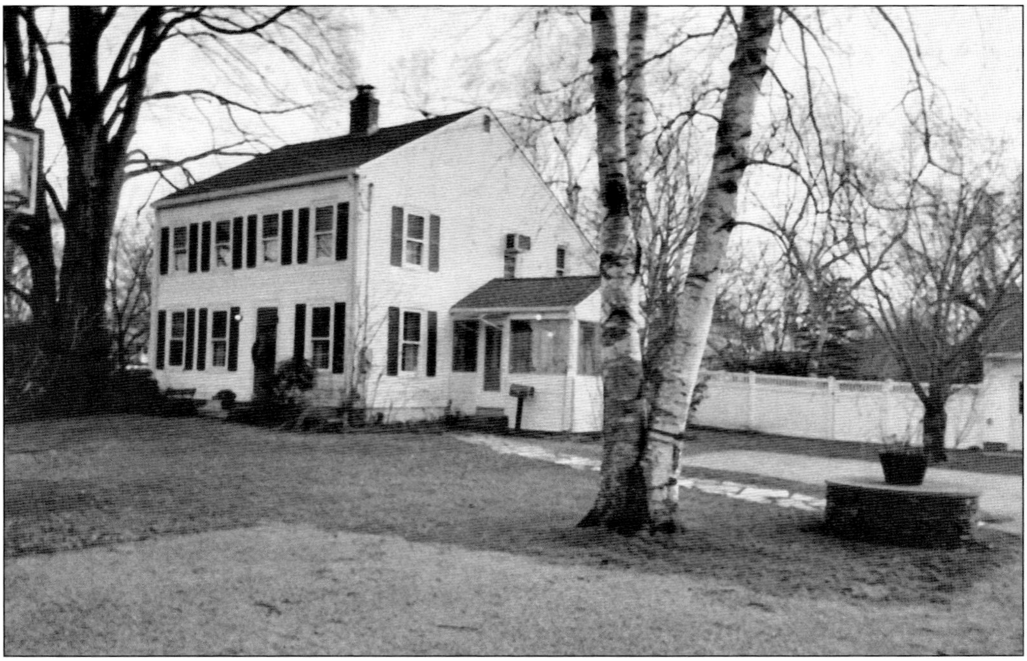

The Lewis Whitmore house at 20 Riverview Road was built in 1787. This house is reputed to have been a stop on the Underground Railroad. A small building in the rear was the site of a post office in Rocky Hill that was moved there from the corner of Washington and Old Main Streets. Henry Whitmore, Rocky Hill's postmaster in the 1840s, owned this house in 1869.

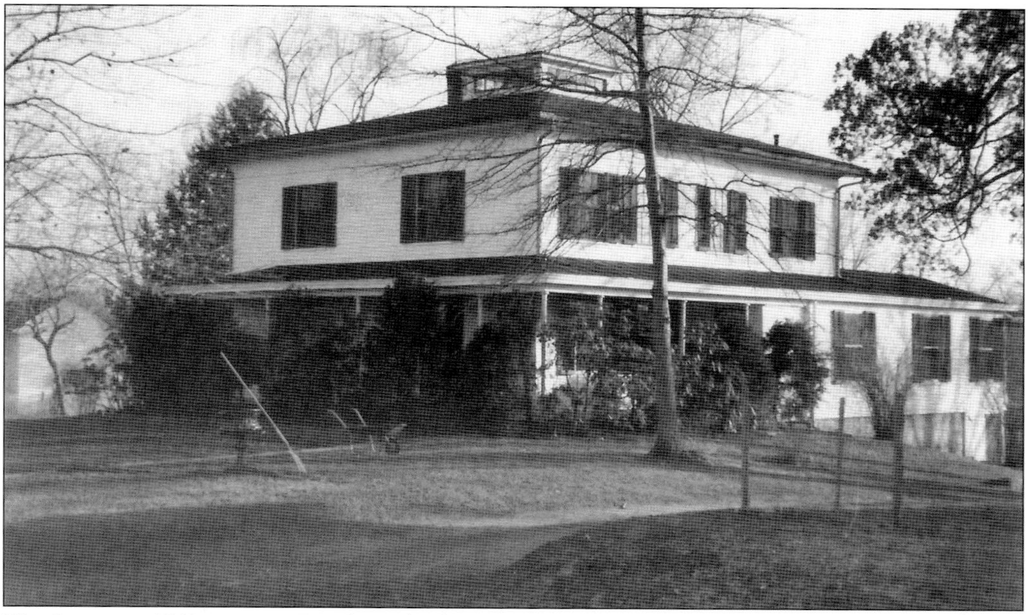

The house at 42 Riverview Road was built in 1853. It was the home of Congregational minister Louis Burton Rockwood and served as the social library from 1855 to 1866. It is rumored to have been a stop on the Underground Railroad. Ferry captain Henry Hale owned the house in the 1950s. He and his family were noted shad fishermen and ferrymen on the Connecticut River.

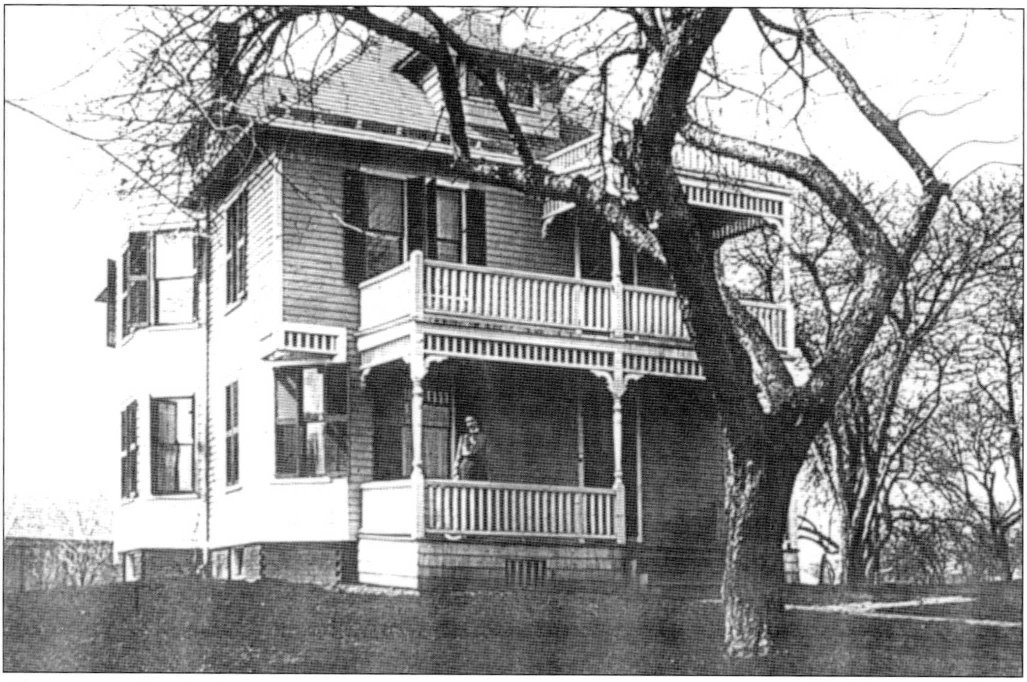

The Dennis family bought the land on which 48 Riverview Road stands in 1883. The house was built in 1900. William Dennis, a reporter for the *Hartford Courant*, contributed to *Wethersfield and Her Daughters* in 1934. Dennis and his wife toured the Far East in 1939. In 1940, they were reported as war refugees in Switzerland. Dennis's book *Glittering Horizons*, published in 1940, recounts his experiences on this harrowing trip.

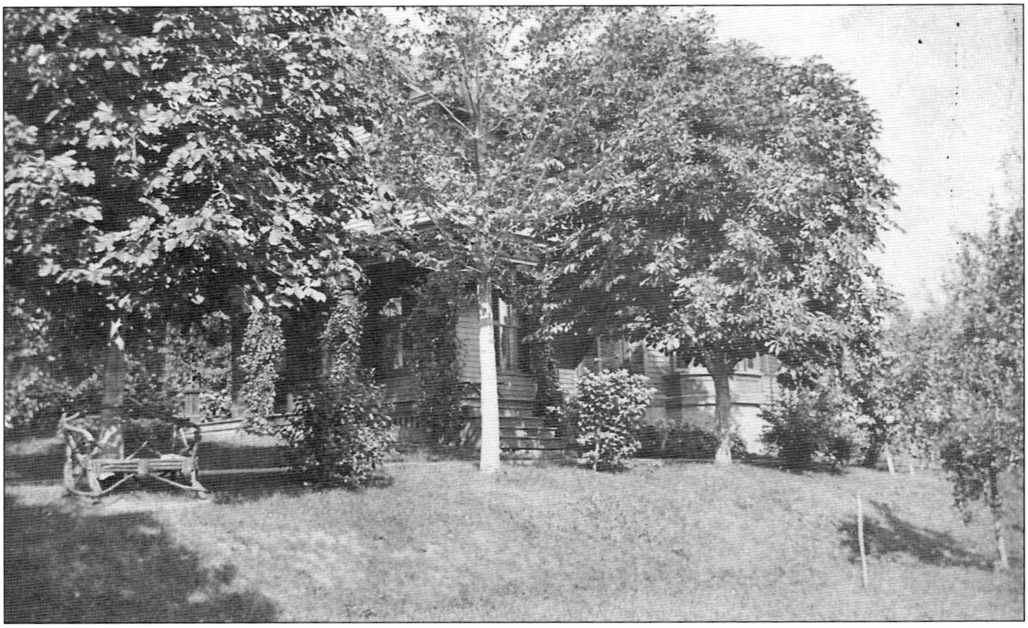

This house at 51 Riverview Road was built in 1865. At the turn of the 20th century, it was owned by Eugene Belden. He and his father, Seabury, operated the last shipyard in Rocky Hill, located north of Hog Brook, in the late 19th century.

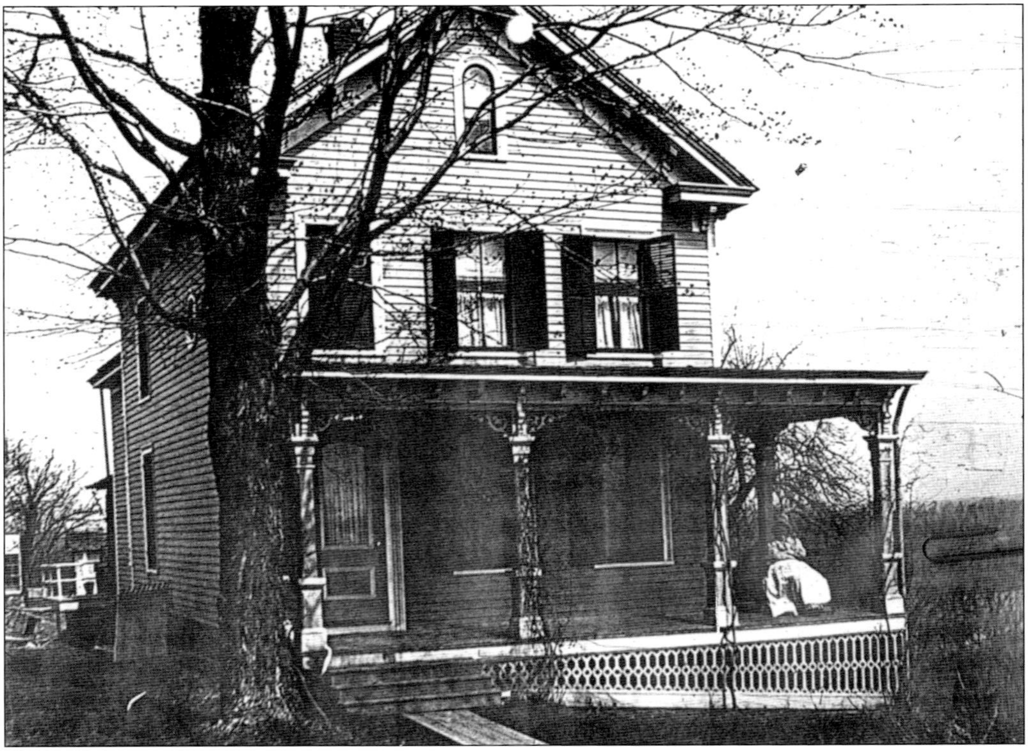

The house at 53 Riverview Road was owned by George Belden, who worked at the Belden Shipyard. He was not a member of Seabury and Eugene Belden's immediate family but may have been a relative. He became a local builder and built many Rocky Hill homes in the early 20th century.

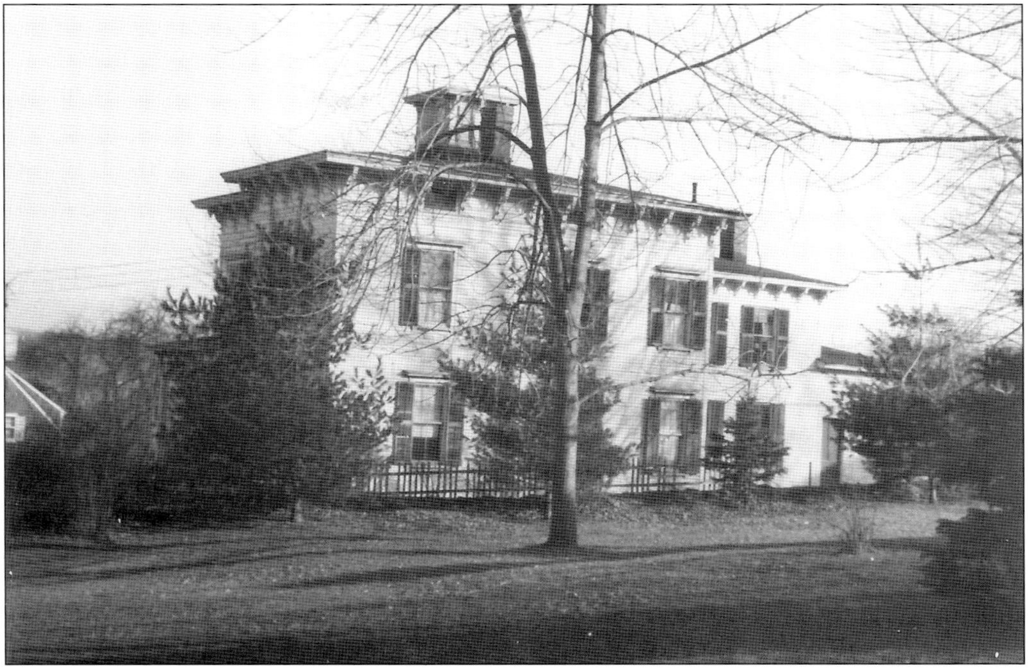

The house at 54 Riverview Road was built in 1880 by Jason A. "Gus" Robbins. He owned a large apple orchard across Riverview Road and was one of the richest people in Rocky Hill. During World War I, his wife, Jane, gained notoriety as a suffragist and opponent of the war. Jason died in 1925, and Jane sold the house to the Hall family, who owned it until 1969.

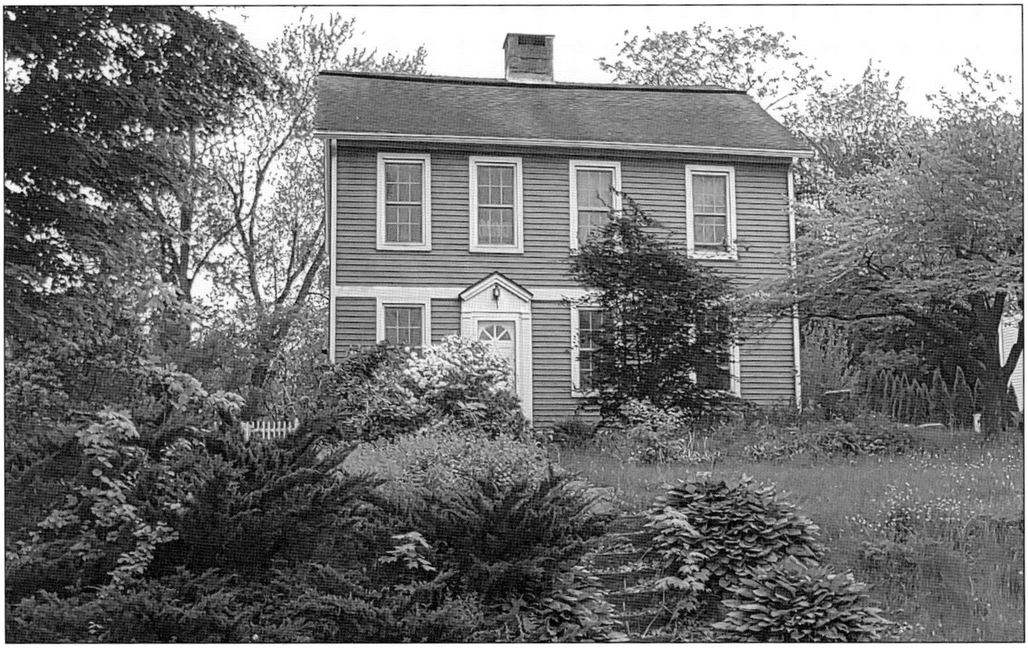

The house at 60 Riverview Road was built in 1793. It belonged to sea captain William Webb. When he died, the house was left to his daughter Belinda Webb Goodrich. The 1820 US Census shows one slave girl living here. The Gradual Emancipation Act of 1797 would have required that she be freed on her 21st birthday.

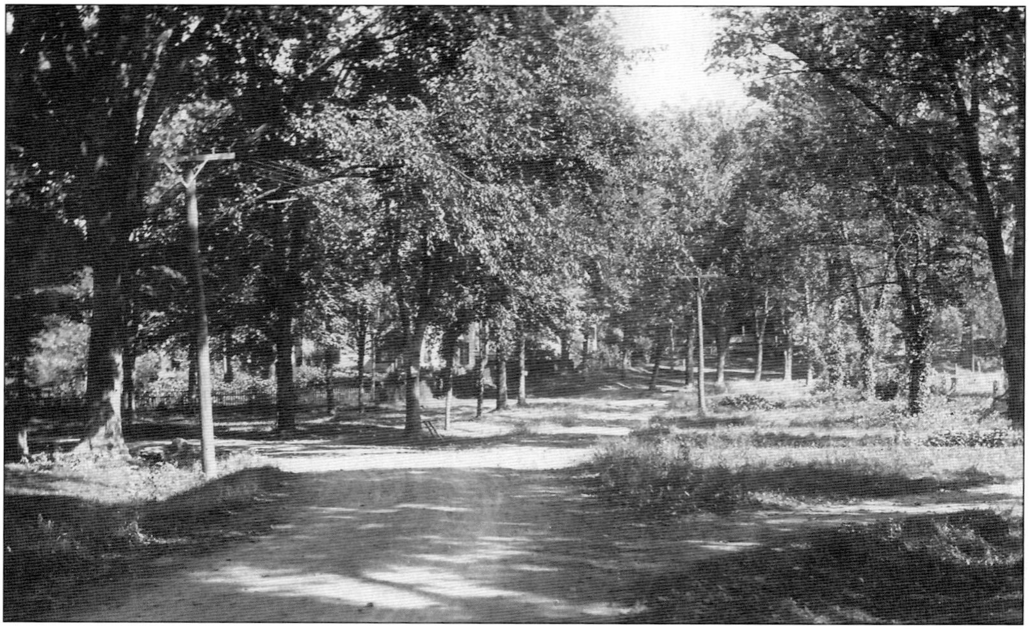

This photograph of Washington Street was taken in the late 1890s or early 1900s. The road turning left is modern Old Main Street. The road going straight is Riverview Road. Washington Street is the dirt path going off to the right. Washington Street was once known as New Street, then Mudd (or Mud) Lane. There is a question of when it stopped being a dirt path and become a thoroughfare.

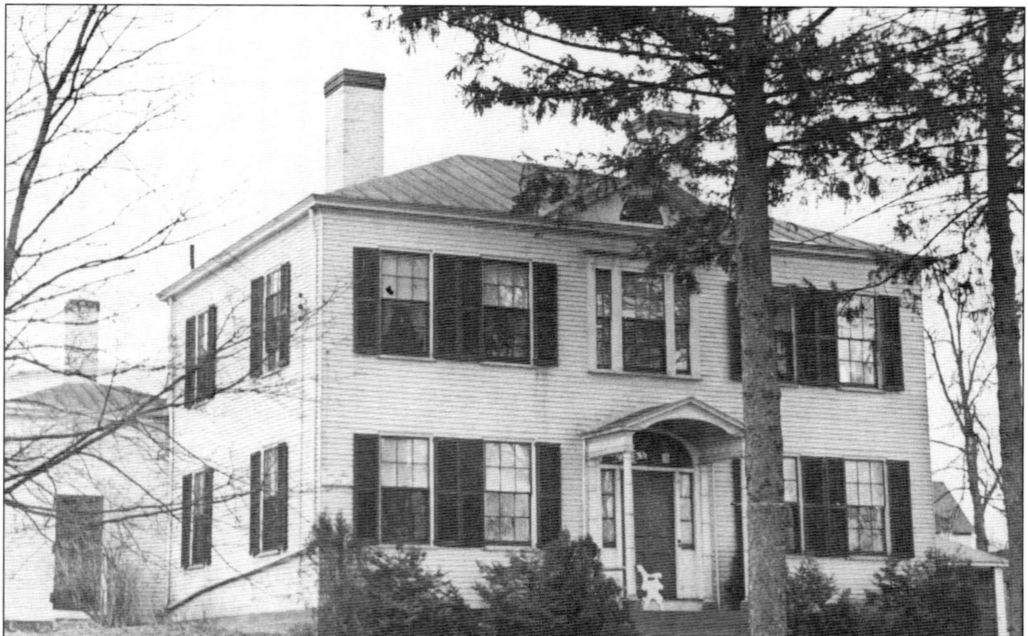

The house at 12 Washington Street was built in 1808. Horace Merriam lived here at the turn of the 20th century. He owned a grocery store on the east side of Main Street just south of Glastonbury Avenue. He was the great-great-grandson of Burrage Merriam, the second minister of the Rocky Hill Congregational Church.

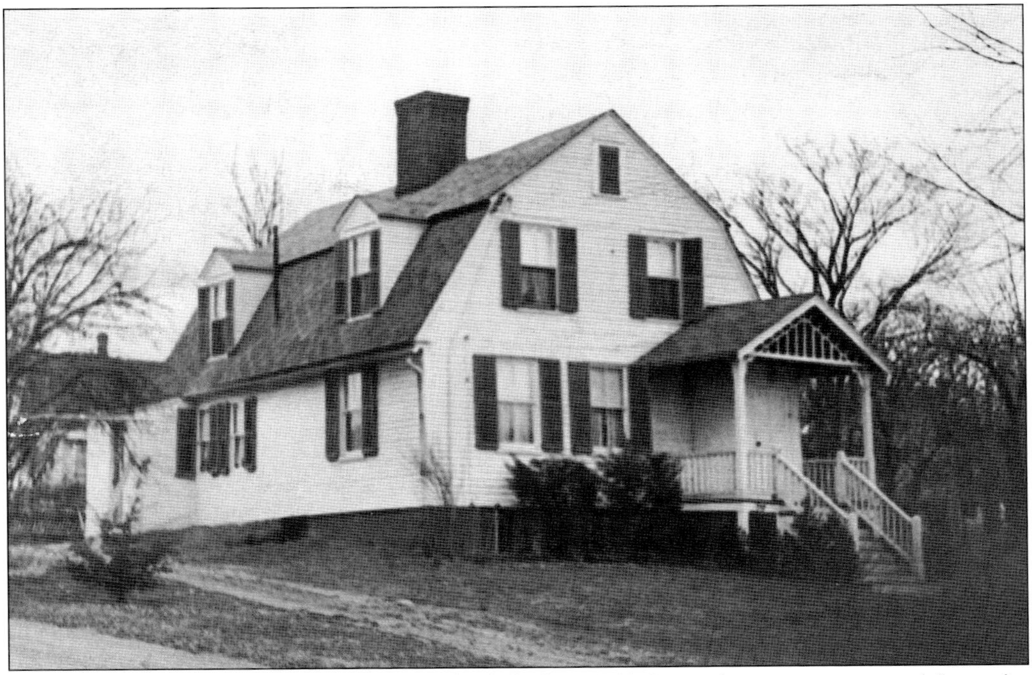

The house at 14 Washington Street was built before 1765. Legend says it was moved from the riverfront. The stoop facing the street was added because the original stoop on the side faced a proposed road from Belden Lane to Riverview Road that was never built. Blacksmiths James and Walter Wilcox lived here in the late 1800s. They were employed at the Welles and Wilcox Edge Tool Manufacturing Company on Dividend Brook.

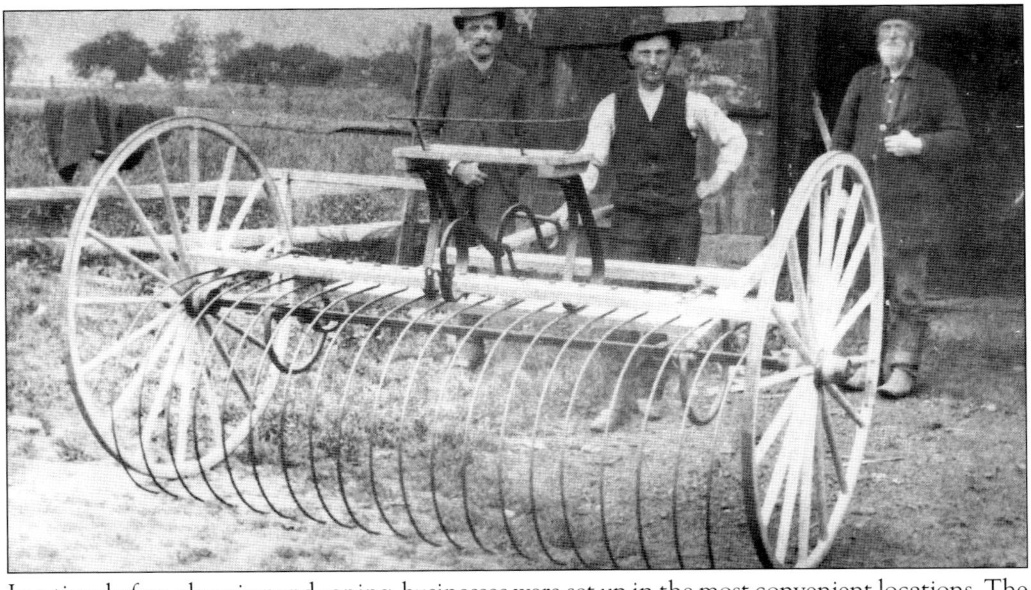

In a time before planning and zoning, businesses were set up in the most convenient locations. The Risleys lived at 17 Washington Street, and their blacksmith shop was at the corner of Washington Street and Glastonbury Avenue (then Ferry Road). George Risley Sr. is on the right, and George Risley Jr. is in shirt sleeves.

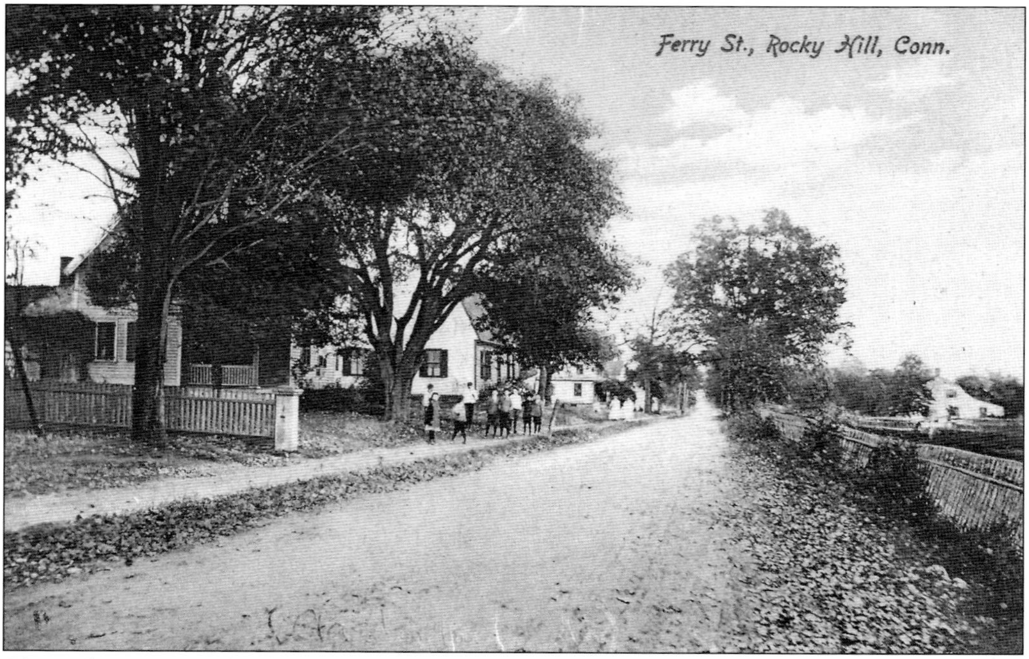

Glastonbury Avenue has been a main road to the riverfront and ferry from early times. It has been known as Griswold Lane and, more recently, Ferry Street. Today it is part of Connecticut Route 160. This picture was taken around 1911 from the corner of Main Street. Travelers on Route 160 are surprised by the choice of turning back or boarding the Rocky Hill Ferry and crossing the river.

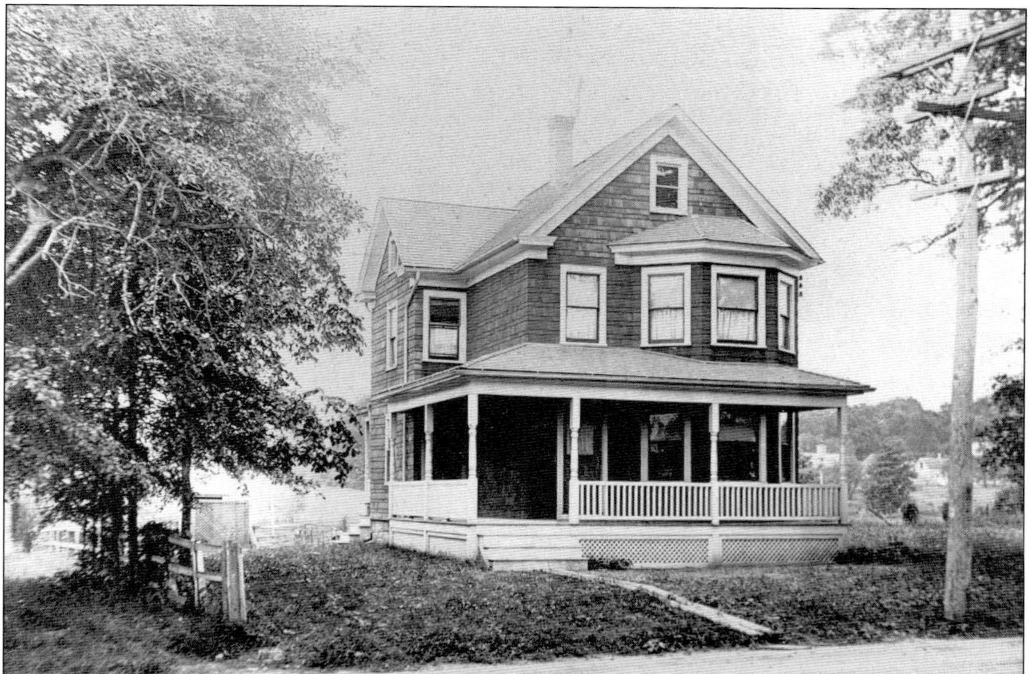

The Elwood Backe house, at 25 Glastonbury Avenue, was built in 1913 and is said to be the first house in Rocky Hill to have electricity. Elwood Backe was the stepson of noted Rocky Hill entrepreneur Elwood F. Belden. (Courtesy of Mike Martino.)

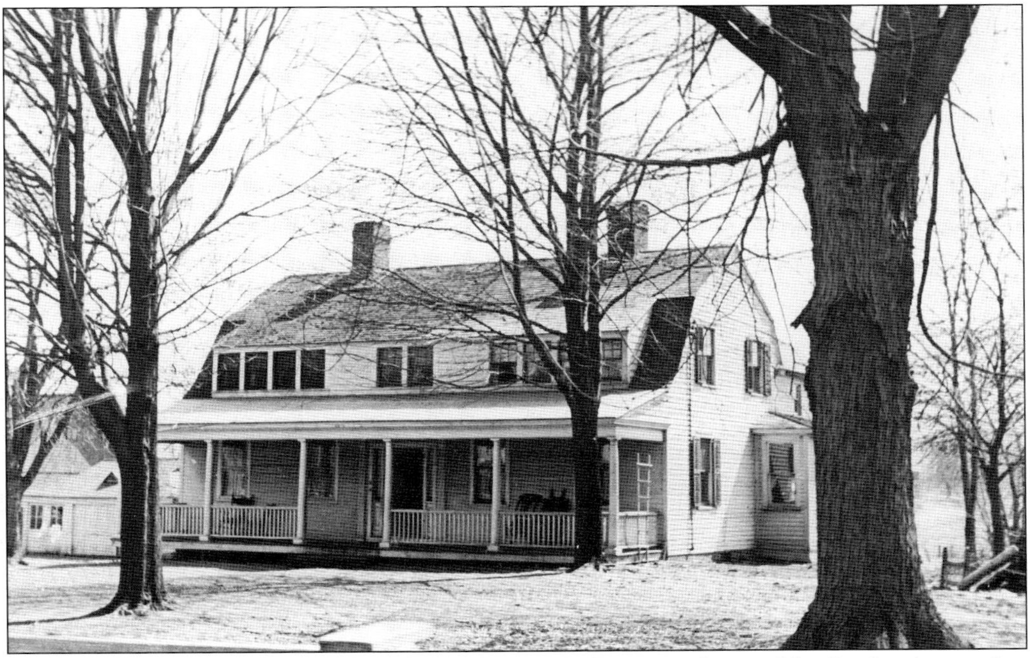

The Burdett house, at 29 Glastonbury Avenue, is a replacement for an older Burdett house that burned down. It is said to be an exact replica of the original. The original was a farmhouse built in 1892. There was once an extensive farm behind it. Today this is an apartment complex that has been converted to condominiums.

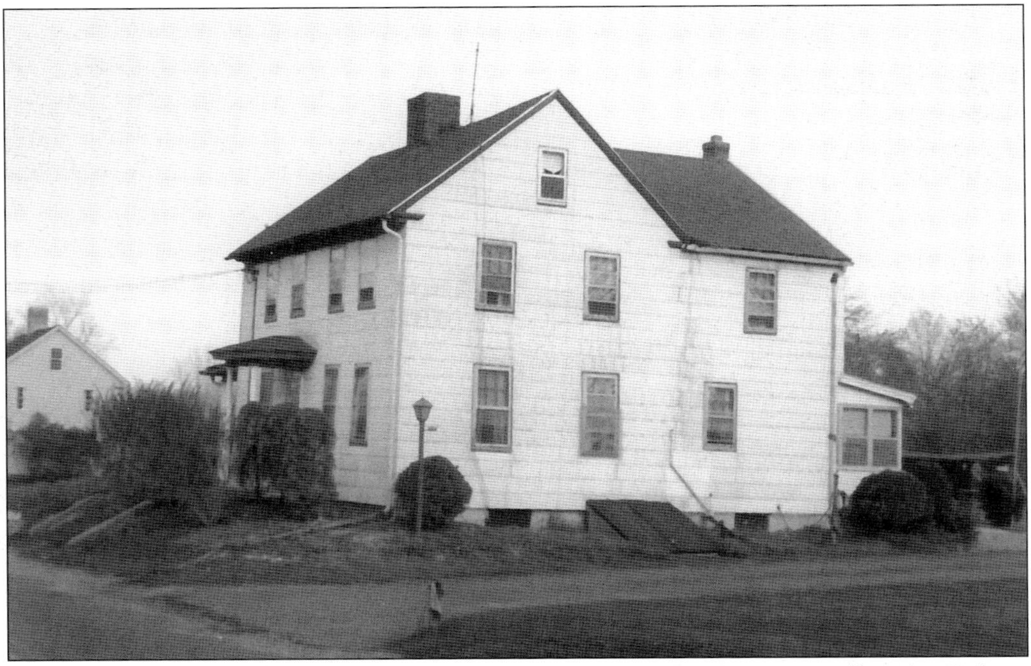

Nicholas Cady built 41 Glastonbury Avenue in 1770. The National Register calls it the William Bradley House, but William Bradford is the only owner in a title search with a similar name. In the 20th century, it was owned by World War I veteran Dominick Spadaccaini. He bought it in 1928, lost it to bankruptcy during the Depression in 1935, and regained ownership in 1947.

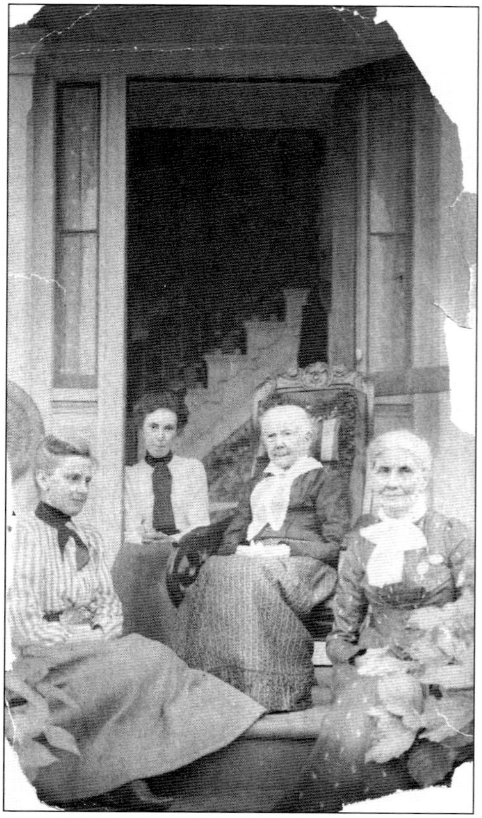

The house at 51 Glastonbury Avenue was built in 1800. It is called the Griswold House and was owned by Martin J. Griswold from 1874 until 1915. The doorway and staircase in this picture exactly match 51 Glastonbury Avenue as it appears today. The women, relatives of Martin J. Griswold, are Elizabeth Griswold, Mrs. Augustus Adams (née Martha Griswold), and "Ida" Mabel Adams, the daughter of Augustus Adams and Martha Griswold.

This photograph looks west up Pratt Street, once a favorite sledding site and for many years a major access route to the riverfront. The street was rerouted to the north when the railroad tracks came through. At one time, it ended on land granted to Thomas Williams in 1661 for a shipyard. Many descendants of Thomas Williams owned property at the east end of Pratt Street.

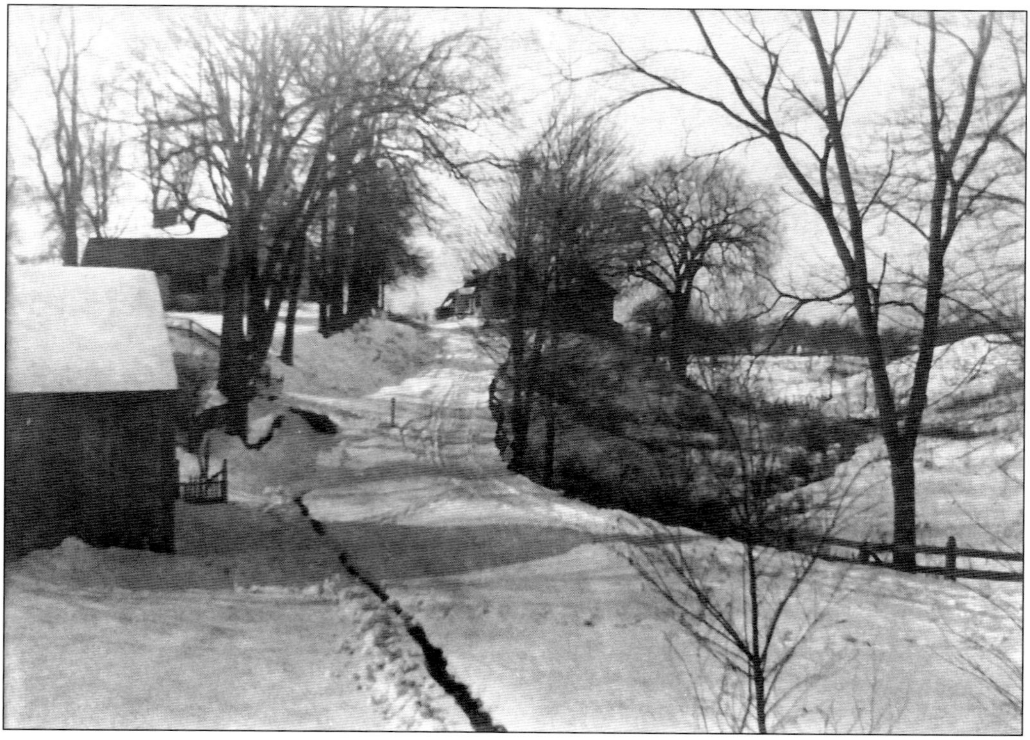

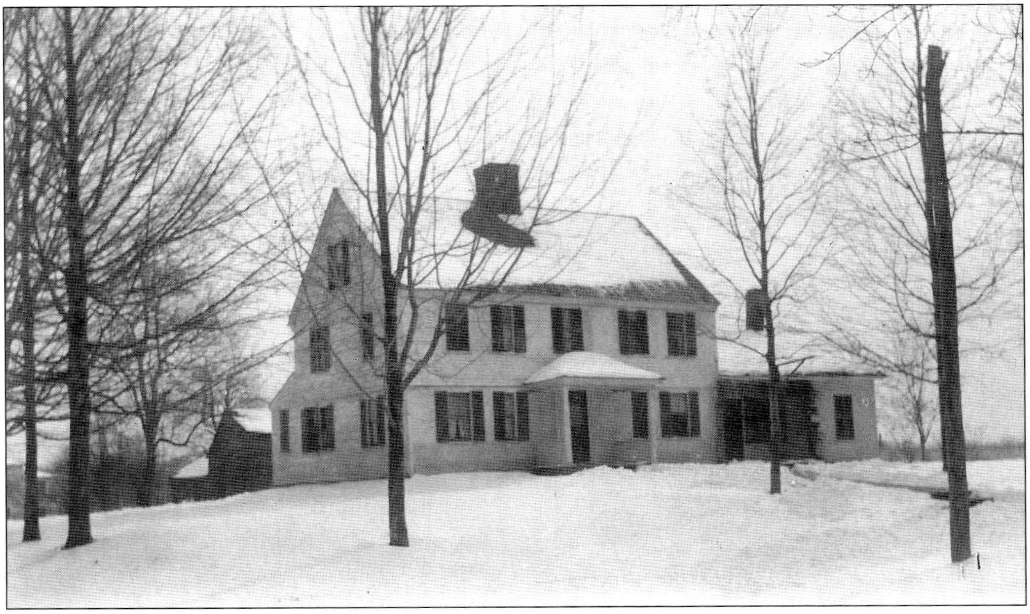

The house at 1 Pratt Street was built in 1716. It was the home of Benjamin and Mary Deming in 1730/31. Their daughter, Baby Deming, who died at birth, was the first person buried across Dividend Road in Center Cemetery. In 1760, it was owned by the sea captain and slave owner Elisha Williams. Charles Yeager, railroad agent, postmaster, and constable, owned the house in the first half of 20th century.

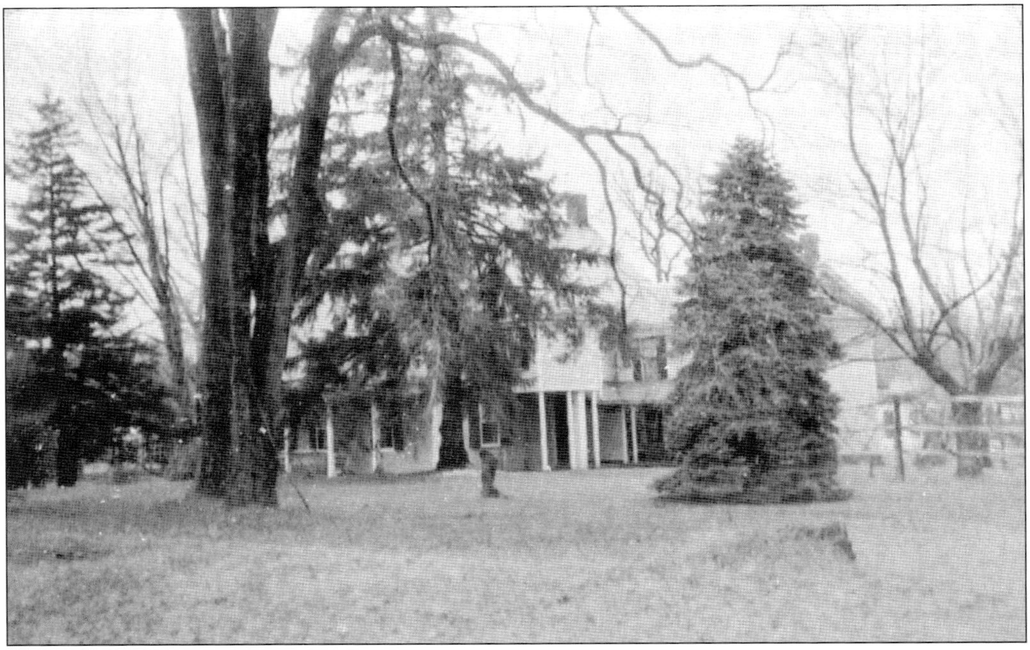

This was the Bulkeley Mansion, later the Edward Stevens Mansion. The house was razed in 1965. In 1971, W.T. Grant Plaza, which contained a large W.T. Grant's store, a post office annex, and a bank, was opened on this site. The shopping center was abandoned in 1974. The land was bought by Ames Department Stores, which operated its headquarters here until it was abandoned in 2002. (Courtesy of Mike Martino.)

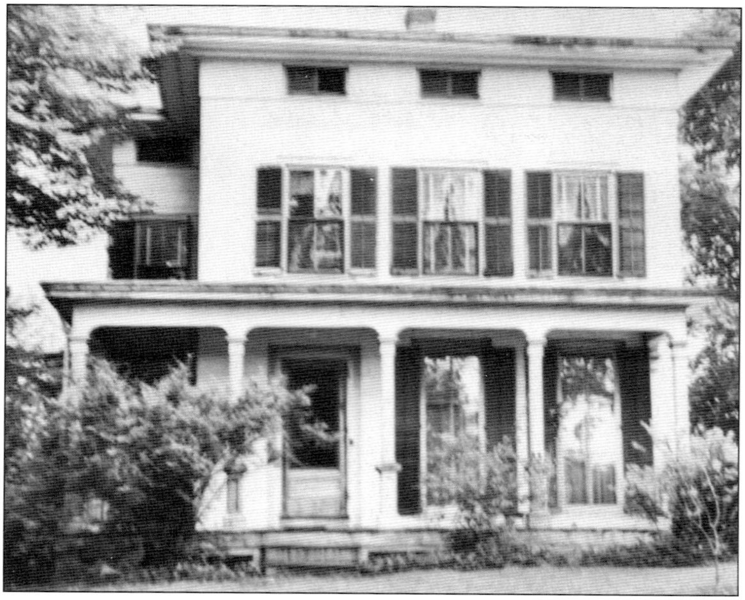

The home at 11 Pratt Street was built in 1805. It was acquired by James Halligan, an Irish immigrant, who willed it to his son Frank in 1896. Lawrence Kelley owned it until 1930. He sold it to Emma Bennett. She sold it to Henri Merineau in 1949. His daughter Yvette married Chester Lane, who lived at 22 Pratt Street, in 1936. Their daughter Nancy married Douglas Robbins of the historic Robbins family.

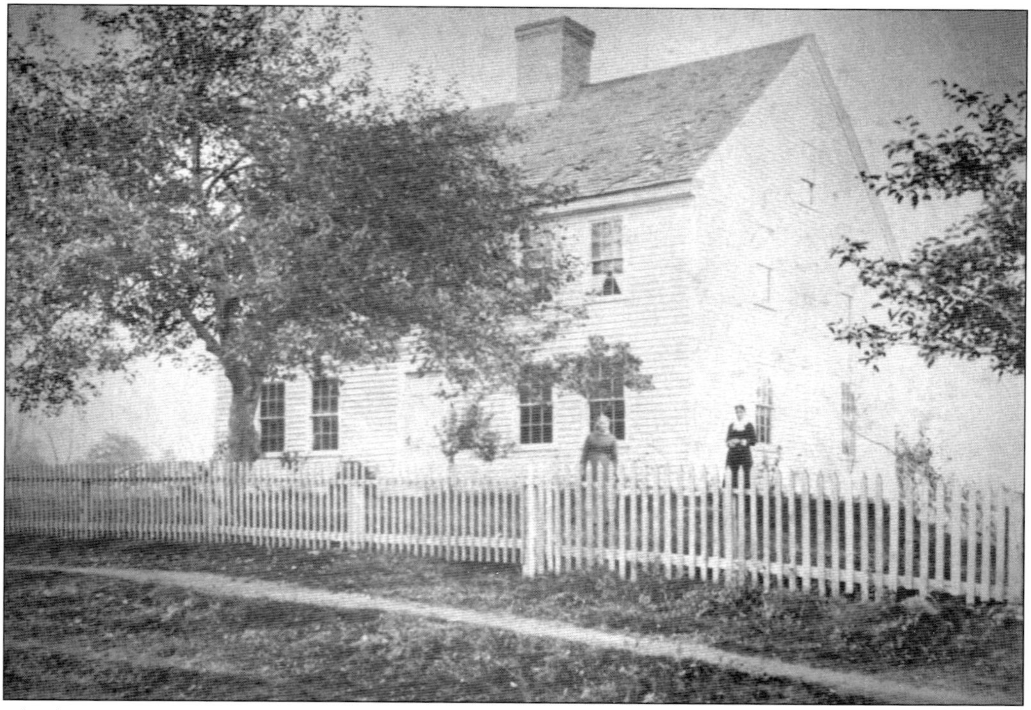

The house at 22 Pratt Street was built in 1800. The Thayer family acquired it in 1844. Abigail Thayer married William LeVaugh, and this became the LeVaugh house in 1855. The LeVaugh family sent three sons to the Civil War. The Lane family bought the house in 1919 and lived here until 1930, when they sold it. They bought the house back in 1945 and lived here until 1999.

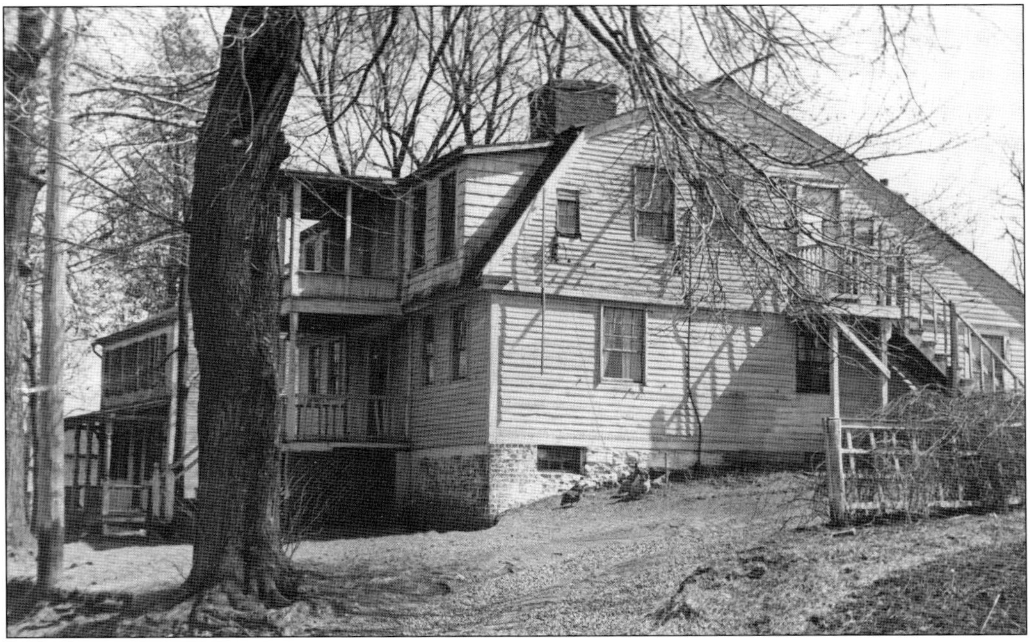

The house at 53 Pratt Street was built in 1770 for Elijah Hinsdale. It was owned by Dr. Joseph Higgins in 1794. Dr. Higgins was a member of the Hartford County Medical Society when he died of consumption (tuberculosis). He was married to Nancy Williams, the third great-granddaughter of Thomas Williams. The house is greatly changed today. The porch and dormers, which weren't original to the house, are gone.

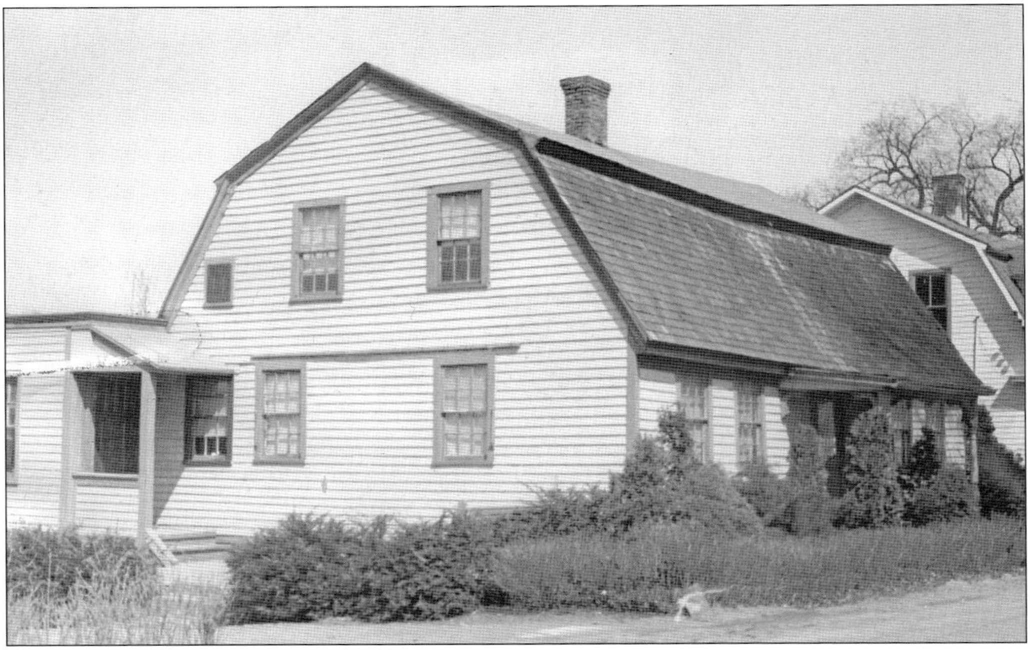

Samuel Williams built 54 Pratt Street in 1745. Legend claims it was moved here from the riverfront. William Dickenson of Farmington, Connecticut, took ownership in 1763. He deeded the property to his brothers George and Noadiah Dickinson in 1767 with the proviso that Sarah, widow of Samuel Williams, had use of half the house during her lifetime.

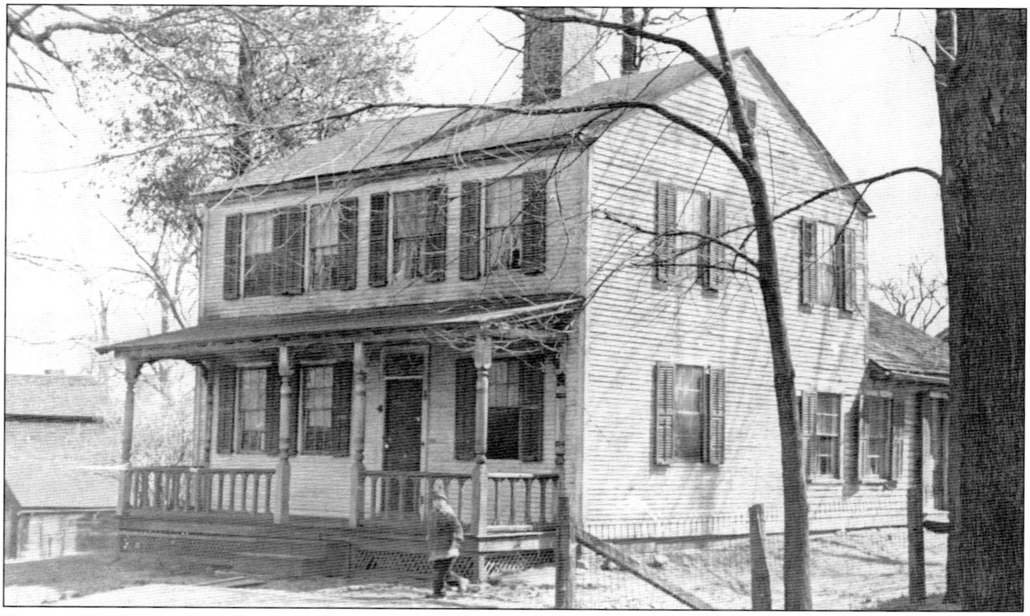

Daniel Williams was the grandson of Thomas Williams, grantee of the first shipyard. Daniel built the house at 55 Pratt Street in 1749 and sold it in 1792 to Hezekiah Whitmore, a shipwright. He built the schooners *Friendship* and *Brutus* and was master of the Middletown-built schooner *Caret*. Robert Sugden Jr. owned the house in 1869, possibly as an investment. Sugden was co-owner of the Pleasant Valley Foundry at Dividend Brook.

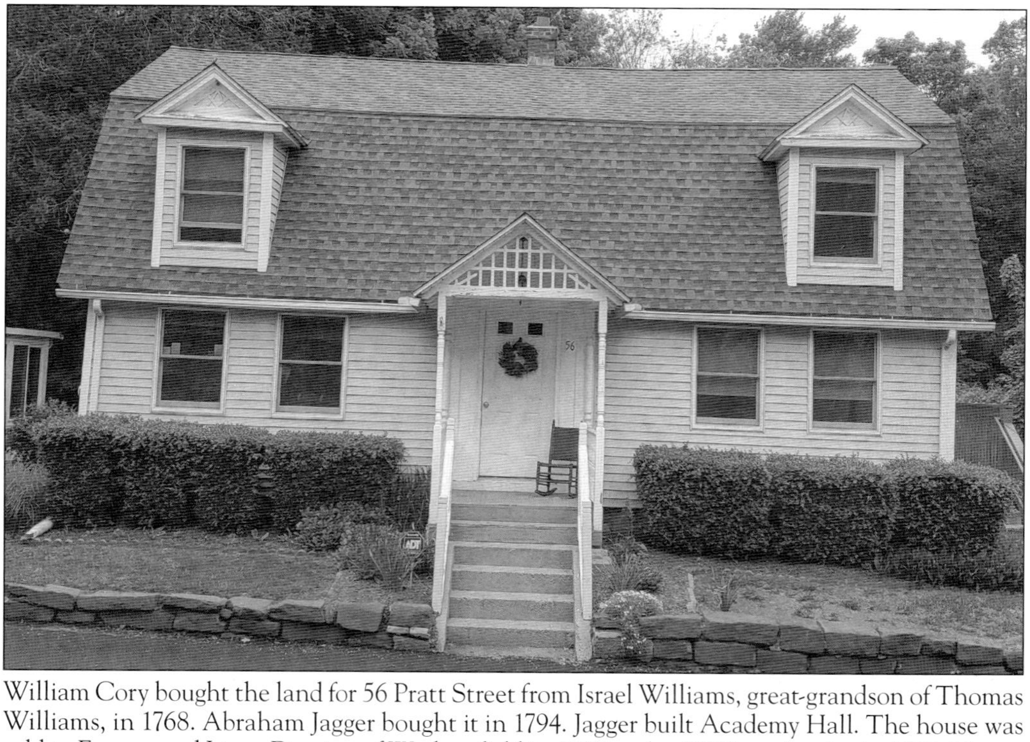

William Cory bought the land for 56 Pratt Street from Israel Williams, great-grandson of Thomas Williams, in 1768. Abraham Jagger bought it in 1794. Jagger built Academy Hall. The house was sold to Erastus and Linus Deming of Wethersfield in 1830 and to William Appley in 1889. Notice the Masonic symbols in the dormers. Masonic rites were held in this house during the 1890s.

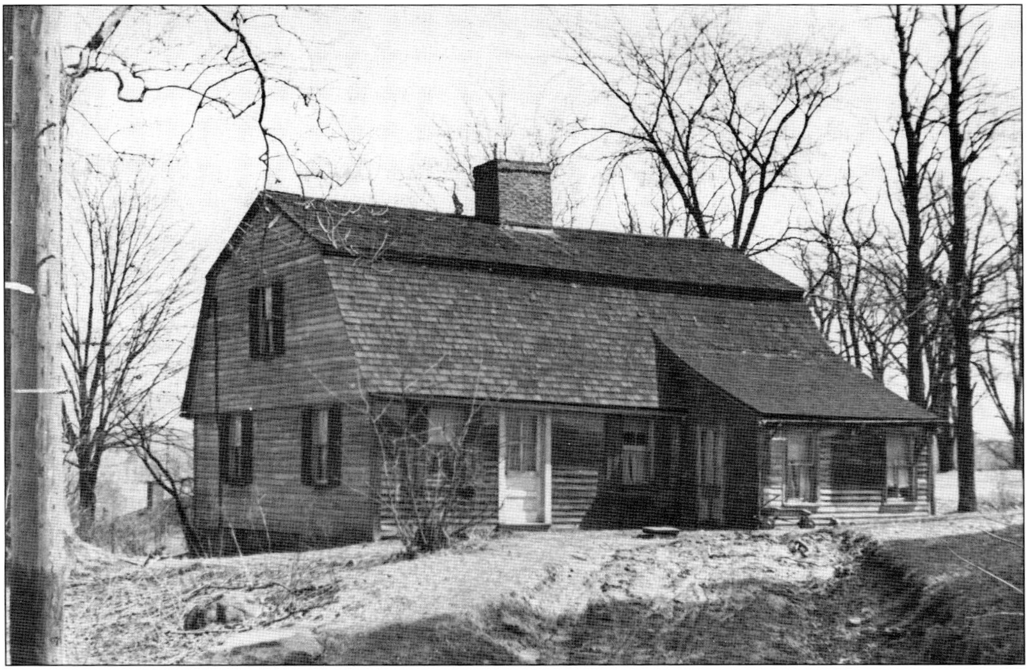

The house at 57 Pratt Street was built in 1730. This land was deeded to Daniel Williams by his brother Ephriam in 1724. The original deeded land ran down to the Connecticut River and must have included the Thomas Williams Shipyard.

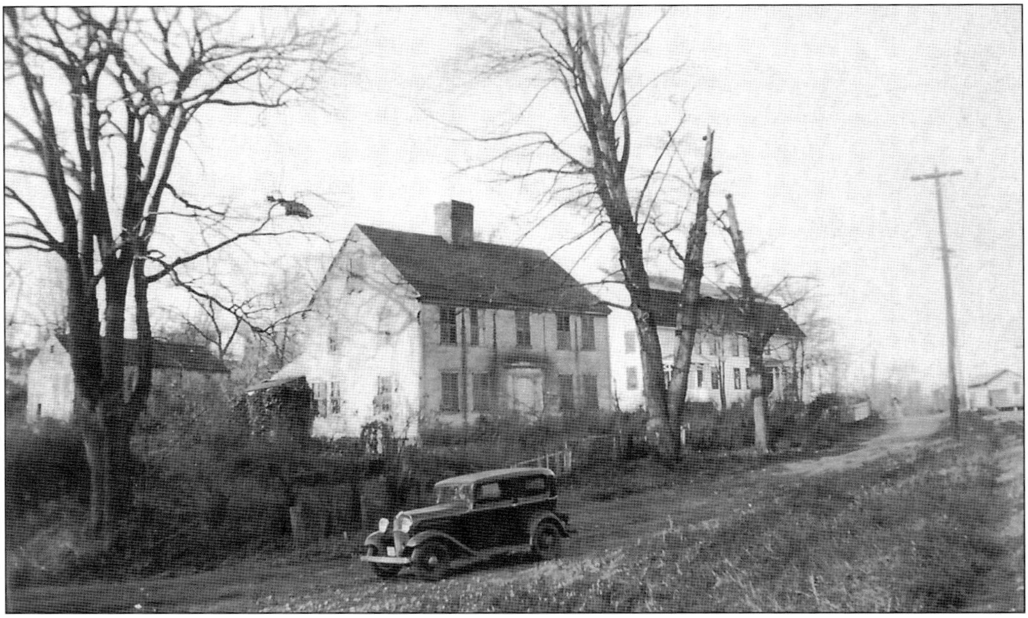

Jacob Williams, the first owner of 72 Pratt Street, was a sea captain and ship owner. The house was partially built from an old ship. In 1934, a jar was found containing a history of this house written in 1884 by Mary Ann Grimes. She was a spiritualist and promised to be present when the jar was opened. It is unknown if she showed up.

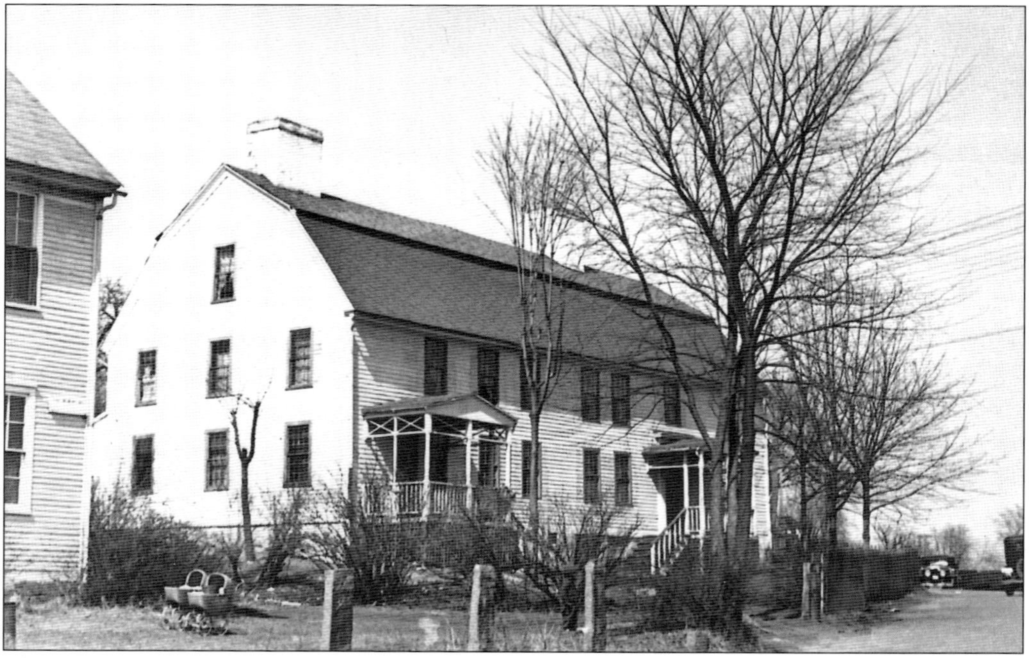

This house was built in 1754 by Oliver Pomeroy, a Rocky Hill Revolutionary War sea captain. He became a tavern owner and store keeper. Polly Dickinson owned it at one time. She was renowned for parties, including sleigh parties ranging around the river towns, apparently involving lots of drinking and good times. The house was moved to Sherborn, Massachusetts, in 1938.

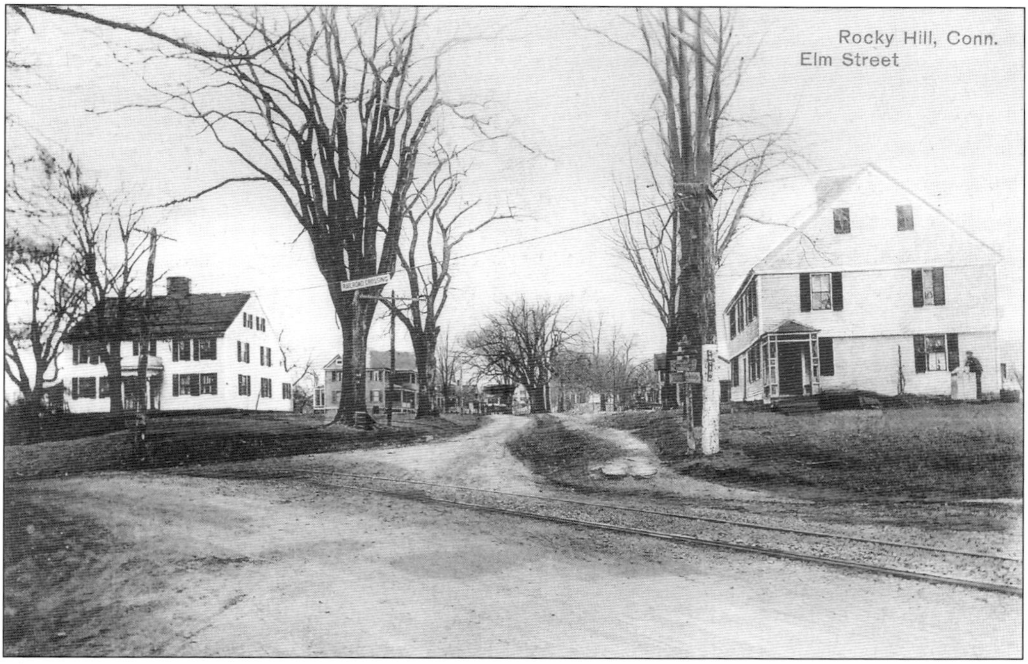

Elm Street forms the middle section of Connecticut Route 160 in Rocky Hill. For much of its history, Elm Street was dotted with Colonial farm houses that were once backed by farms. At least one large schooner was built on Elm Street and transported, with great difficulty, to the river.

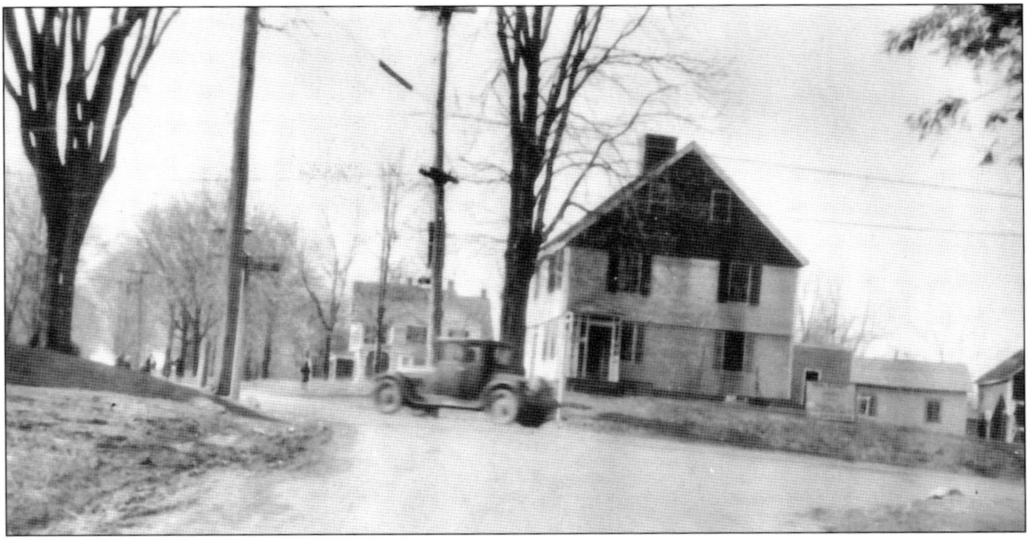

This photograph shows the east side of the McNamara house, at the northwest corner of Main and Elm Streets. It was the first house in Rocky Hill to have a telephone. It was torn down around 1930 in preparation for the Silas Deane Highway. The land where the house once stood is now in the middle of the highway. (Courtesy of Mike Martino.)

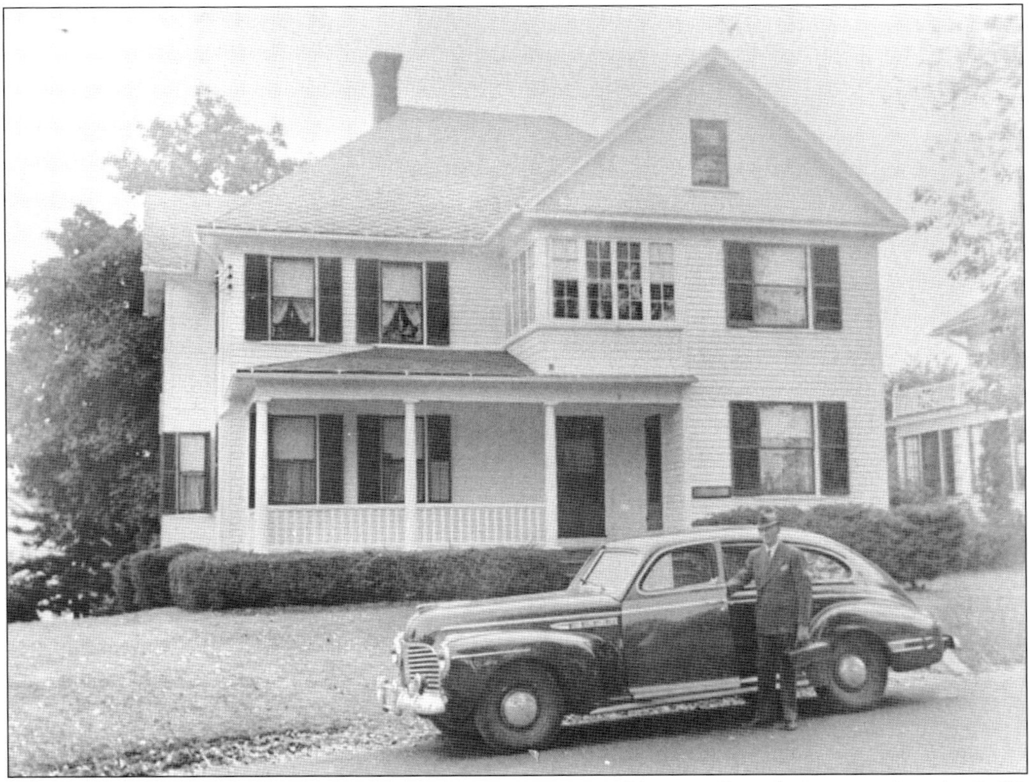

This house was the home and office of Dr. Oran Moser and his son David. Oran was Rocky Hill's beloved country doctor from 1903 to 1953. David took over his practice in the second half of the 20th century and also served as Rocky Hill's first mayor when the town went from a selectman to a mayor/town manager form of government in 1967. (Courtesy of Mike Martino.)

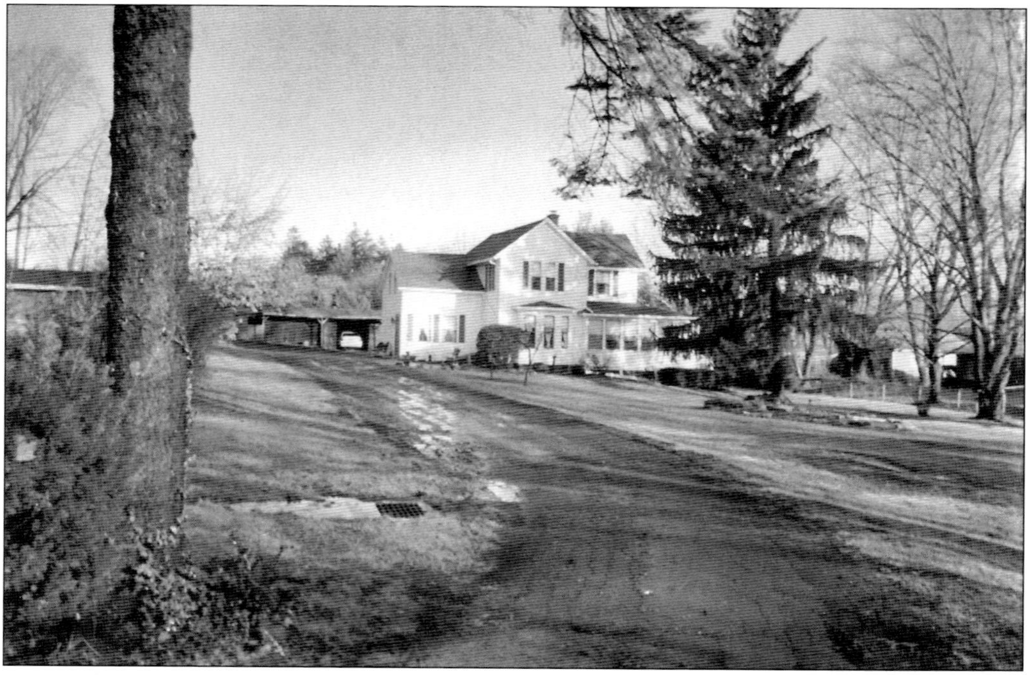

Dan Taylor owned 53 Elm Street. When Captain Dan was a ferryman in the US Army, he guarded the Apache chief Geronimo on Angel Island in San Francisco Bay. During the 1936 Connecticut River flood, he was washed out into the river on the Rocky Hill Ferry, which was tethered by a tenuous mooring line. He was marooned without food or water for several days before being rescued.

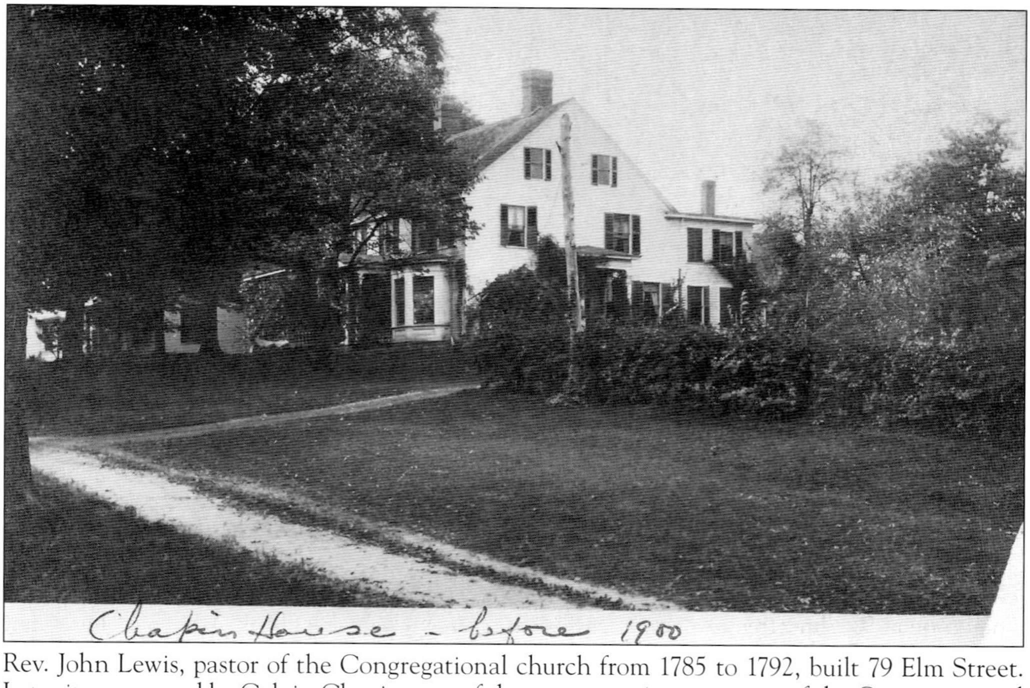

Rev. John Lewis, pastor of the Congregational church from 1785 to 1792, built 79 Elm Street. Later it was owned by Calvin Chapin, one of the most prominent pastors of the Congregational church, who made many contributions to Rocky Hill. This photograph was taken about 1902.

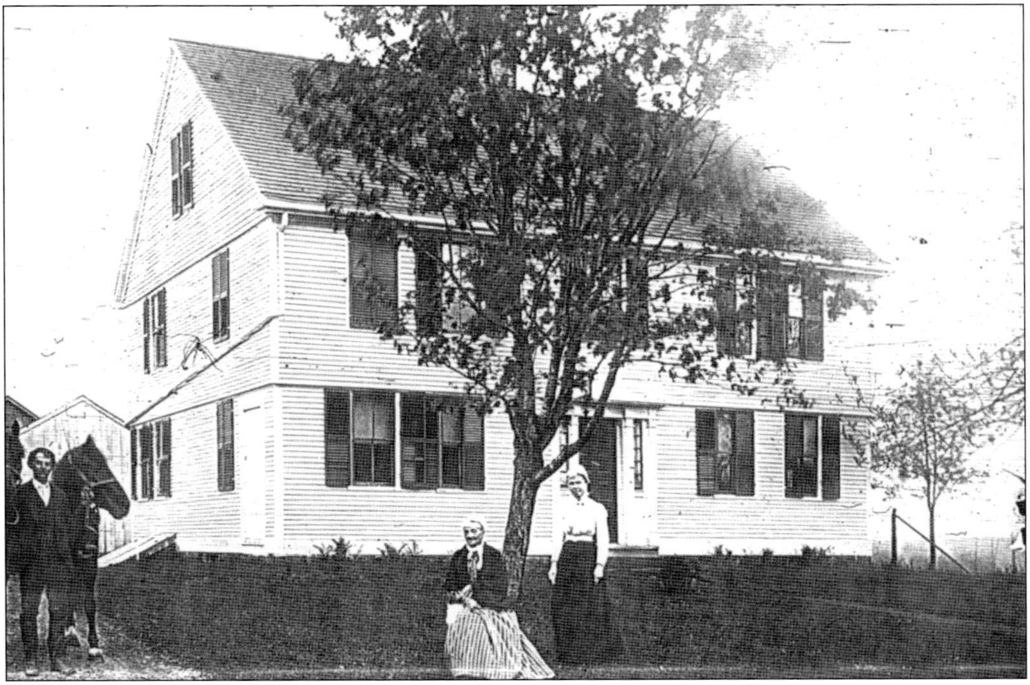

Eliel Williams, slave owner Elias Williams's son, built 82 Elm Street in 1769. A hidden space in the attic may have been used as a hiding place on the Underground Railroad (there seems to have been a difference of opinion in the family about slavery). This was later the home of Alice Williams, an honored school teacher in Rocky Hill who lived to be 103.

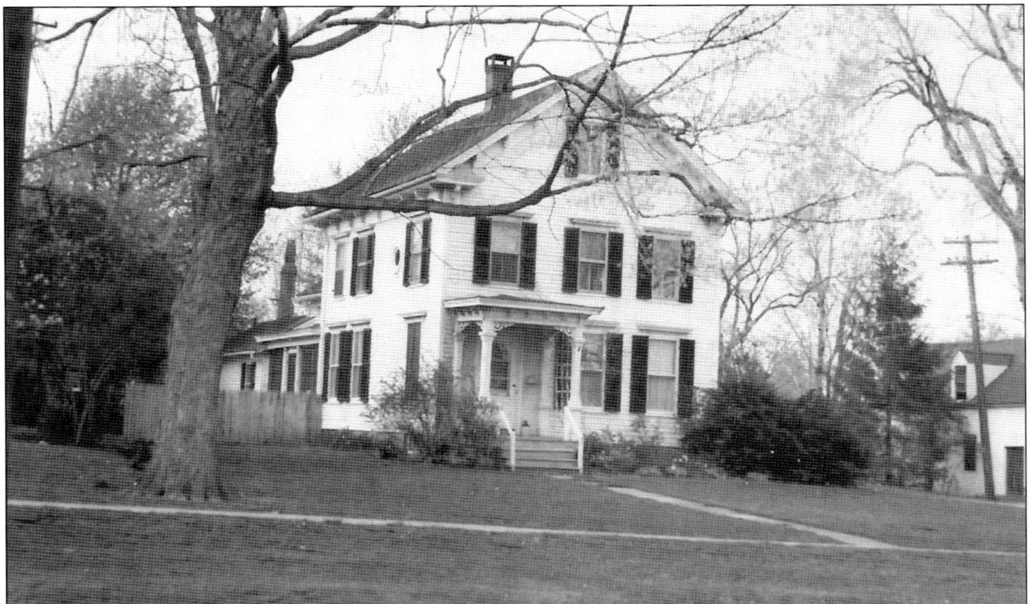

The house at 93 Elm Street was built in 1860. Its owner, Samuel Ashwell, served in the Union cavalry during the Civil War. He was taken prisoner in Virginia. Paroled due to poor health, he returned to Rocky Hill and became a prosperous farmer. He occupied many positions in the town government. The street across from his house is named Ashwell Avenue in his honor.

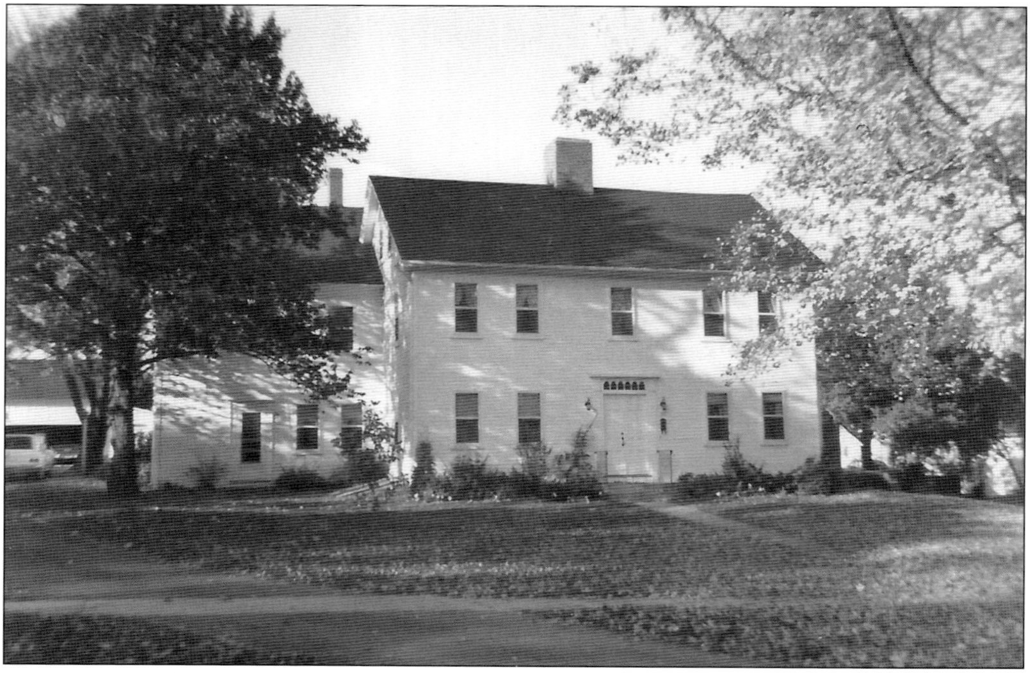

The house at 103 Elm Street was built in 1808 and was once the farmhouse for a large farm. Washington Williams owned this house in the late 19th century. He was the son of Eliel Williams, who built 82 Elm Street. It was owned by Frank Churchill in the first half of the 20th century. Churchill was a prosperous farmer and volunteer fireman, held several town positions, and served in Connecticut's general assembly.

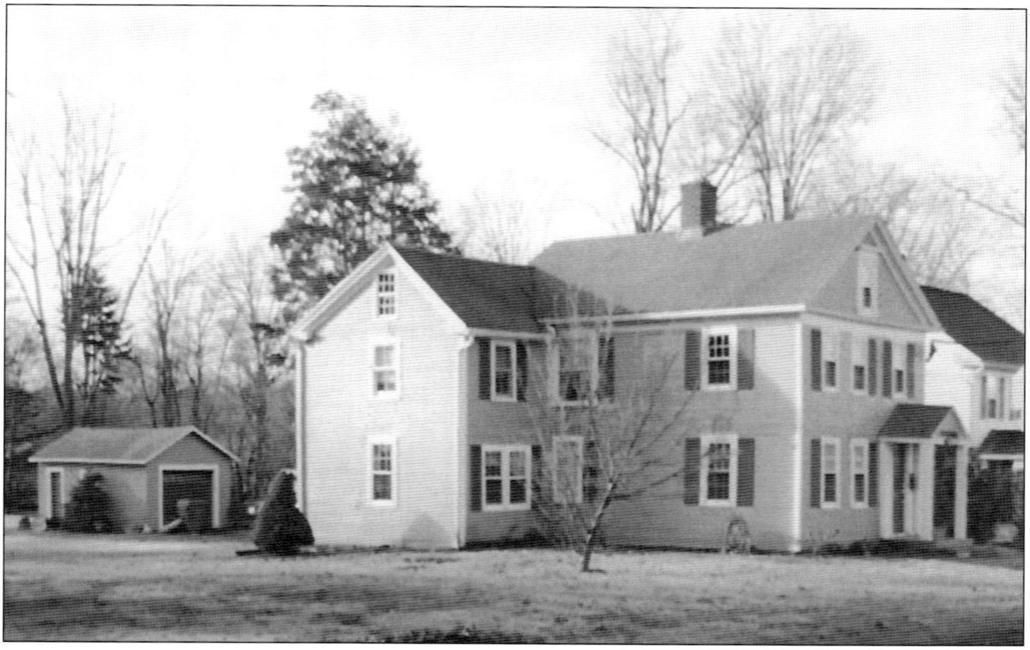

The Dimock family has owned 150 Elm Street since it was built in 1844. The siding at the back of the house came from the old Congregational church, which was demolished to make way for the current church in 1808.

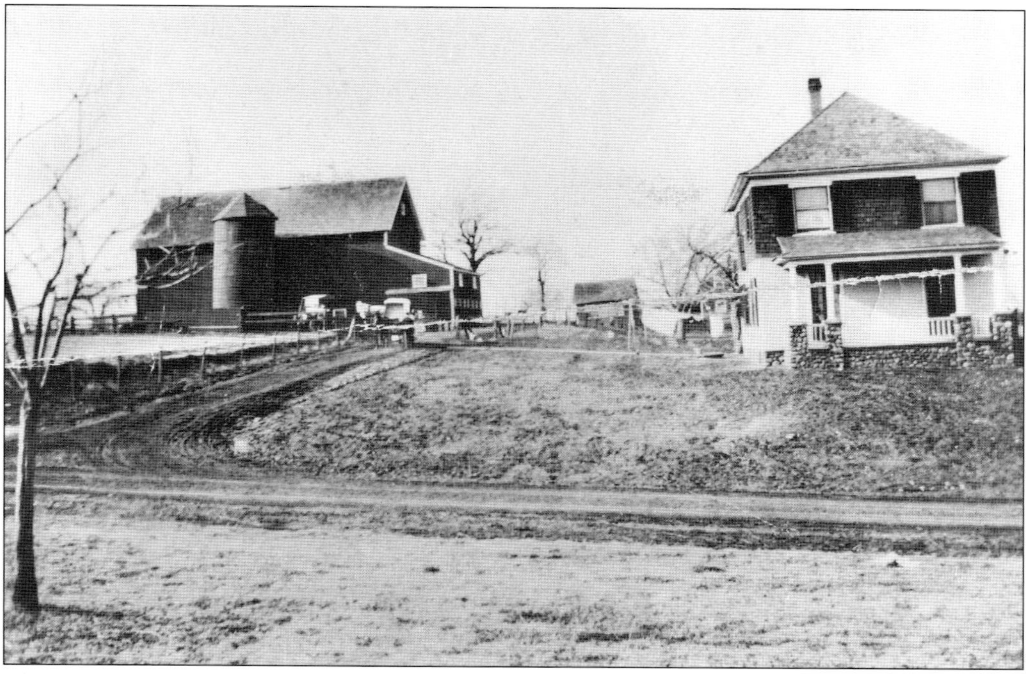

The Gilbert farmhouse, at 730 Elm Street, belonged to Charles S. Gilbert and was located at the northeast corner of the Elm Street and Gilbert Avenue intersection. The house still exists today. (Courtesy of Mike Martino.)

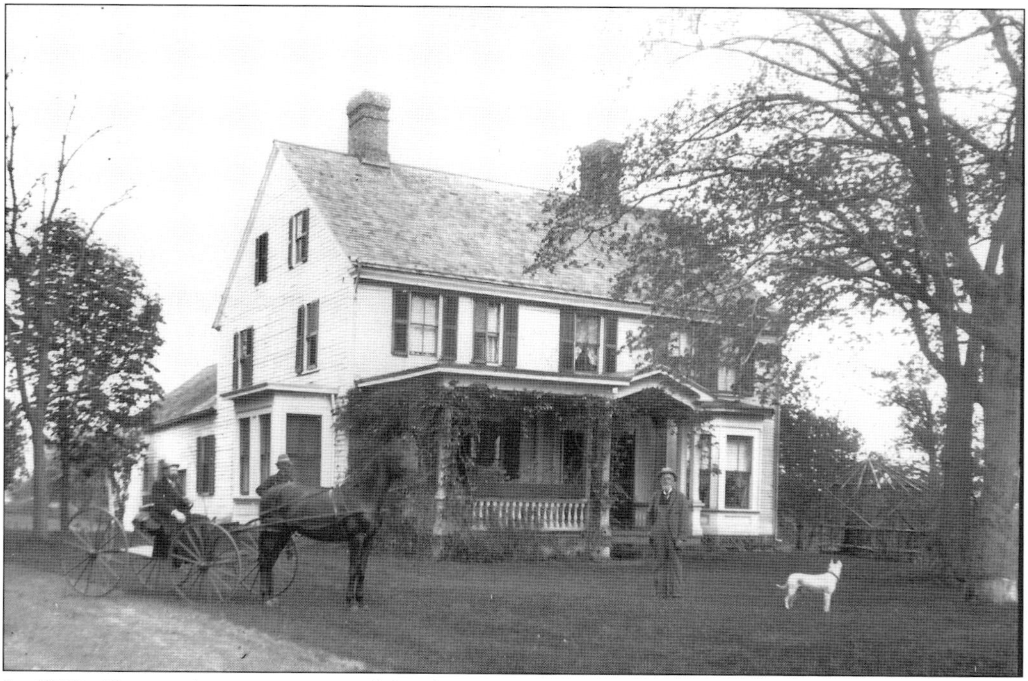

In 1903, Chapin Avenue contained five houses. It was a gravel road that ran from Elm Street to modern Mountain View Drive. The Sunnycrest Trust sold several building lots on Chapin Avenue in 1953. This may have resulted in the street going through to Parsonage Street. Today, the street serves as the staging area for town events such as the Memorial Day parade.

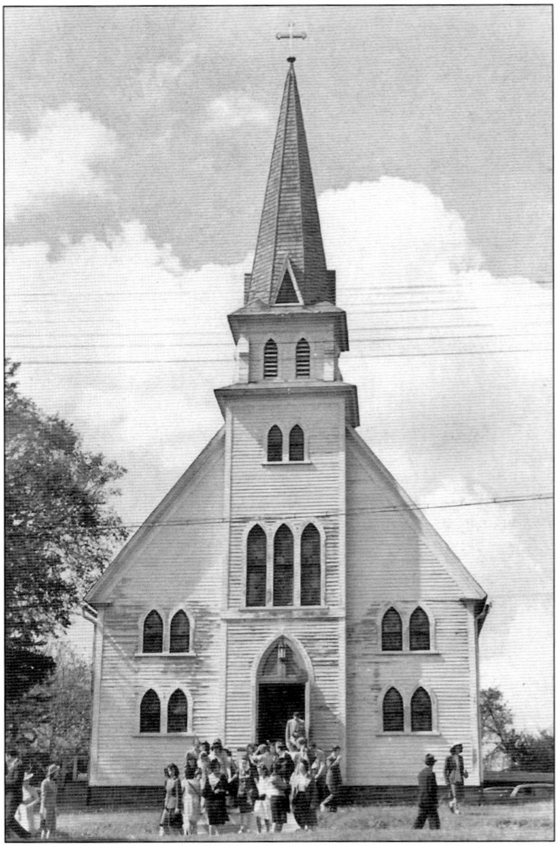

St. James Roman Catholic Church was dedicated in 1883 on the lot south of 12 Chapin Avenue. It was an inconvenience for many farm workers who lived on Parsonage Street, because Chapin Avenue ended at Mountain View Road. It was necessary to drive down to the "center" and up Elm Street to St. James Church. The church relocated to Elm Street in 1961.

This house was built in 1880. The number on the house is 17 Chapin Avenue, but its tax address is 2245 Silas Deane Highway. A private road next to the house runs east past several commercial buildings to the highway. The house once belonged to the Elmore family, and the industrial buildings belonged to the Elmore Company, which made concrete structures, primarily burial vaults.

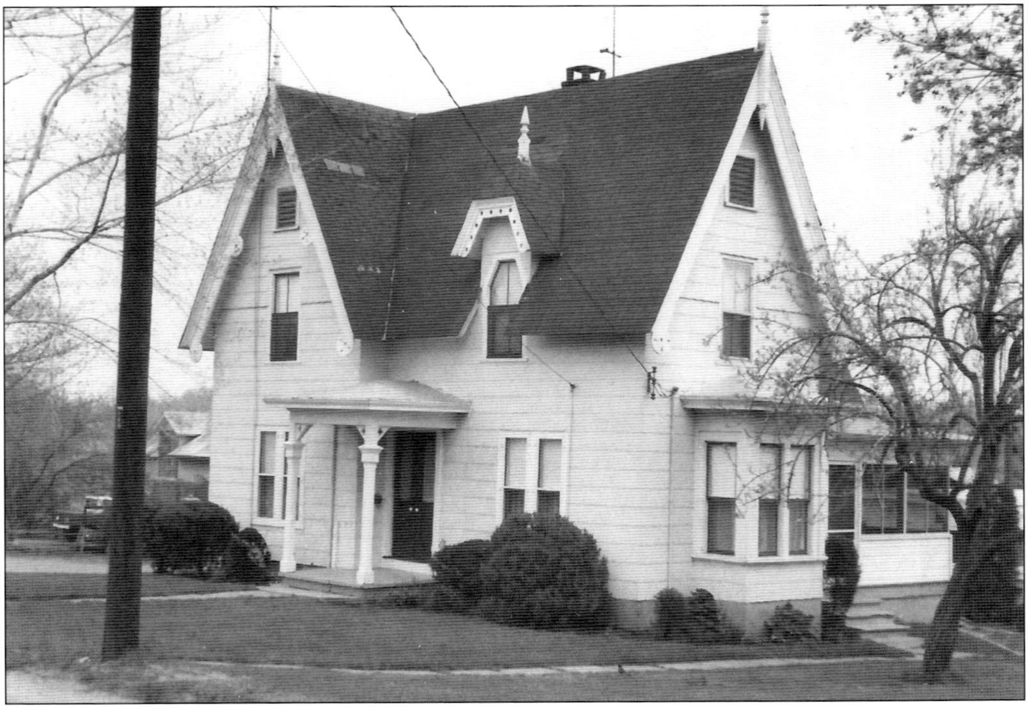

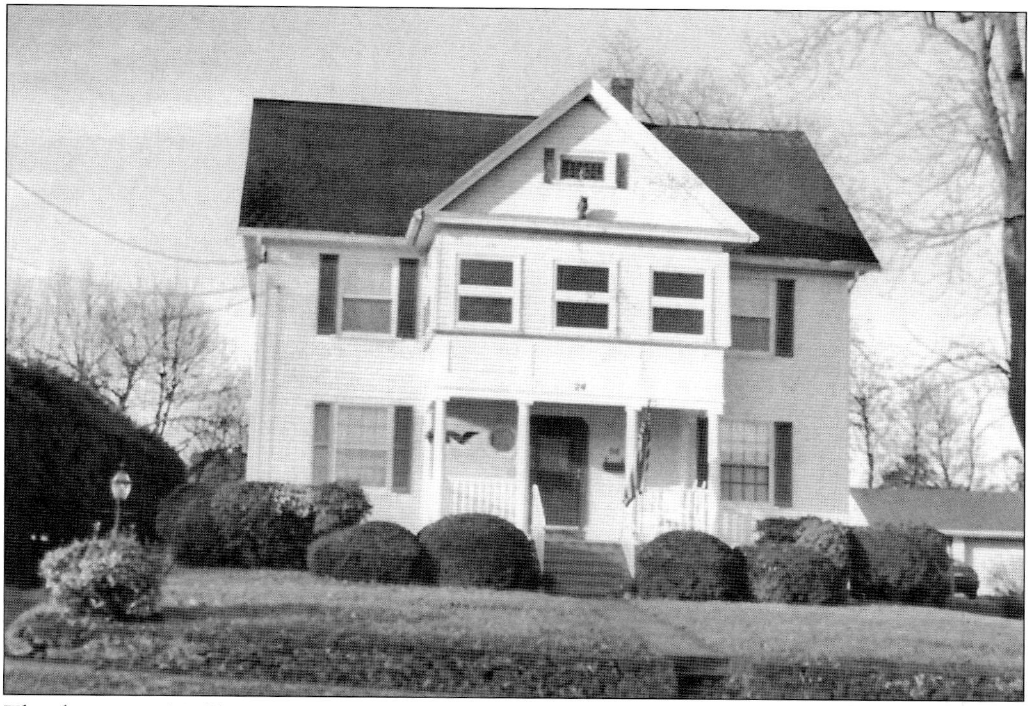

This house at 24 Chapin Avenue was built in 1908 as a memorial for the 100th anniversary of the construction of the present Congregational church. Pastor Frank P. Waters was its first occupant. The house served as lodgings for the pastors from 1908 until 1967, when the church sold it as a private residence.

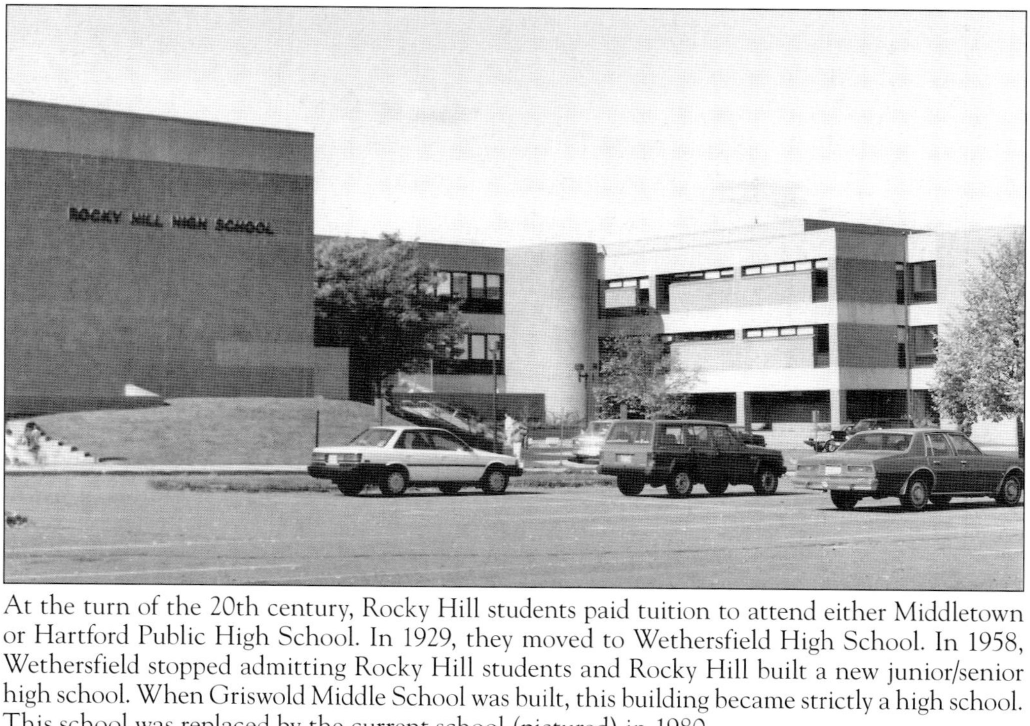

At the turn of the 20th century, Rocky Hill students paid tuition to attend either Middletown or Hartford Public High School. In 1929, they moved to Wethersfield High School. In 1958, Wethersfield stopped admitting Rocky Hill students and Rocky Hill built a new junior/senior high school. When Griswold Middle School was built, this building became strictly a high school. This school was replaced by the current school (pictured) in 1980.

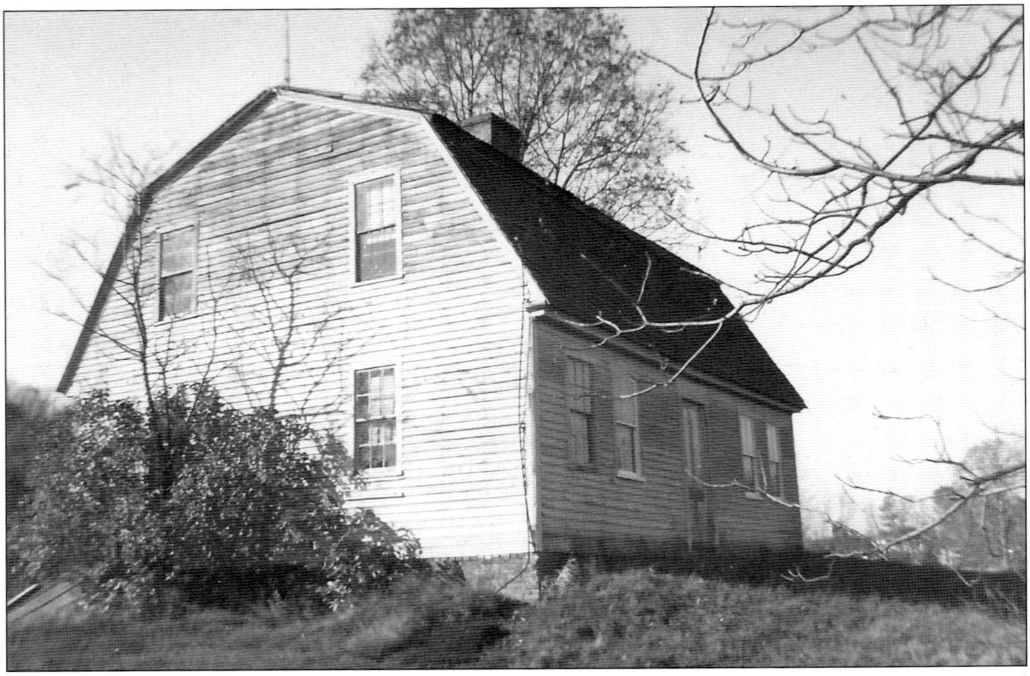

The house at 1 Webster Lane was built in 1730. It is known as the Webster House and was located on the Webster farm off Elm Street. The gambrel Cape section still exists, although the size of the house has doubled due to modern additions.

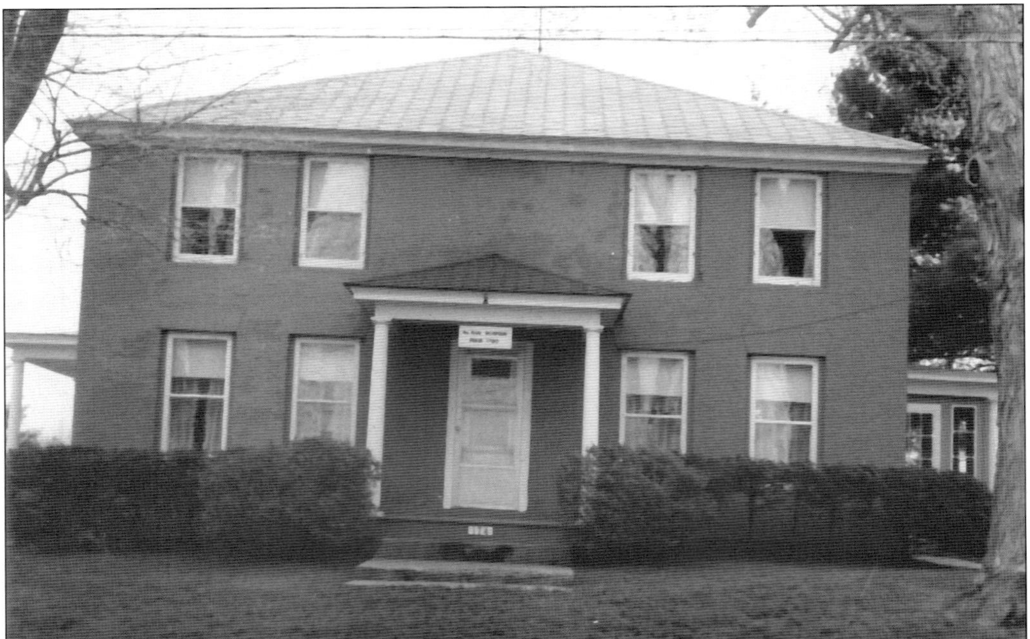

When the Rocky Hill Congregational Church was established in 1722, a grant of 60 acres was made for parsonage land, including a lane that is now Parsonage Street. Until the 1960s, much of the land along Parsonage Street was occupied by farms. Elias Dickinson built 174 Parsonage Street (pictured) in 1790. He acquired the land from Samuel Boardman to settle a debt.

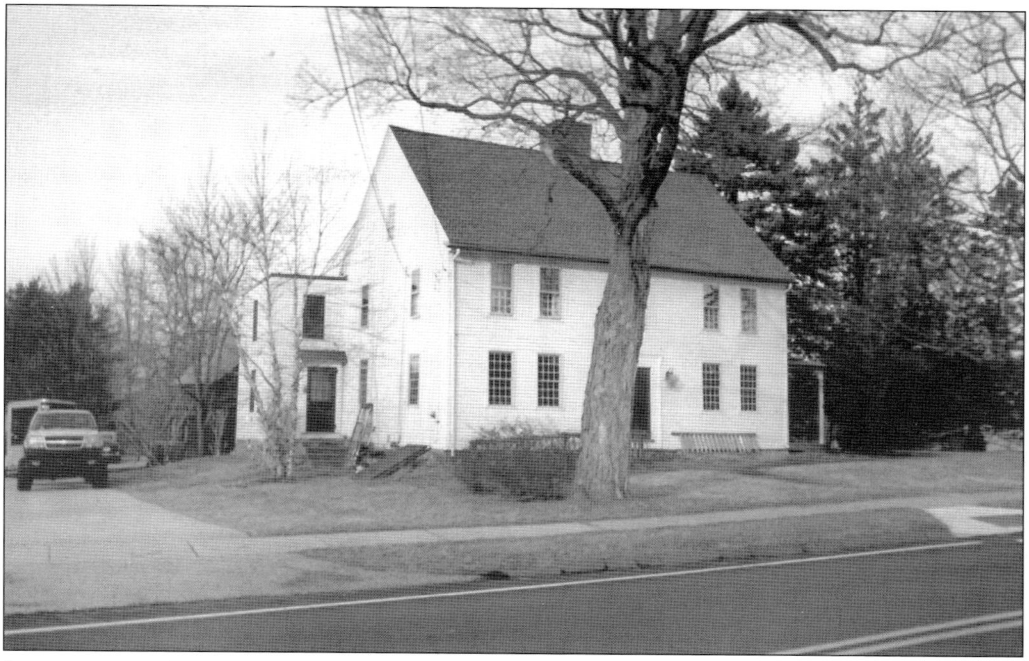

Per town records, 189 Parsonage Street was built in 1790. It was Horatio Robbins's farmhouse in the mid-19th century. He willed it to his son Russell in 1860. Russell sold it to Albert Deming Griswold in 1864, and it became the William F. Griswold farmhouse in 1898. In the 1960s, the farm was sold for private housing and public use.

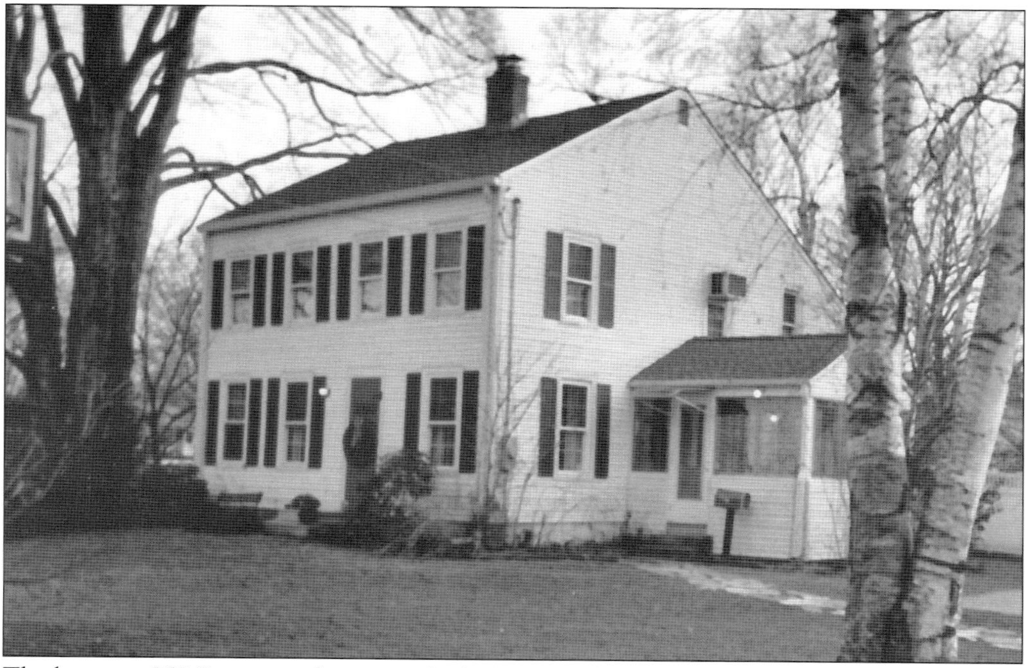

The house at 250 Parsonage Street was built in 1856. The property was originally on an 11-acre tract of farmland. It was sold to Jeremiah Murphy in 1864 and stayed in the Murphy family until 1906. Jeremiah's wife, Margaret McCarthy Murphy, quit claimed the property to Ellen Connery, her niece, reserving life use for herself. The land was subdivided into building lots in 1937.

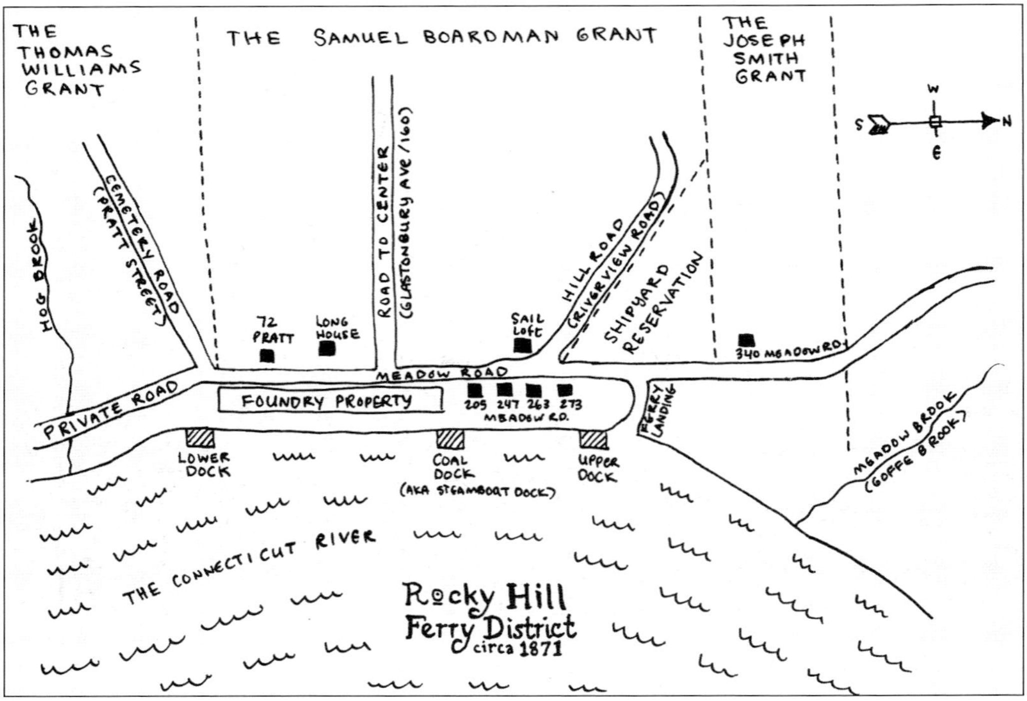

Wethersfield ceded four land grants in this area between 1650 and 1667: the Samuel Boardman Grant, the Thomas Williams Grant, the Joseph Smith Grant, and the Shipyard Reservation. Over time, these grants, except for the Shipyard Reservation, were divided into smaller parcels. This map is a work in progress, is not to scale, and will change based on further research. (Courtesy of Jennifer Duff Creations.)

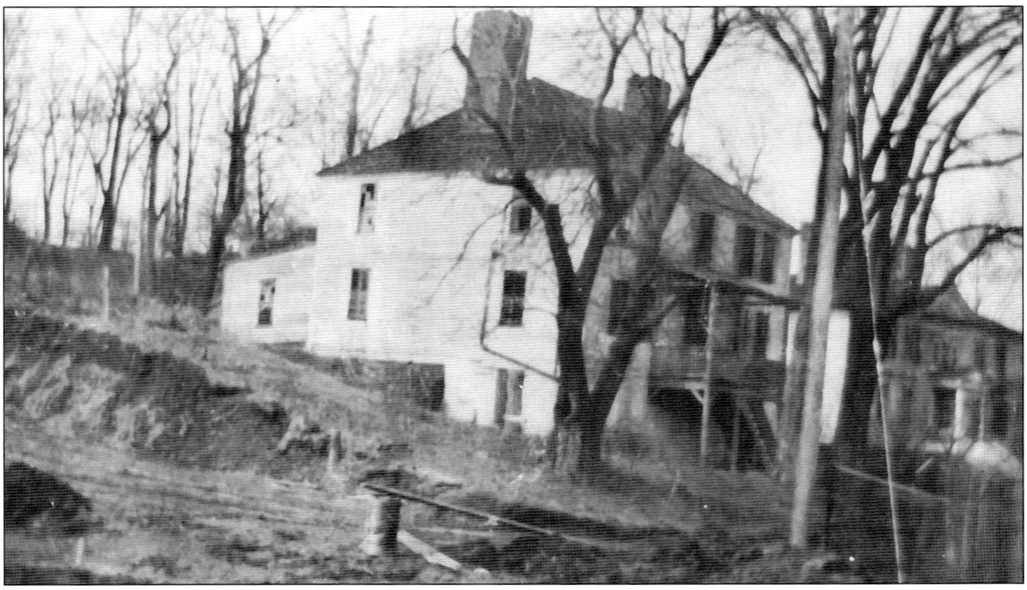

This house north of Hog Brook was built for Asa Deming in 1785 and was owned by several shipbuilders, including Deming (around 1800) and Seabury Belden (around 1900). Its last owner in Connecticut was Winfield Honiss. In 1935, it was dismantled and moved to Needham, Massachusetts. It moved to another Needham site in 1988.

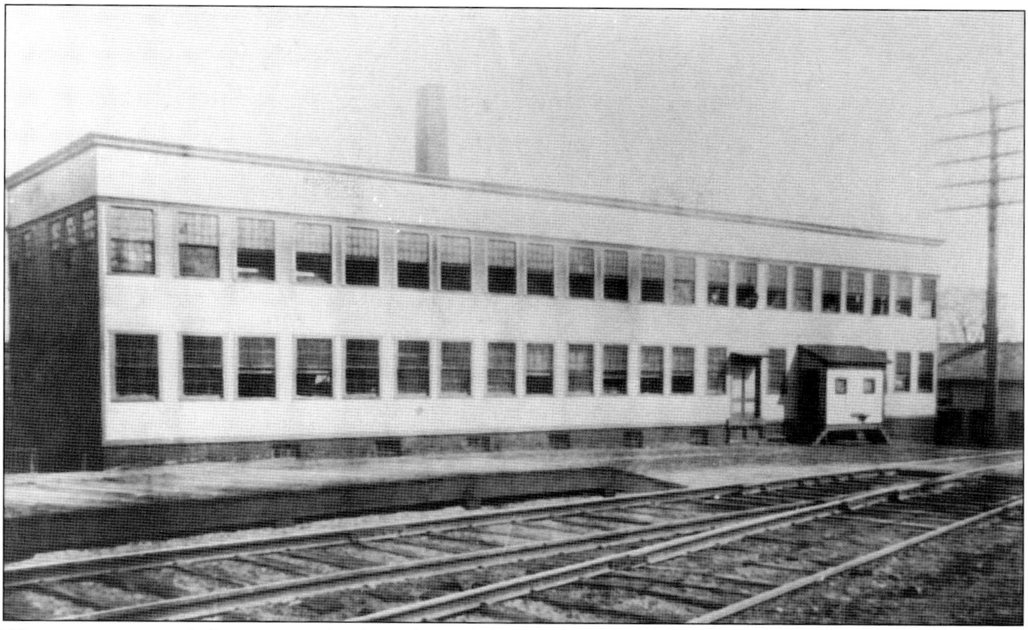

The site commonly known as the foundry was located on the riverbank at the end of Glastonbury Avenue. In the maritime era, it was several lots and contained dwellings, stores, and shops. At various times, it has been Pierce Hardware, Hart Hardware, the Rocky Hill Foundry, Champion Manufacturing (pictured), Austin Manufacturing Company, the Foster-Merriam Foundry, and the Connecticut Foundry. Today, the site is abandoned and is scheduled for redevelopment.

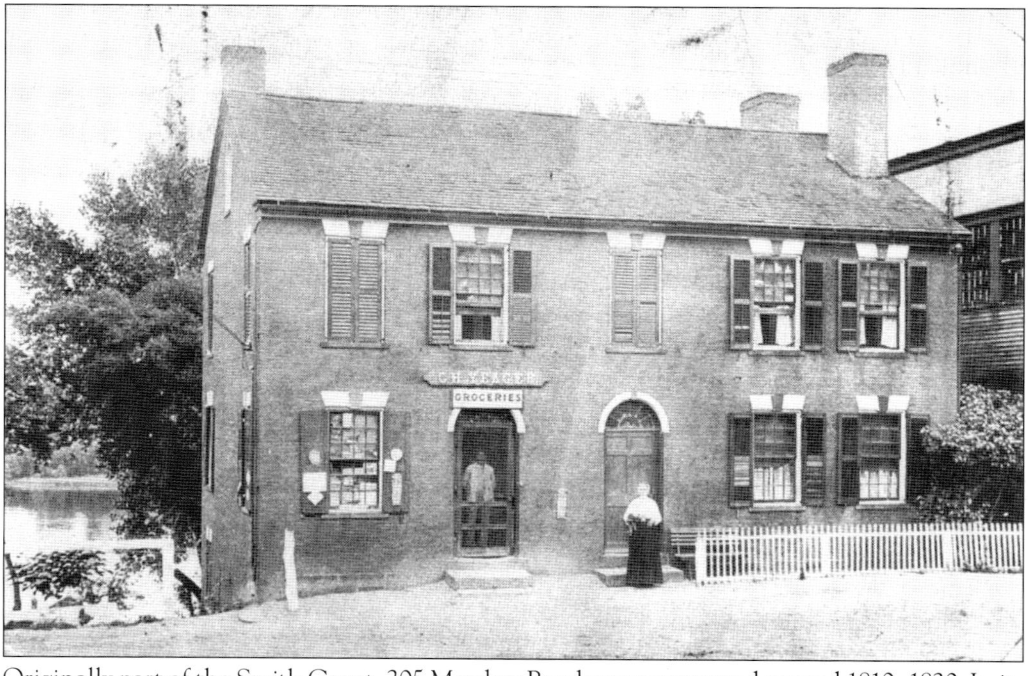

Originally part of the Smith Grant, 205 Meadow Road was constructed around 1810–1820. In its early history, it was a tavern for seafarers. For most of the 19th century, it was owned by Abijah Collins, a shipbuilder, and his heirs. At the turn of the 20th century, it was the Yeager House and Store. It was torn down in 1953. The lot is now part of the foundry property.

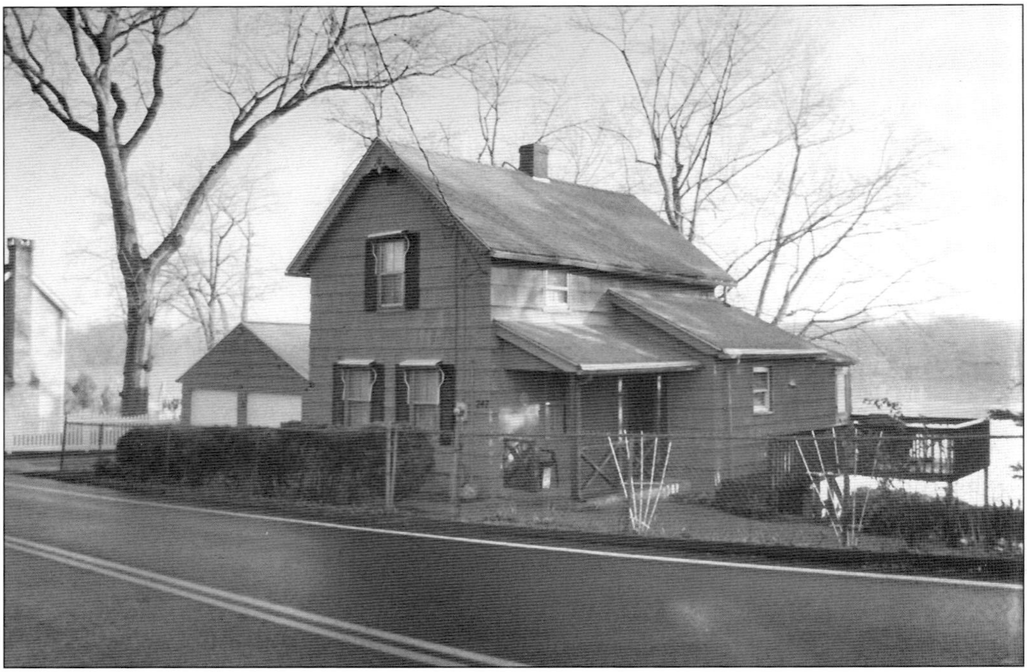

The Smith Grant was awarded to Joseph Smith in 1672. His granddaughter Abigail Grimes (née Smith) came into possession and oversaw the distribution of the land grant lots to family members and purchasers for most of the 18th century. She lived to be 90, dying in 1792. The current house (pictured), at 247 Meadow Road, was built in 1890.

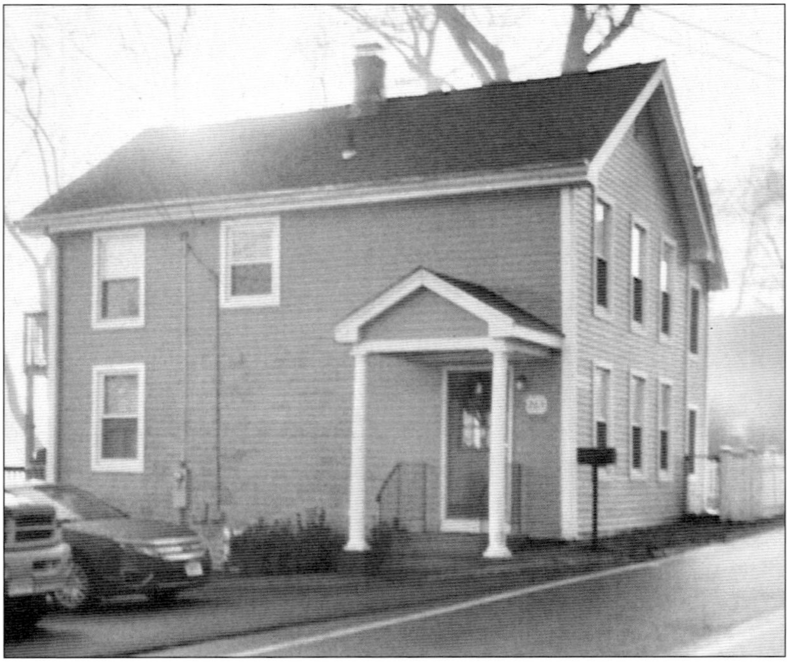

Lots on the river were prime real estate, often containing several homes, stores, and other buildings; 263 Meadow Road was one of these. In addition to serving as the home to the heirs of Abigail Grimes, it has been home to the Stanley store, the Grimes store, and probably others. The current house was built about 1800.

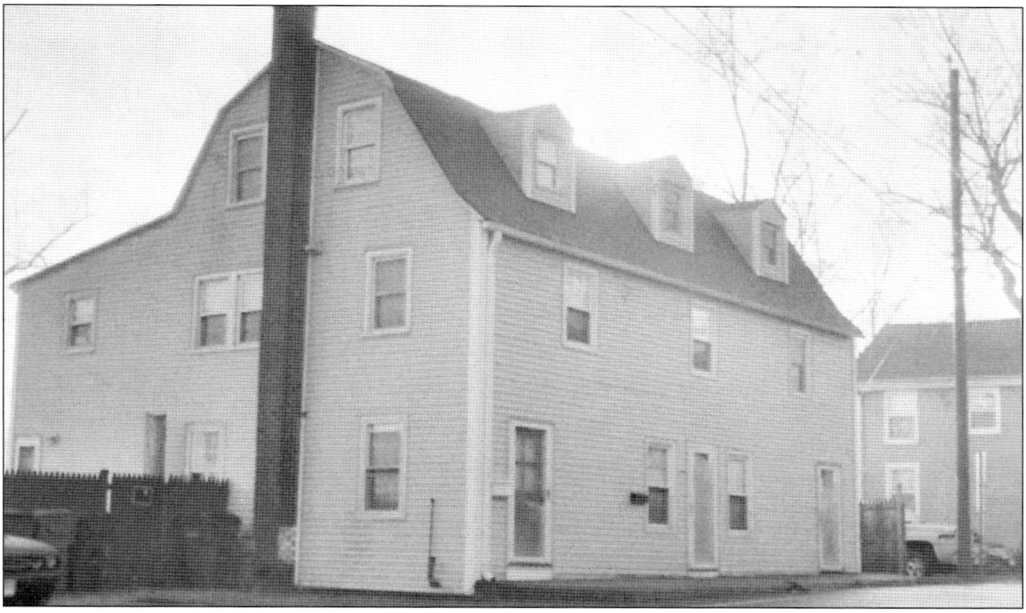

The land on which 273 Meadow Road stands has changed hands several times. Its proximity to the ferry landing has made it valuable property. It has been owned by the Town of Wethersfield, the Town of Rocky Hill, and several private citizens. A c. 1910 photograph shows this as a wooded lot. The Hale family of rivermen acquired this property in 1945 and built the house shown here.

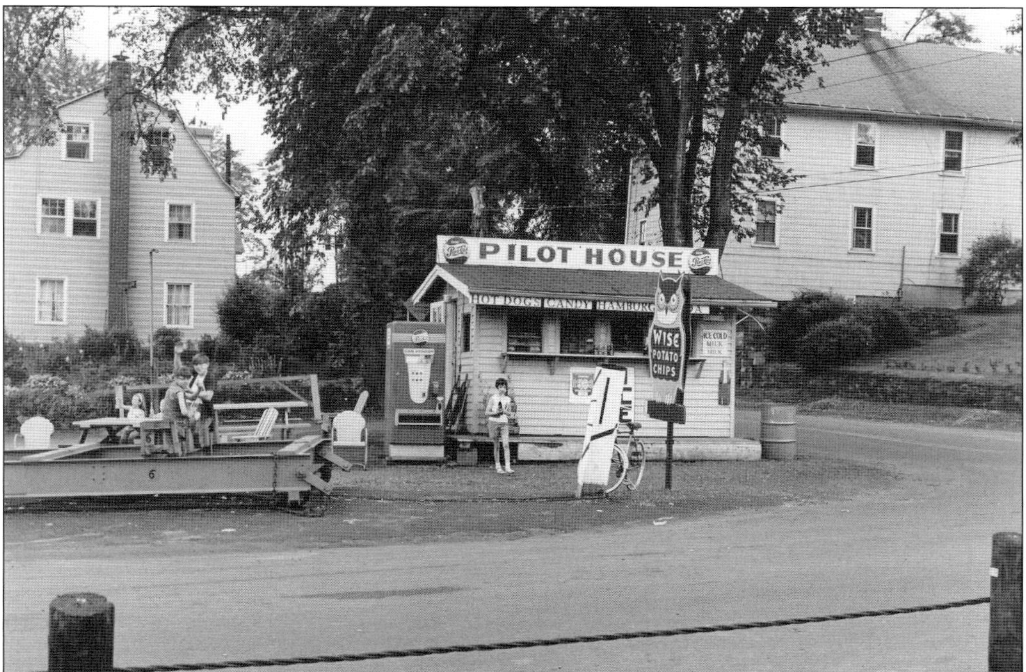

In 1951, the Hale family opened a small take-out establishment that sold shad caught fresh from the Connecticut River. In recent years, another popular local eatery, Mitchell's, ran a summer facility at this spot. A small riverfront restaurant, Shad Row, has operated on this site since 2014. (Courtesy of Mike Martino.)

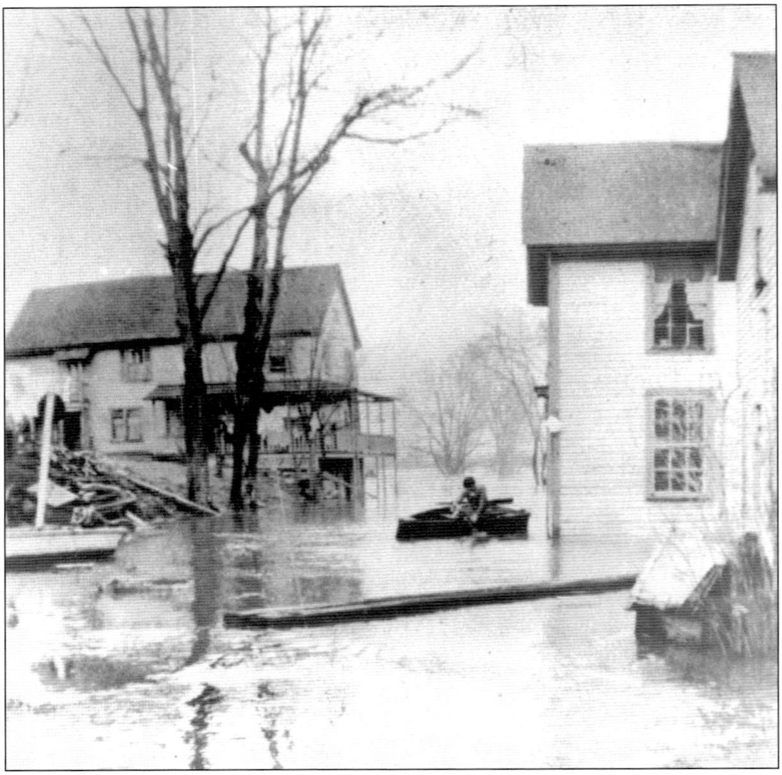

The Sail Loft House (left) was constructed at 276 Meadow Road in 1800. It faces the Connecticut River. During Rocky Hill's maritime heyday, this building also served as the Yankee Hotel & Tavern. It was sometimes used as a store. Sails were hung in front as they were worked on (before the porch was added). This picture was taken after the 1936 flood. (Courtesy of Mike Martino.)

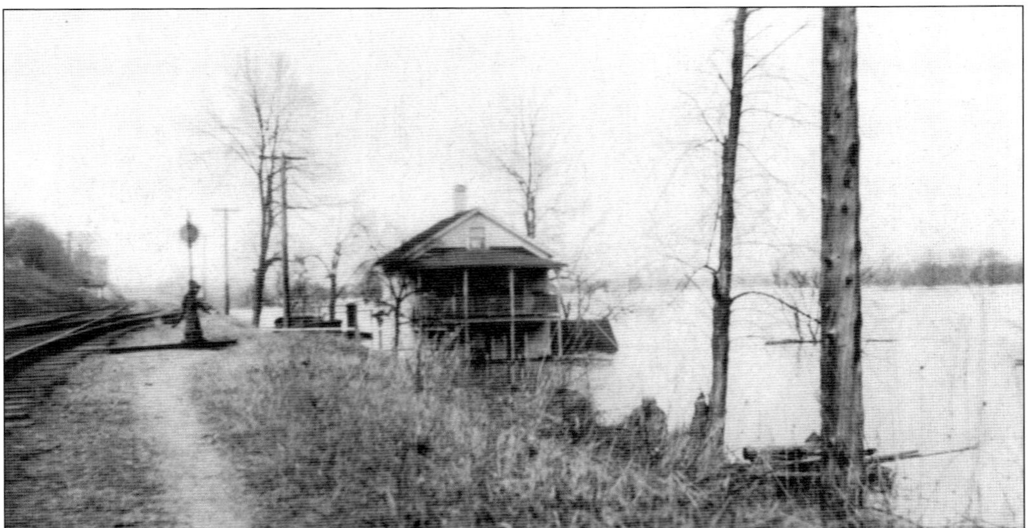

At one time, 340 Meadow Road was on the northern border of the Shipyard Reservation. The house sits high on a hill overlooking Ferry Park and the river. This picture was taken after the 1936 flood and shows how severe it was. The current house was built in 1800. (Courtesy of Mike Martino.)

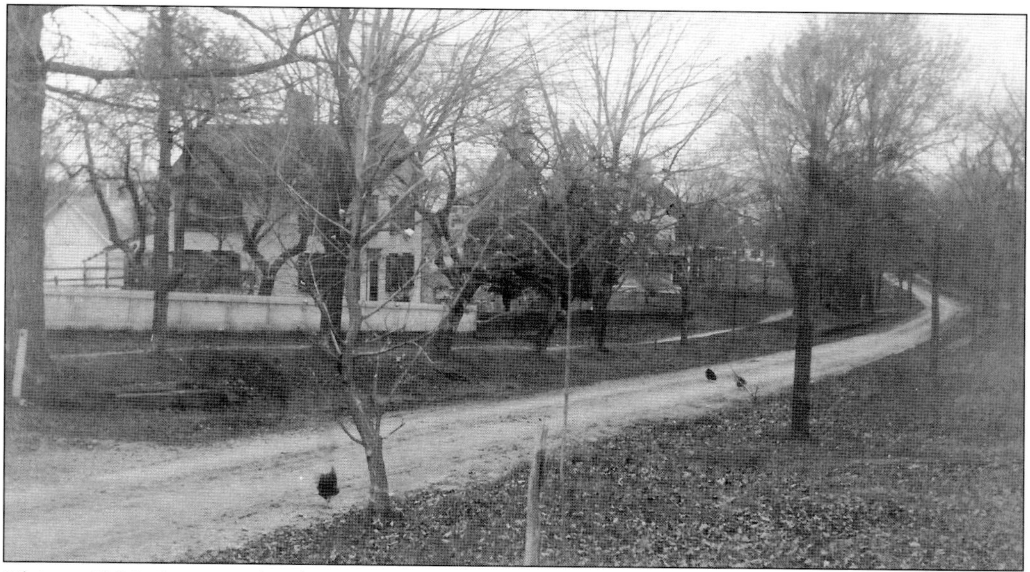

This c. 1900 photograph of Main Street looks north from Grimes Road. Main Street was the primary road from the south into Rocky Hill for most of its history. In 1802, it became part of the Hartford-Saybrook Turnpike. From 1909 through 1930, trolley tracks to Middletown ran down the center of the street. Inns, eating establishments, and gas stations along it once welcomed travelers.

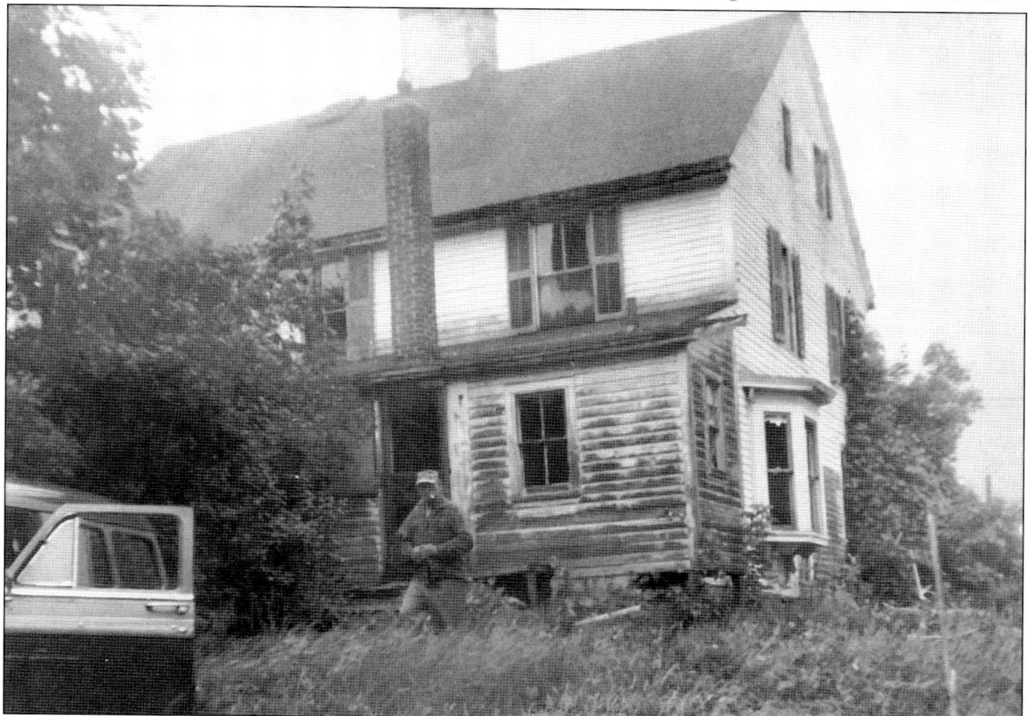

This house, at the southwest corner of the Elm Street–Silas Deane Highway intersection where Best Cleaners is today, was built in 1720 for James Robbins. This photograph shows the house being prepared to be burned for fire department practice drills in 1959. While the house was being prepared, historic artifacts, including a working cap-and-ball pistol from 1840, were found hidden in the rafters.

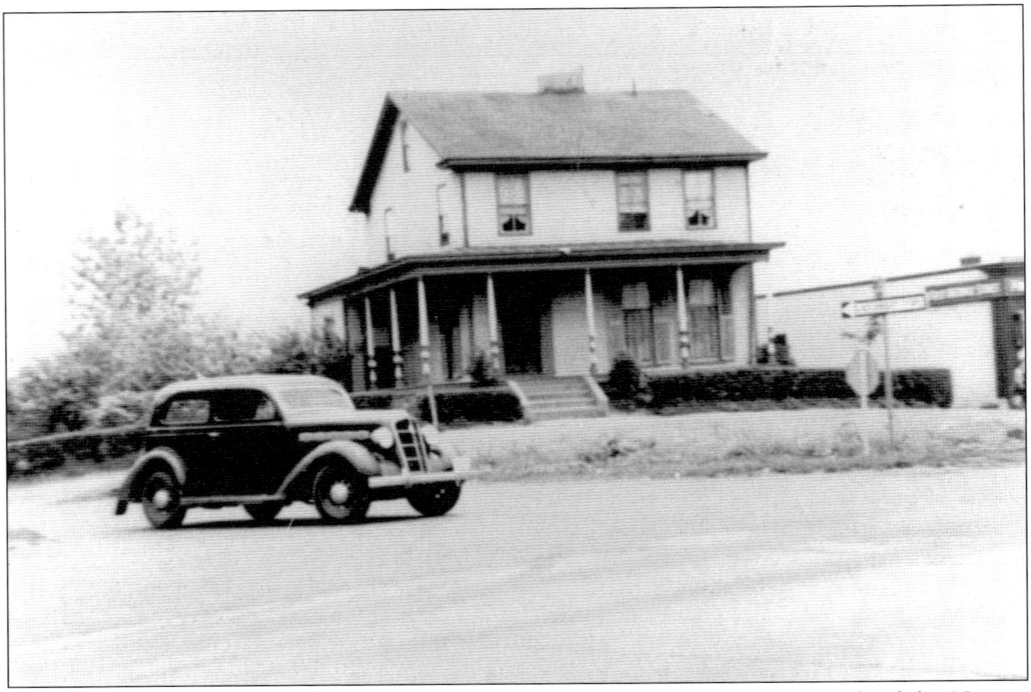

At 2344 Main Street, this house once stood on the east side of the street north of the Horace Merriam Store. This was the home of the Nevicos, a large Italian family. Several of the Nevico sons served in World War II. (Courtesy of Mike Martino.)

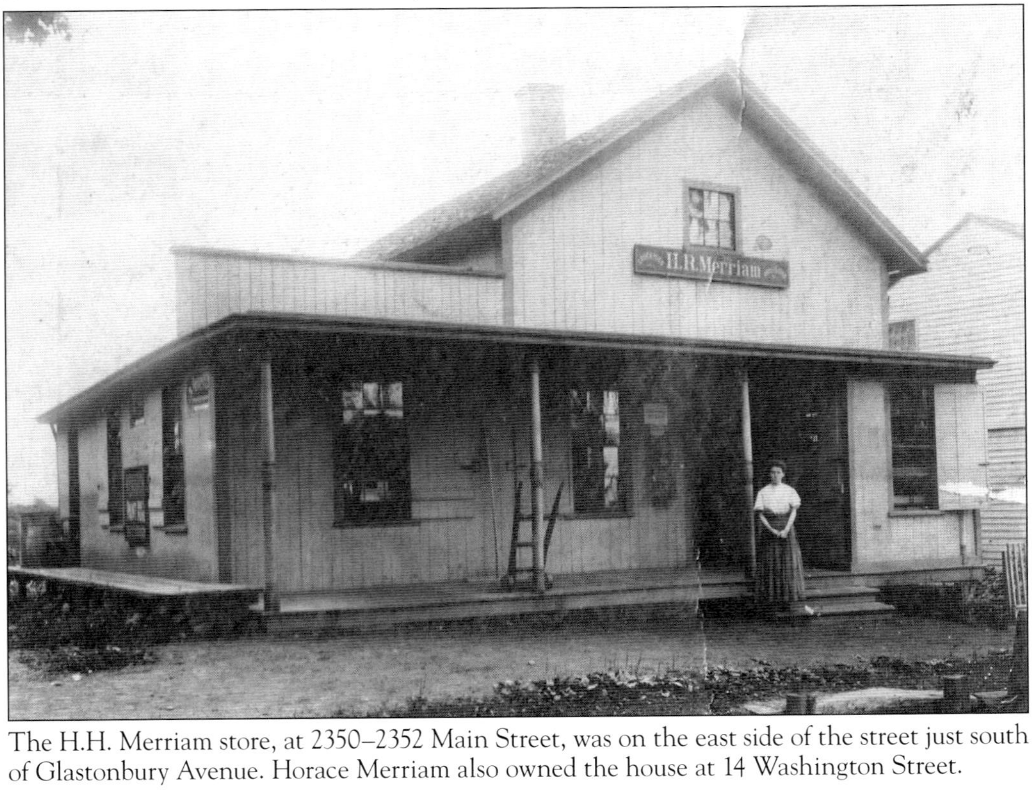

The H.H. Merriam store, at 2350–2352 Main Street, was on the east side of the street just south of Glastonbury Avenue. Horace Merriam also owned the house at 14 Washington Street.

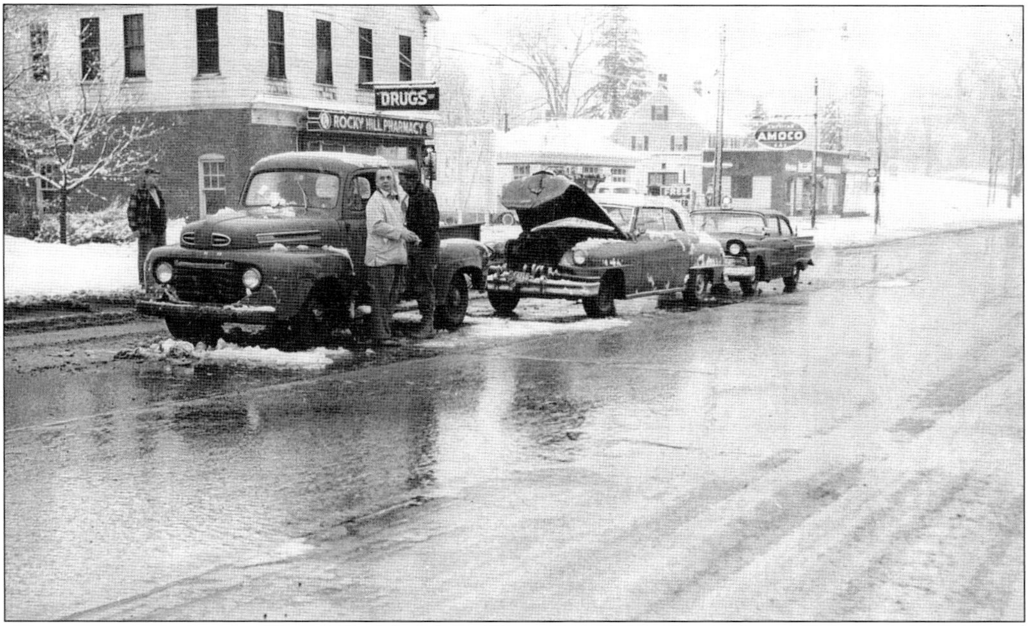

Weather is often a factor in Rocky Hill. This fender bender happened on March 4, 1958, in front of the Rocky Hill Pharmacy during an ice storm. The Rocky Hill Police Department's 1957 Ford cruiser is on the scene. The buildings are the Rocky Hill Pharmacy, Zacchio Brothers Garage, a hair salon, and a hardware store. (Courtesy of Mike Martino.)

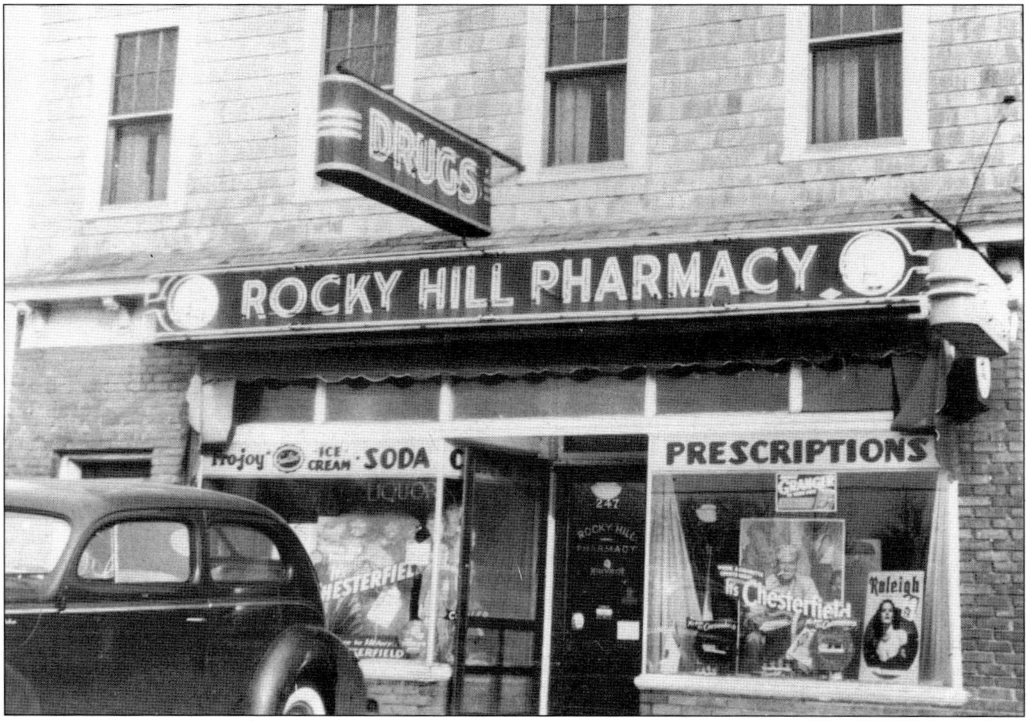

This photograph of the Rocky Hill Pharmacy at 2390 Main Street was taken in 1943. It was a typical drugstore from the 1940s that filled prescriptions, had a soda fountain, and probably sold alcohol (except on Sundays). Note the heavy emphasis on cigarette sales. (Courtesy of Mike Martino.)

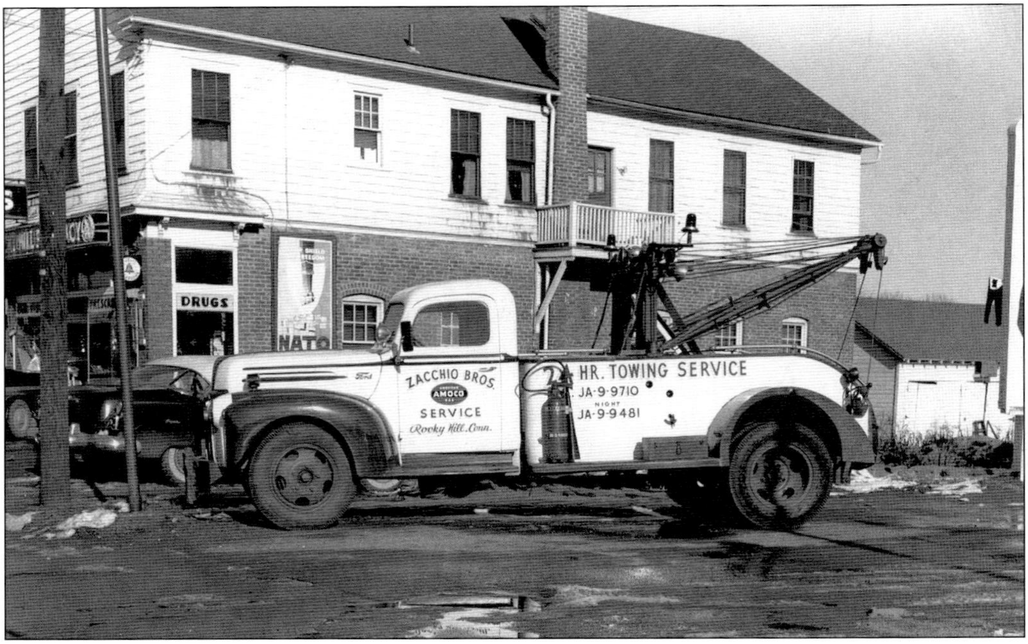

The wrecker at Zacchio Brothers Garage at 2400 Main Street stood ready to respond to emergencies such as the fender bender on the previous page. (Courtesy of Mike Martino.)

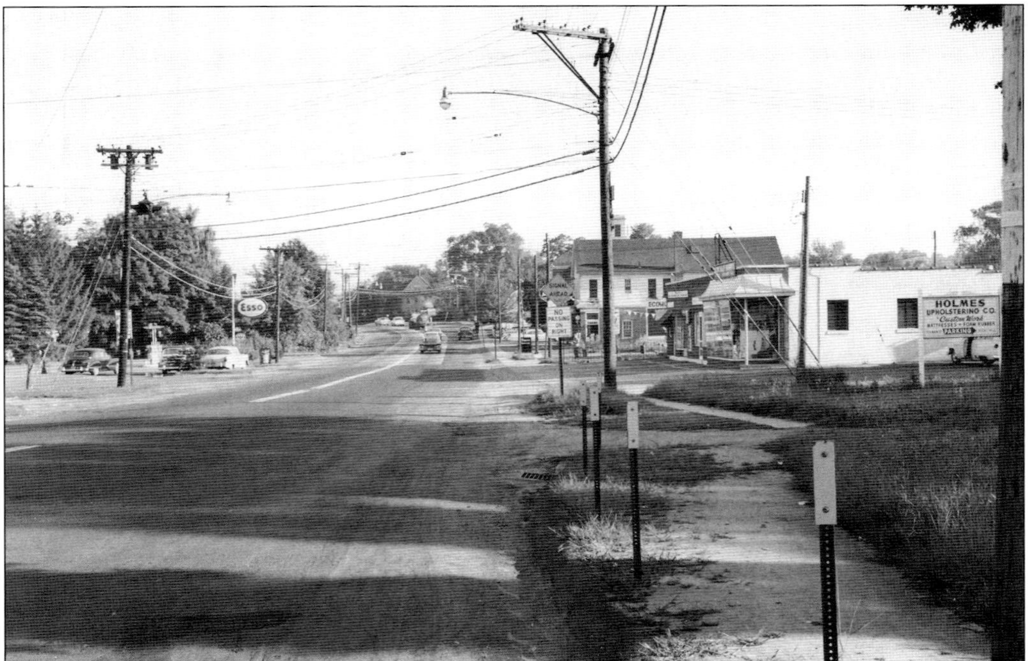

This multi-business complex across Main Street from Garden Street at 2410–2414 contained, from left to right, Holmes Upholstering, Main Street Barbershop, Molly's Beauty Shop, and Connecticut Valley Hardware. This photograph was taken in 1961. The building was demolished in 1971 to make way for the W.T. Grant Plaza. This was in turn replaced by Ames Department Store headquarters, which was abandoned in 2002. (Courtesy of Mike Martino.)

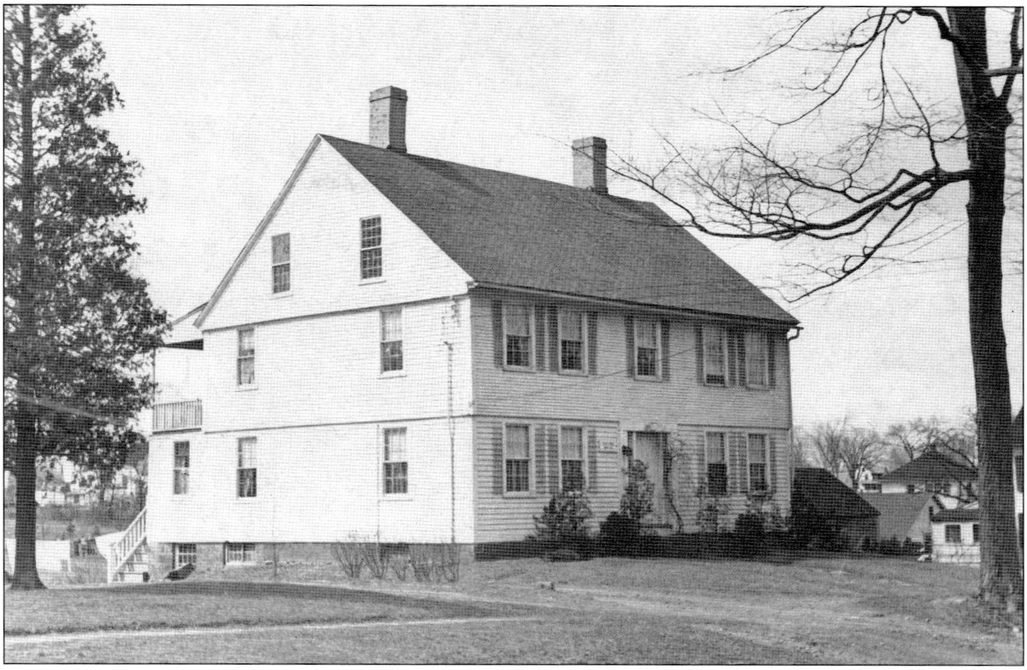

The building at 2473 Main Street was constructed around 1750. An early owner was John Gibbs, who purchased the land from David Smith. He deeded it to his son Jacob in 1830. Ownership passed to Albro Griswold, who operated a fulling mill in Griswoldville in 1848. Horace Williams bought it in 1883. He was the third great-grandson of Thomas Williams, grantee of the Thomas Williams Grant.

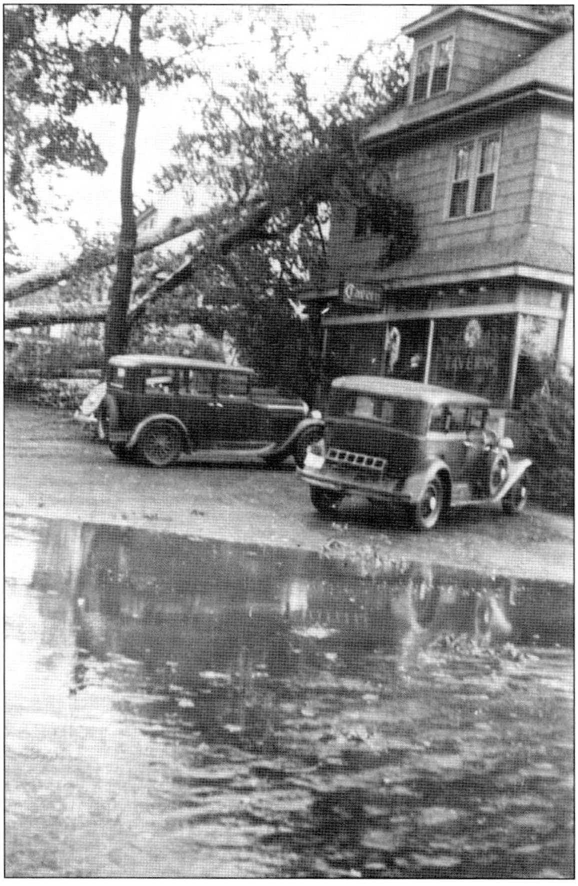

Trees are down and leaning on the Rocky Hill Tavern building at 2427 Main Street, on the corner of Garden Street, after the 1938 hurricane. This site became the popular Frank's Restaurant and is the location of the CVS pharmacy today. (Courtesy of Mike Martino.)

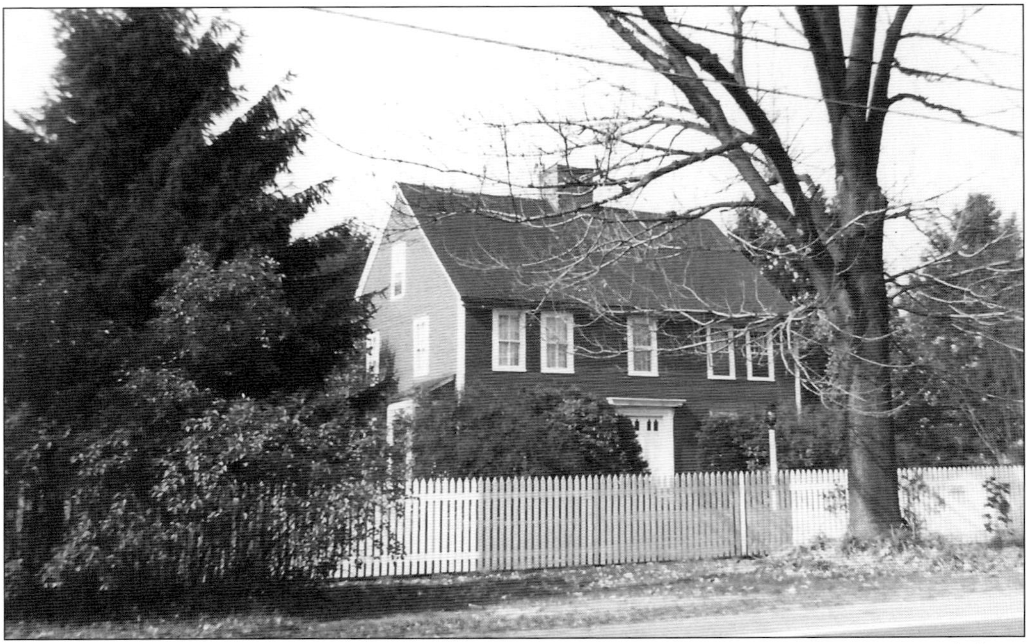

The Valley Hotel at 2519 Main Street was erected in 1780. Located on the Post Road, later the Hartford-Saybrook Turnpike, it was a popular place for travelers and pleasure-seekers from Hartford. Post riders stopped here. It served as the post office in 1812. The town library operated here from 1896 to 1899, and library customers rubbed elbows with seekers of alcoholic pleasures.

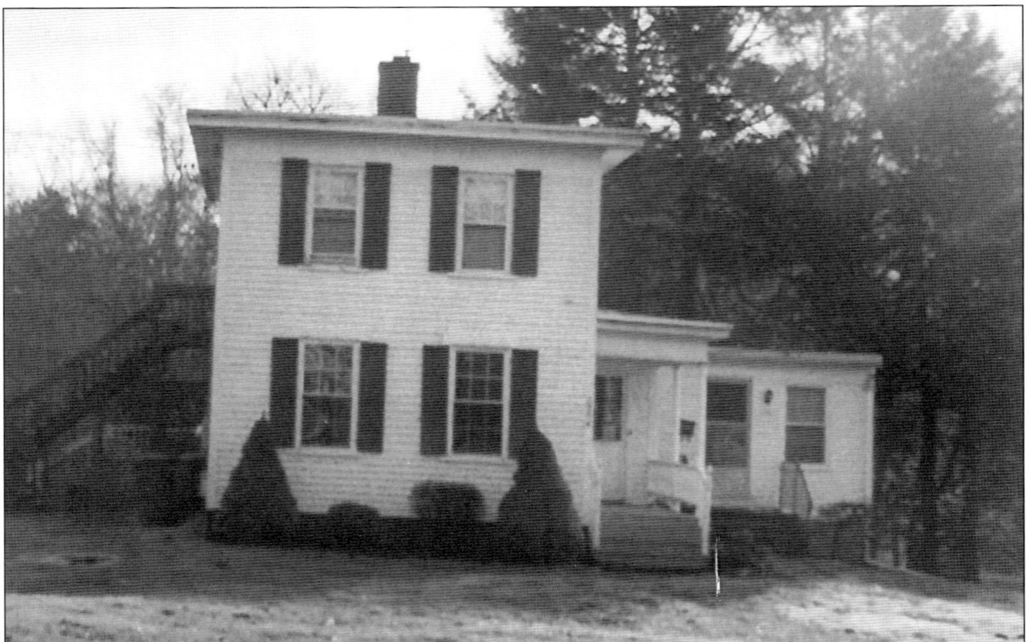

The building at 2594 Main Street, constructed in 1845, was owned by Albro Griswold in 1851. Frank A. Grant, a stonemason, owned it in 1923. When he died, his niece Florence Grant Tallman, whom he had raised, served as executor. Florence was a World War I naval veteran and possibly the orphan sister of Leroy and Frank Grant, who were also Rocky Hill World War I veterans.

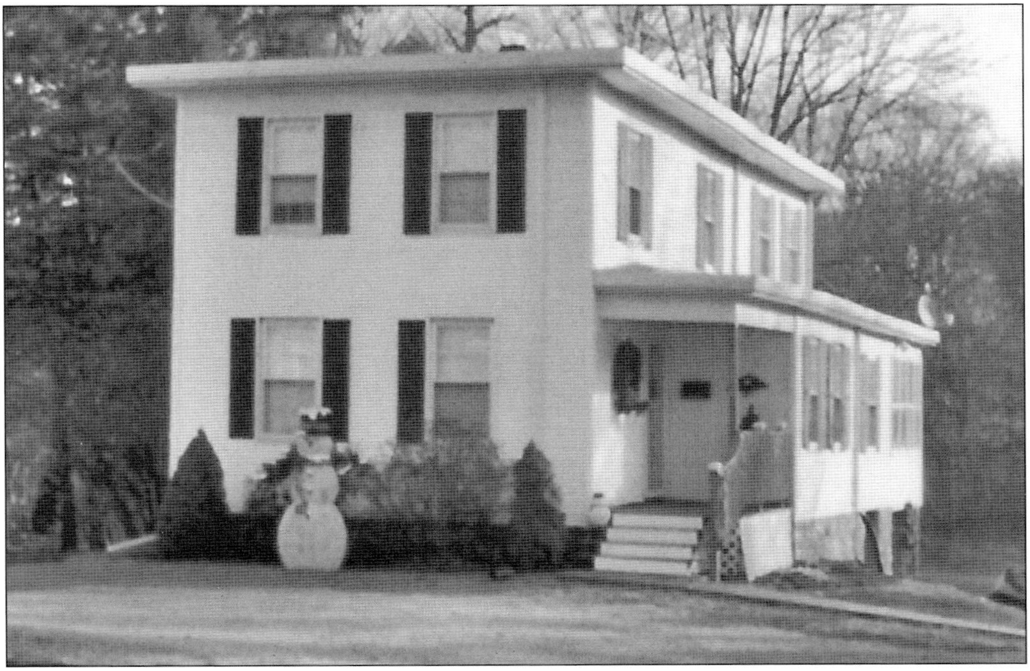

The building at 2606 Main Street was erected in 1846. It was ceded to Ephriam Goodrich by Eleazer Goodrich in 1851. The Goodrich family owned it until 1913, when it was sold by Ephriam's wife, Barbara. In the late 20th century, it was owned by Rocky Hill state representative Richard Tulisano.

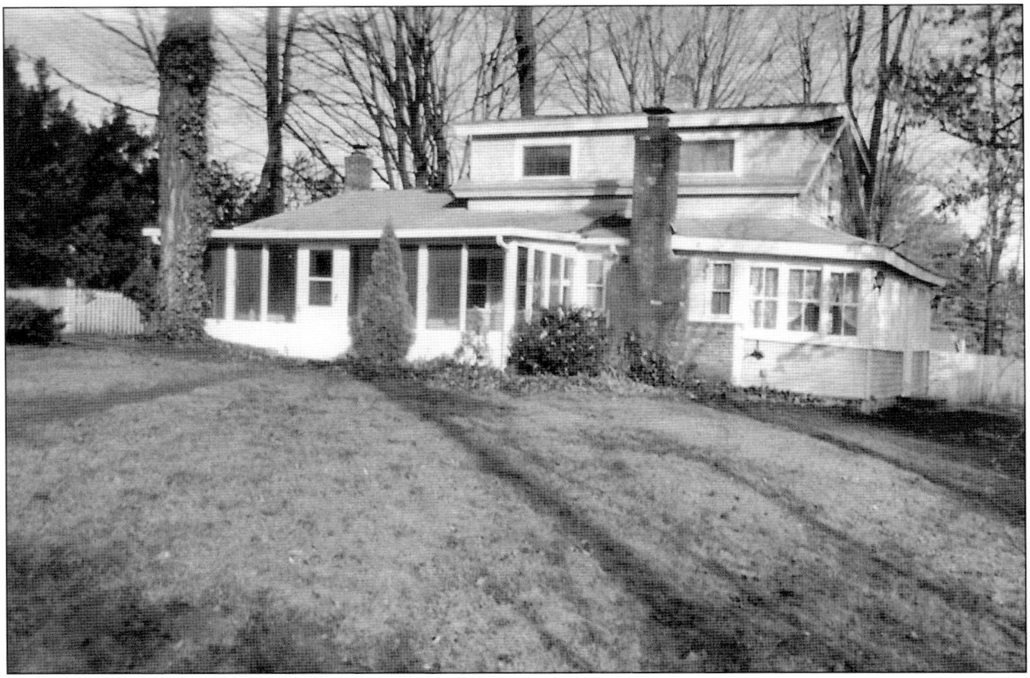

The house at 2773 Main Street was built in 1860. The land it is on was divided into 2773 and 2787 Main Street and sold as two pieces in 1954. Shogoro and Yuki Shinomiya owned it from 1935 to 1940. They were Japanese resident aliens. Shogoro died in 1939. Yuki lived here during World War II and was living in Michigan by 1957. She died in Los Angeles in 1967.

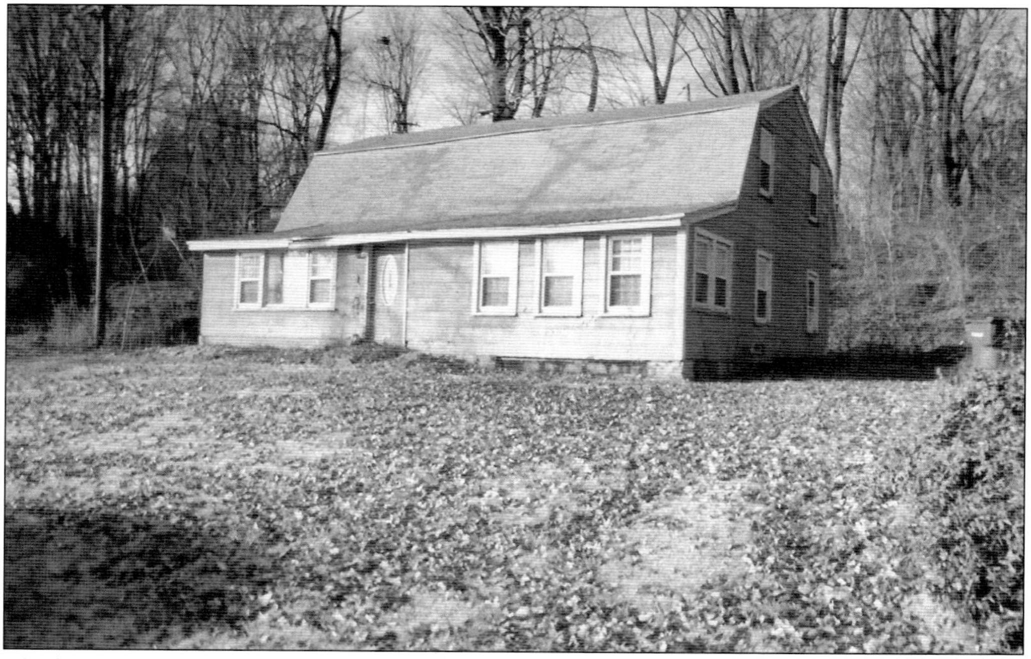

The house at 2787 Main Street is an abandoned piece of history. Built in 1800, it was owned by Joseph Gerritz in 1960. He died on April 1, 1961. Gerritz was a naval veteran of World War I and apparently was called to New London before World War II as a submarine expert. The house seems to be unoccupied today.

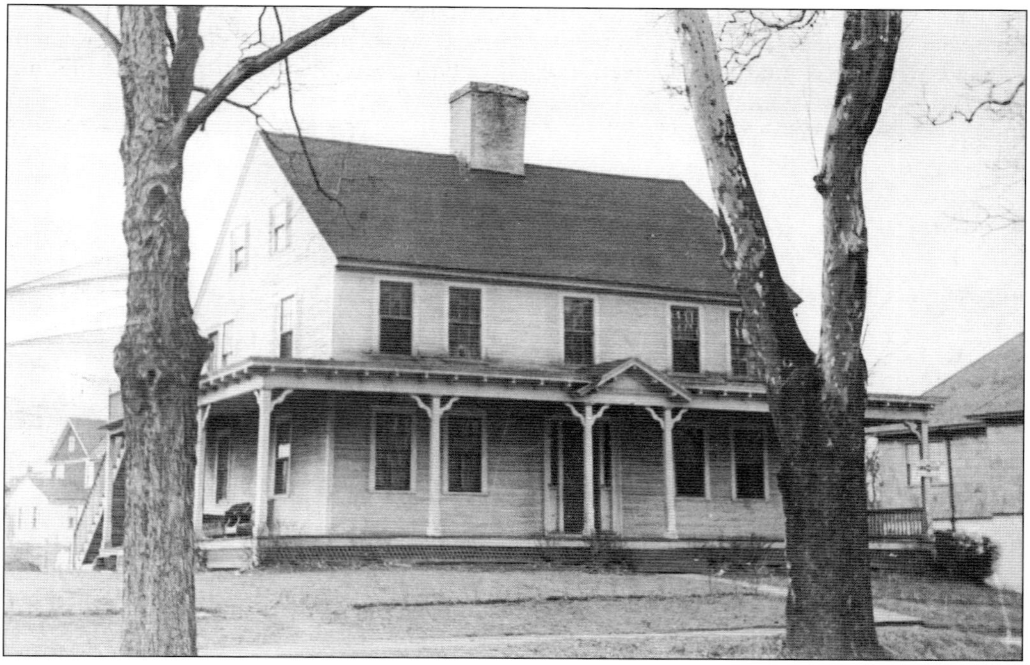

The building at 2816–2818 Main Street was constructed in 1790. The plaque on the front reads "Gershom Bulkeley, 1790." This was either the grandson or great-grandson of Rev. Gershom Bulkeley, the noted clergyman who operated the first Rocky Hill industry, a corn mill, at Dividend Brook. The descendants were father and son.

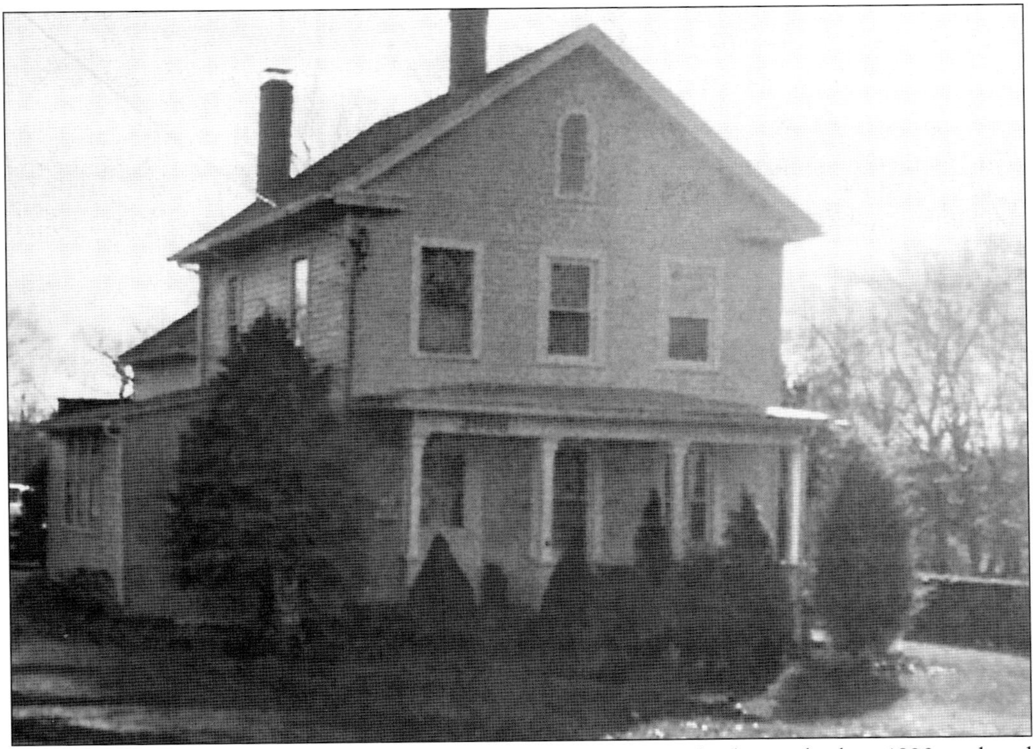

The Halligan family owned 2998 Main Street from 1851 to 1944. This house, built in 1890, replaced an older one. According to a map at the Rocky Hill Historical Society, a large farm called the Halligan Lot was across Main Street from this house and was bounded by Main Street, Cromwell Avenue, West Street, and Brook Street. It seems to have been divided into smaller farms and ultimately into tract housing.

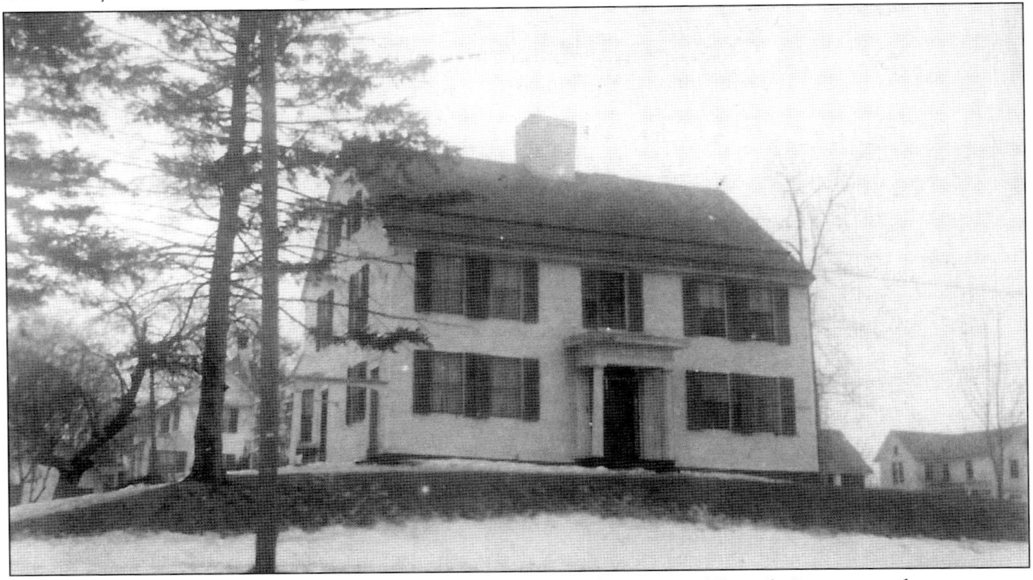

The Rocky Hill Hotel was built in 1776 at the corner of Main and Brook Streets and was once a popular stop on the Hartford-Saybrook Turnpike. It had a checkered past. It was known as a place for drinking and gambling and was raided as a gambling den as recently as 1912.

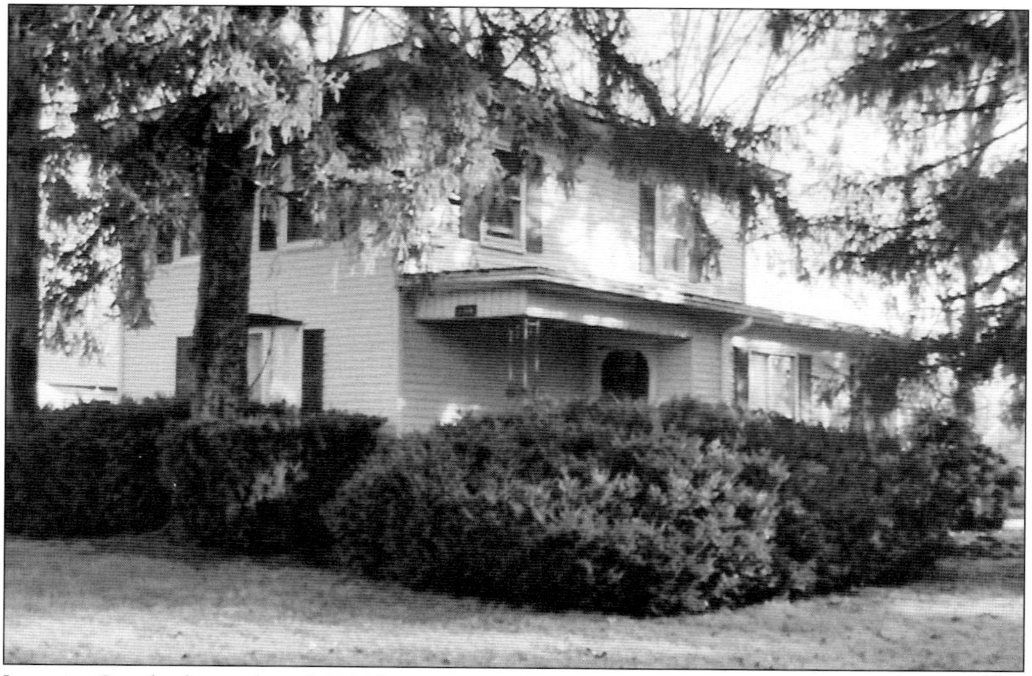

Leveritt Goodrich purchased 3106 Main Street from Cornelius Goodrich in 1866. The current house was built in 1890. The property has an industrial flavor, having been owned by Charles Billing of Billings Drop Forge and the Hartford Electric Steel Company. William Sage Butler, partner with Robert Sugden in the Pleasant Valley Foundry, lived next door.

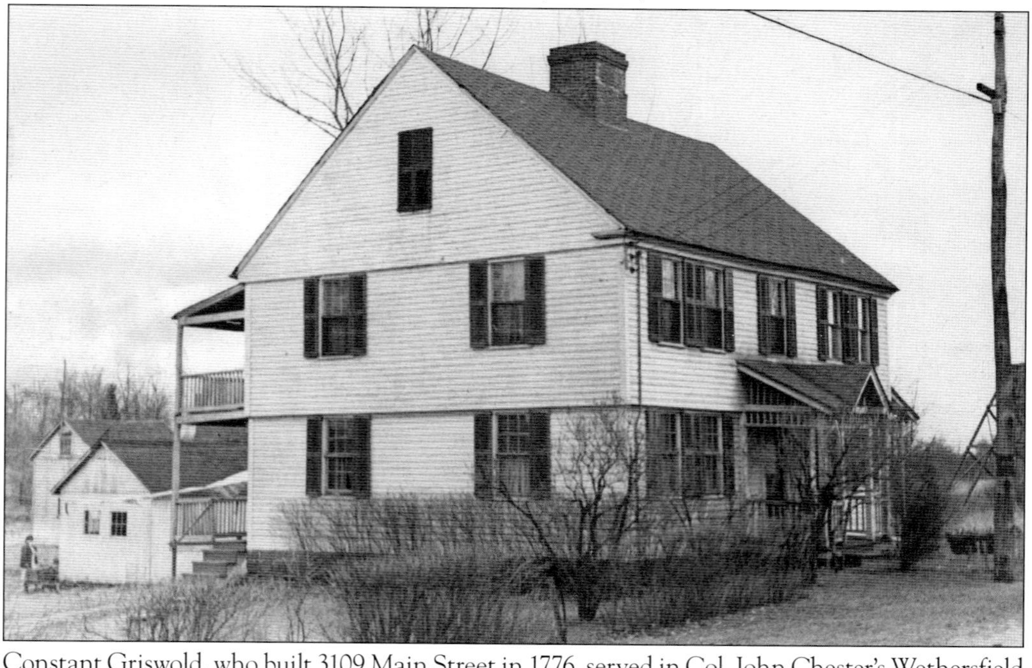

Constant Griswold, who built 3109 Main Street in 1776, served in Col. John Chester's Wethersfield Militia during the Revolutionary War. He was discharged in 1775. His son Ashbel apprenticed with the Danforths, moved to Meriden, Connecticut, and became a famous and wealthy silversmith in his own right.

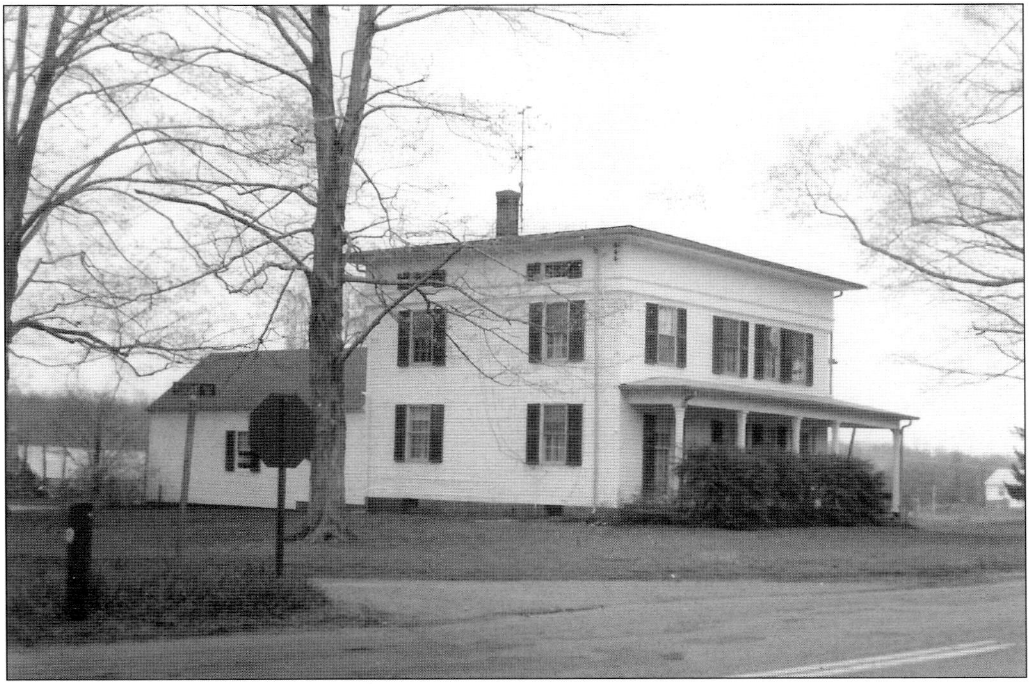

The house at 3220 Main Street was built in 1870, apparently by Robert Sugden Jr., who opened the Pleasant Valley Foundry in 1854. The house is just south of Pleasant Valley Road, which ran to the Sugden-Butler Foundry. Its location made for an easy commute for Sugden. Before Old Forge Road was built, Pleasant Valley Road was a main thoroughfare into town.

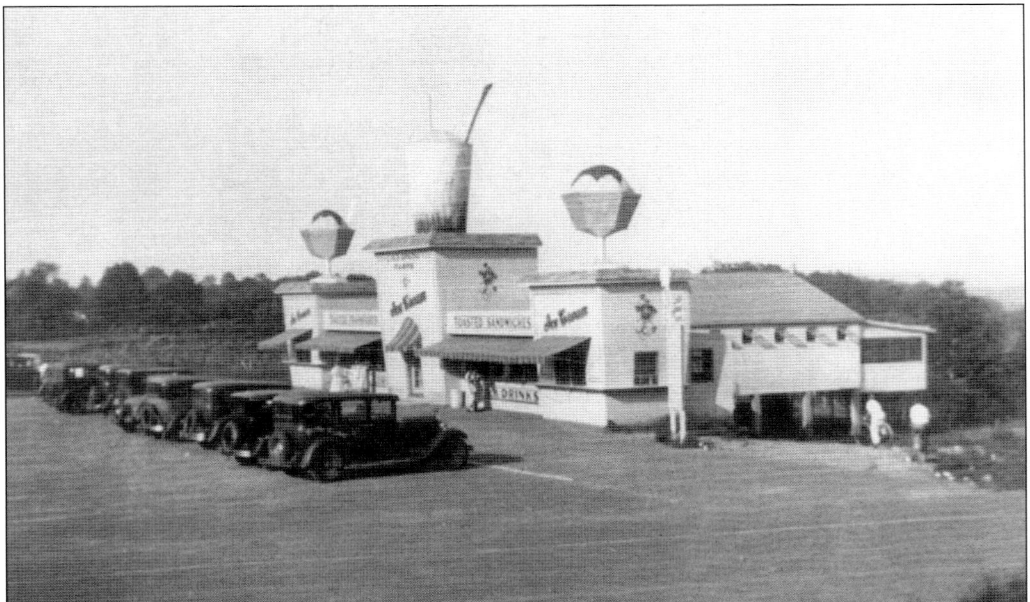

The Cold Springs Ice Cream Shop & Restaurant, at 3272 Main Street, opened in June 1933. The two sundaes were blown down during the 1938 hurricane. The building was Harry Holmes's diner in the early 1940s. In the late 1940s, it became the Fountain Restaurant, which closed in the 1960s. The building is VFW Post 2138 today. (Courtesy of Mike Martino.)

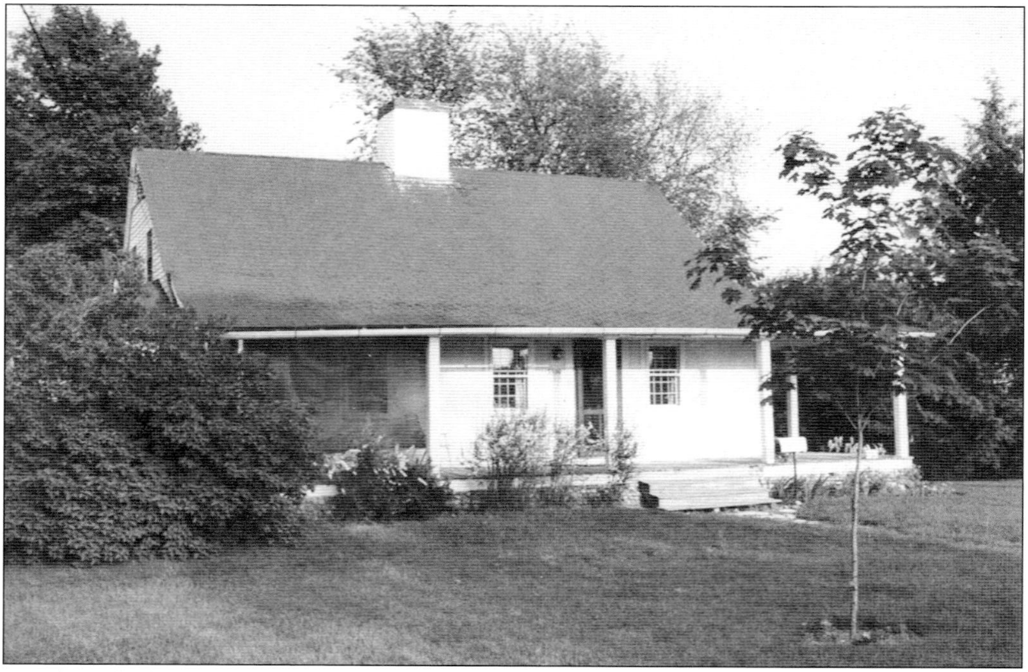

Joseph Butler built 3330 Main Street in 1675; it was improved by his son Charles in 1760. Charles's son Stephen Butler died at sea in 1803. This is one of the oldest remaining houses in Rocky Hill. It is sometimes called the Spencer House. It was deeded to Maria, wife of C. Spencer, in 1874; Walter Spencer sold it in 1907. The house was completely restored in 1957.

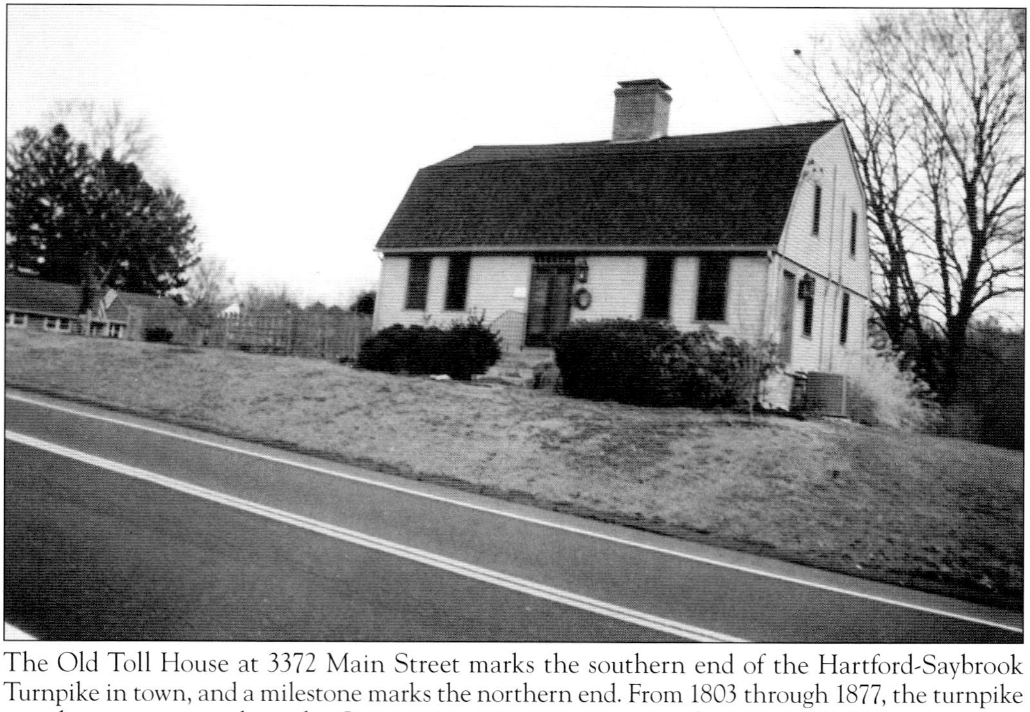

The Old Toll House at 3372 Main Street marks the southern end of the Hartford-Saybrook Turnpike in town, and a milestone marks the northern end. From 1803 through 1877, the turnpike was the main artery along the Connecticut River. It ran up modern Route 154, Route 9, Main Street, Church Street, and Old Main Street in Rocky Hill.

Until 1977, Pleasant Valley Road and Old Dividend Road provided a main avenue into town. Old Dividend Road has since been decertified. (Courtesy of Jennifer Duff Creations.)

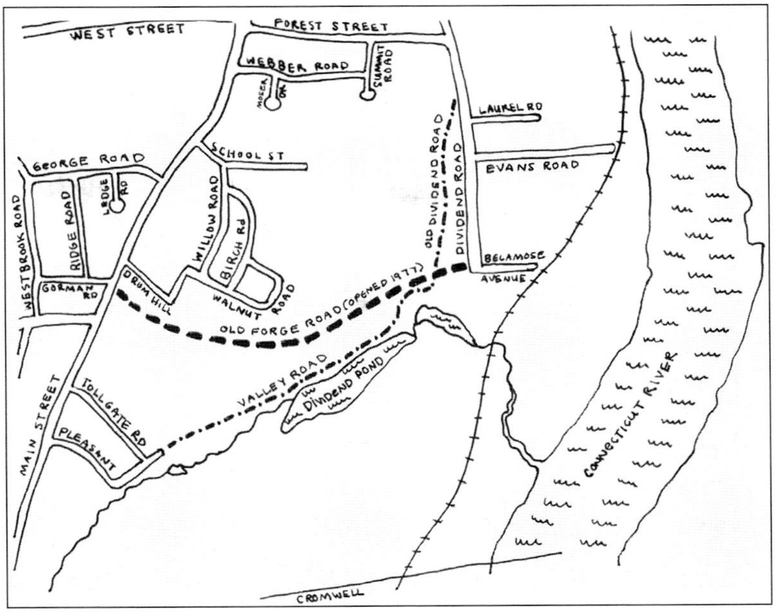

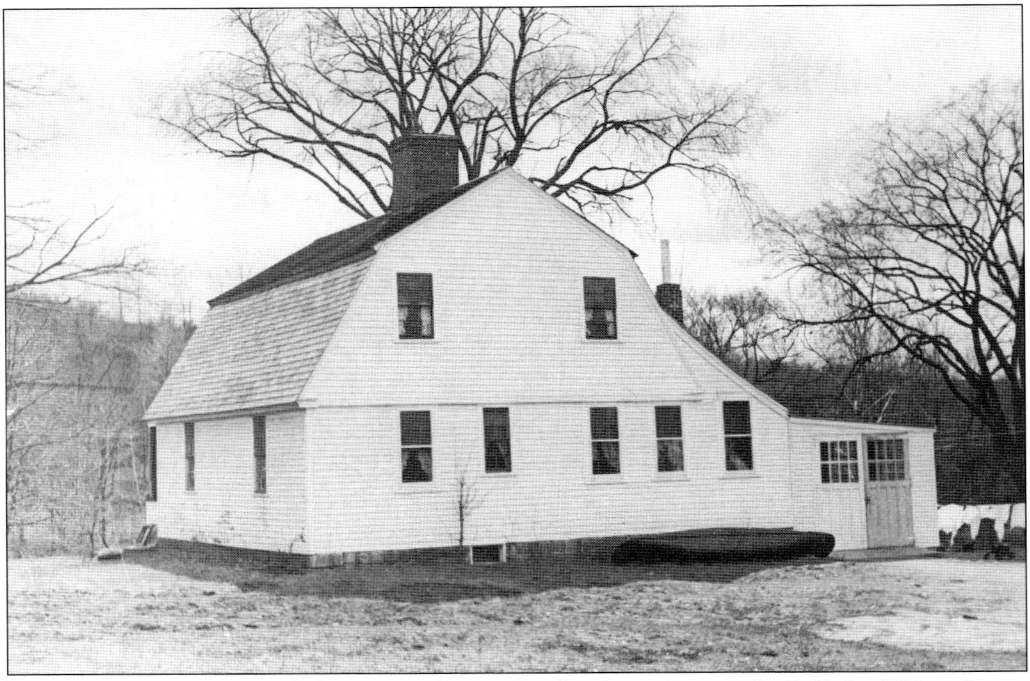

Dividend Road once provided access to the Dividend industrial area. The Bulkeley-Wilcox house (pictured) was located near the entrance to Dividend Park and, at one time, the Wells-Wilcox Edge Tool Company. The plant was immediately adjacent to this house. Co-owner Alfred Wilcox died in 1868 when he was caught and whirled over a spinning shaft. The house is gone today. (Courtesy of Mike Martino.)

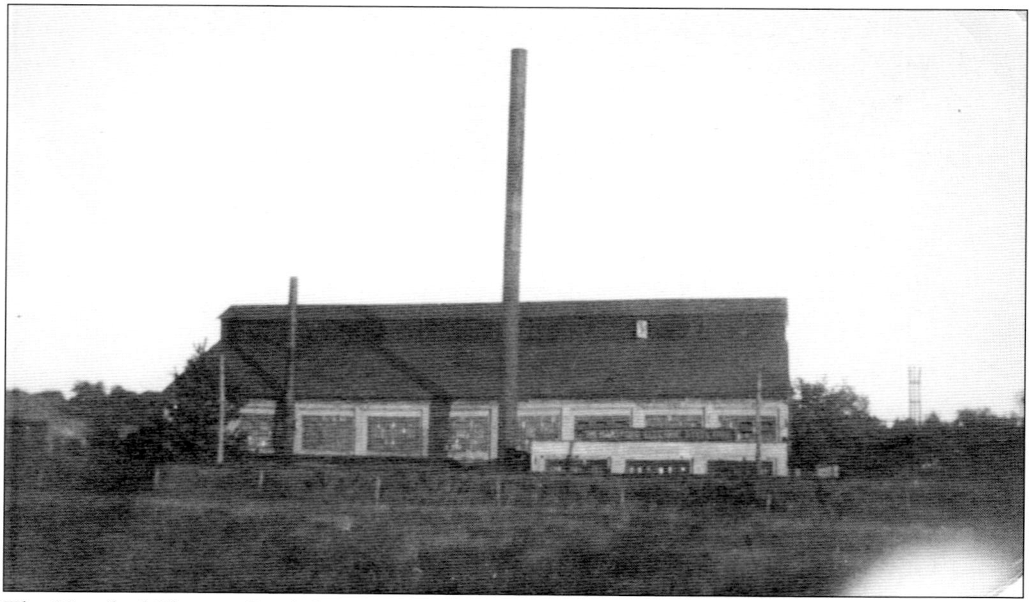

The Hartford Electric Steel Company operated a plant on the riverfront where Belamose Road now ends. The plant was purchased from the Billings and Spencer Company in 1917. It made metal castings for the military during World War I and was acquired by the Belamose Corporation in 1923.

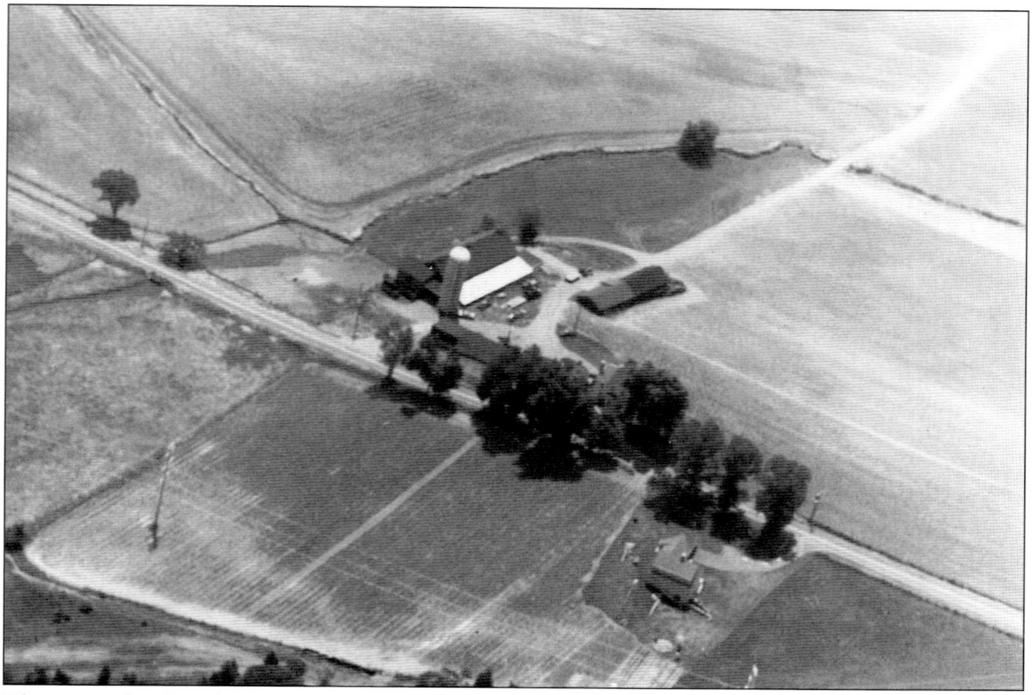

The west side of Rocky Hill was at one time known as "Pumpkin Town." It was a sparsely populated rural and wooded area. In modern times, the west side has given over to strip malls, condos, residential communities, and industrial parks.

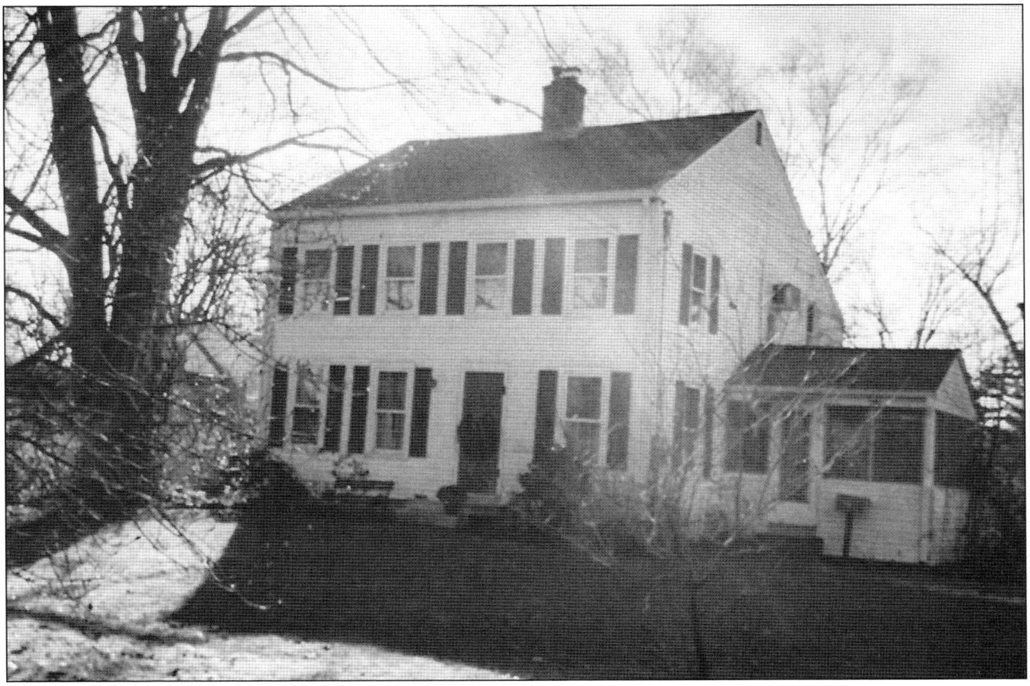

Brook Street, like West and Elm Streets, was laid out in 1692 to provide access to west-side farm lands. The house at 470 Brook Street was built in 1750 on the old Peat Farm. It became a tobacco farm and later a nursery. Western Brook Street was once occupied by the Gardener Nursery (behind the house) and the Collins farm.

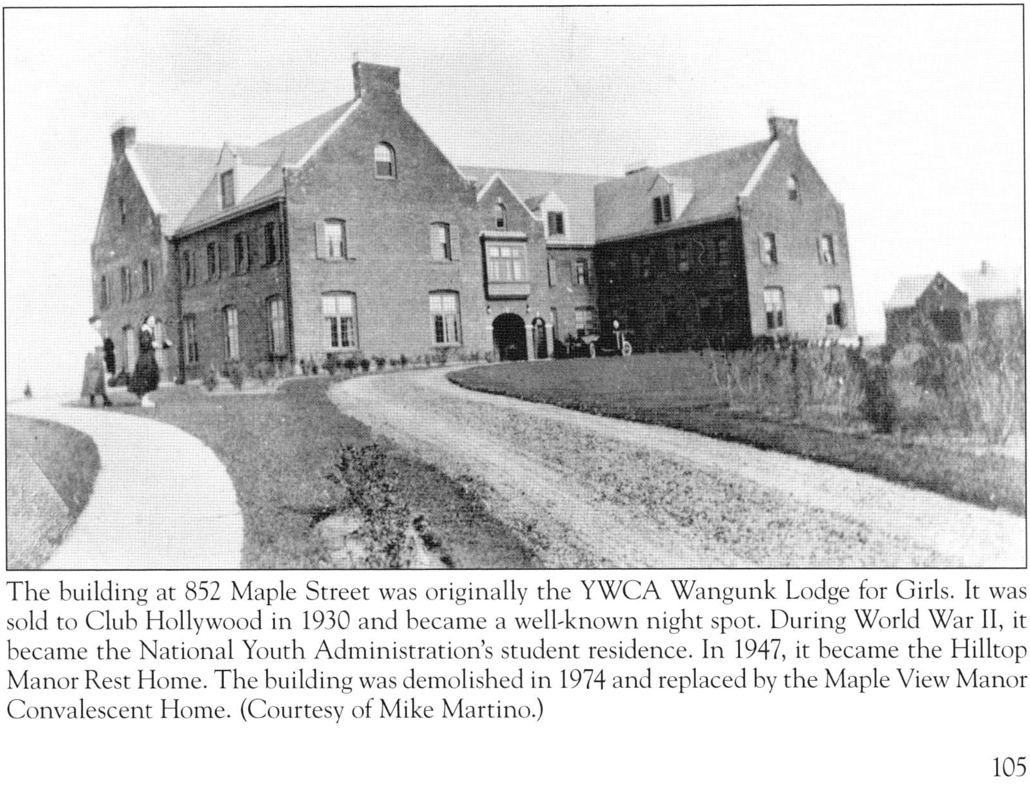

The building at 852 Maple Street was originally the YWCA Wangunk Lodge for Girls. It was sold to Club Hollywood in 1930 and became a well-known night spot. During World War II, it became the National Youth Administration's student residence. In 1947, it became the Hilltop Manor Rest Home. The building was demolished in 1974 and replaced by the Maple View Manor Convalescent Home. (Courtesy of Mike Martino.)

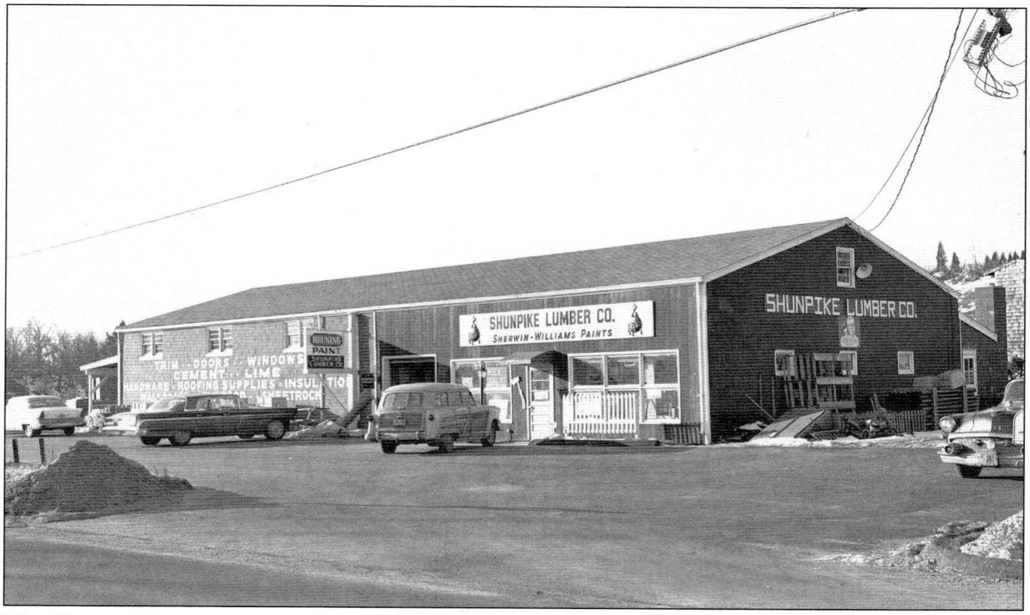

The Shunpike was a major artery on the west side. It was so named because it was used to "shun" tolls on the Hartford-Saybrook Turnpike. It was a country road before the 1980s with few buildings. The modern name of the road is Cromwell Avenue. From 1961 until the 1980s, a main draw on this road was Shunpike Lumber, across from West Street. (Courtesy of Mike Martino.)

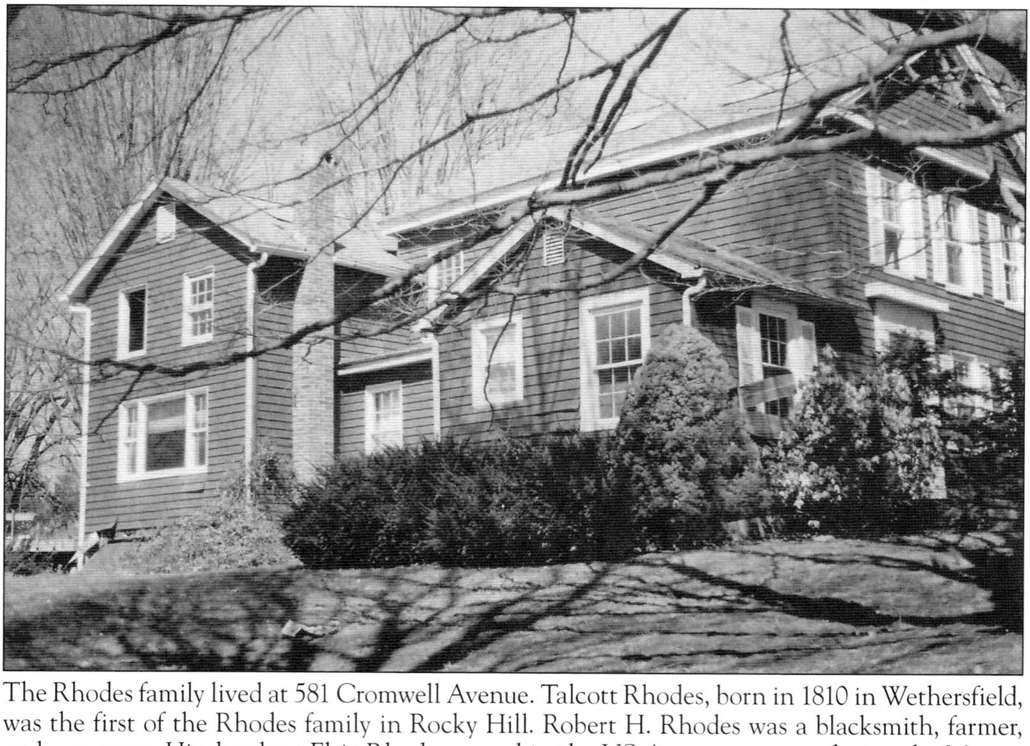

The Rhodes family lived at 581 Cromwell Avenue. Talcott Rhodes, born in 1810 in Wethersfield, was the first of the Rhodes family in Rocky Hill. Robert H. Rhodes was a blacksmith, farmer, and carpenter. His daughter Elsie Rhodes served in the US Army as a nurse during the Meuse-Argonne offensive in World War I. She stayed in the Army and served during World War II. She retired as a lieutenant colonel.

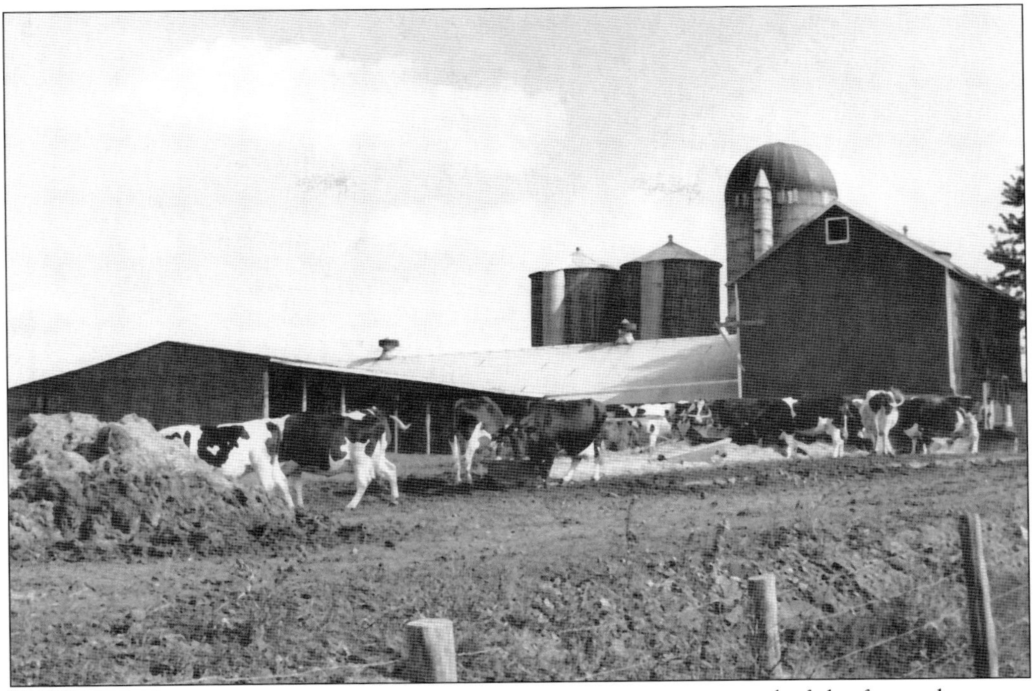

The Meisterling farm, on the far west end of France Street, was typical of the farms that once occupied the west side.

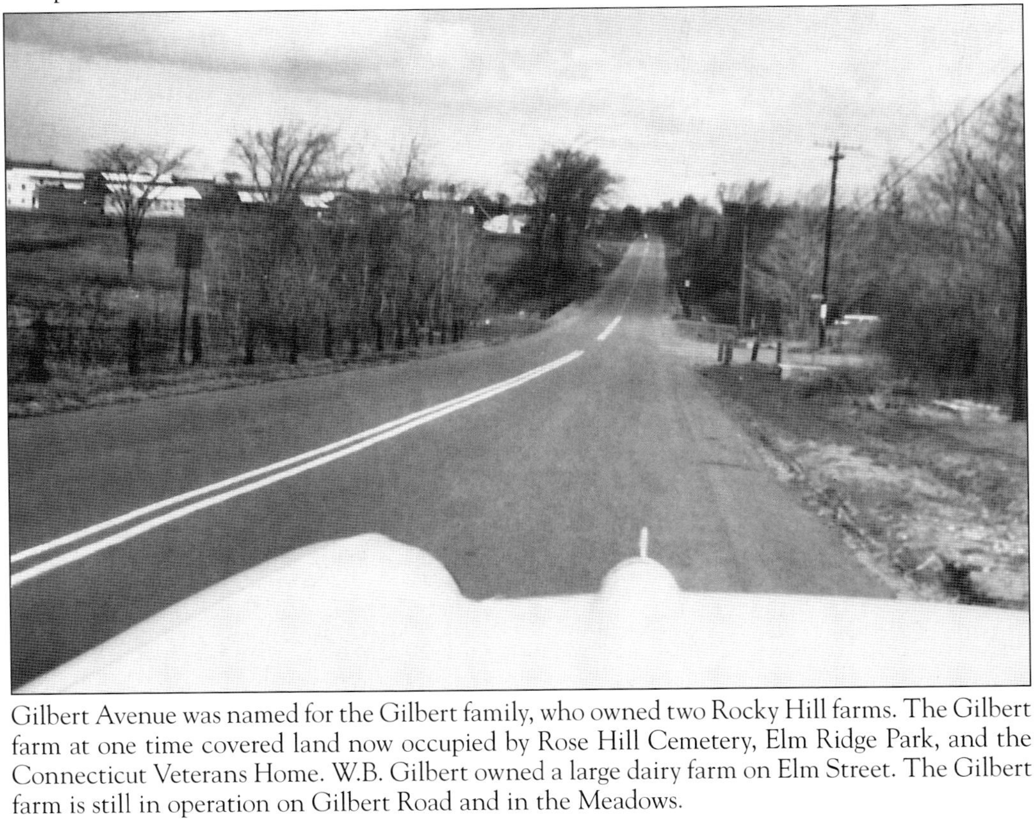

Gilbert Avenue was named for the Gilbert family, who owned two Rocky Hill farms. The Gilbert farm at one time covered land now occupied by Rose Hill Cemetery, Elm Ridge Park, and the Connecticut Veterans Home. W.B. Gilbert owned a large dairy farm on Elm Street. The Gilbert farm is still in operation on Gilbert Road and in the Meadows.

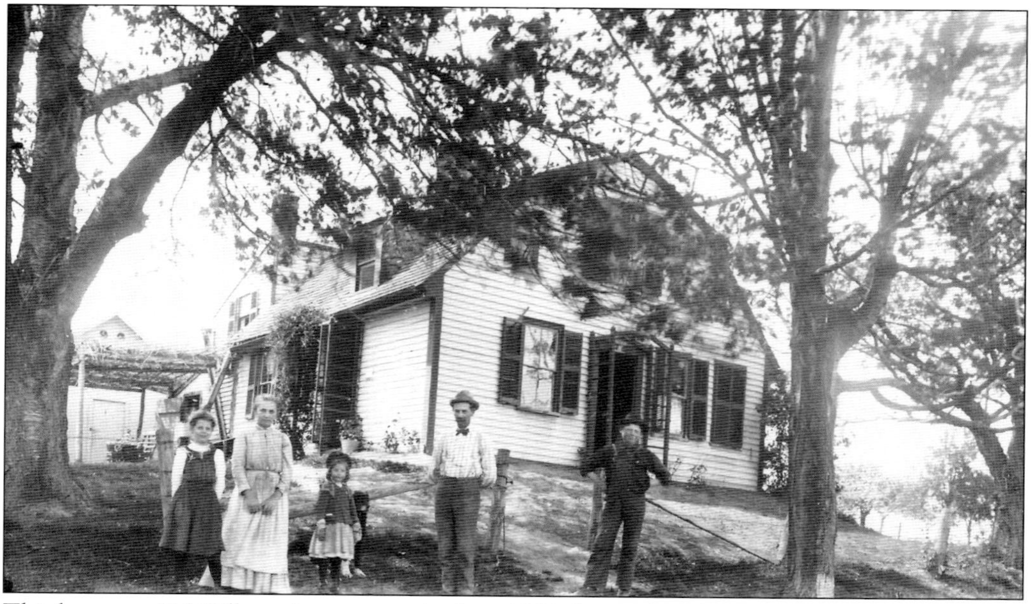

This home, at 114 Gilbert Avenue, was built in 1800. It was the Charles S. Gilbert home around 1902. He was the patriarch of the Gilbert family, which owned much of the farmland south of Gilbert Avenue between Elm and West Streets. The house is occupied by his descendants today.

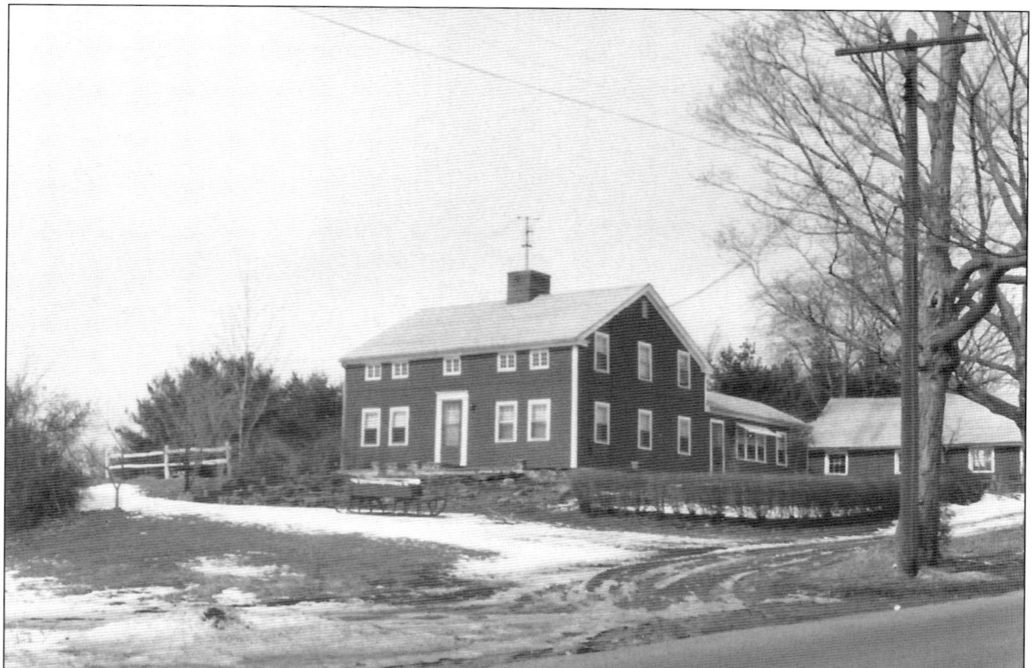

Joseph Jorey, an English blacksmith in Griswoldville who invented a never-slip horseshoe, owned this house at 401 Hayes Road in 1859. Patrick Dillon established a farm here around 1870. It was owned by his son Thomas Dillon at the turn of the 20th century. People with Irish roots settled in Rocky Hill after the potato famine and formed a tight community in the latter half of the 19th century.

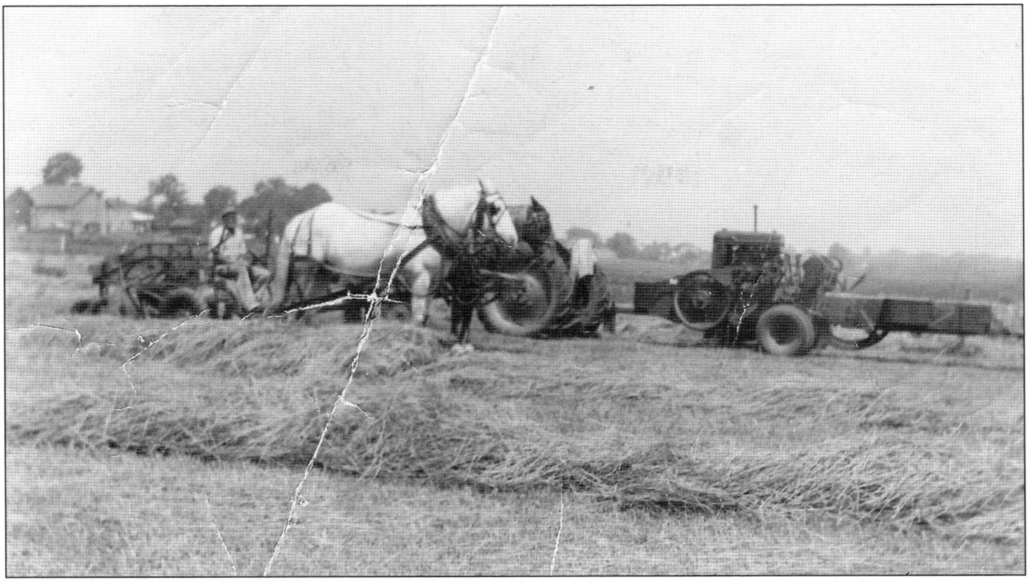

The Hayes family came to Rocky Hill from Ireland and settled on the Hayes Dairy Farm at 360 Hayes Road in the 1860s. The Town of Rocky Hill purchased development rights to the farm in 2014 to preserve farmland and the town's farming tradition. The Hayes family continues to operate the farm. Harry Hayes is shown here with farm equipment in 1953.

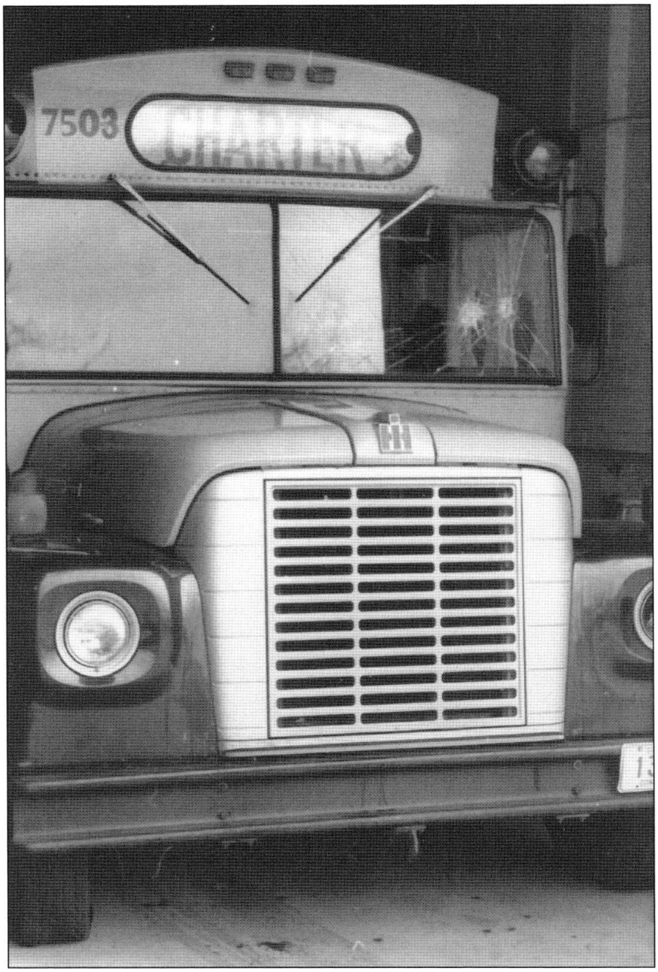

Edward P. Hayes owned and operated school buses in Rocky Hill starting in 1928. Like most businesses, E.P. Hayes had its ups and downs. This photograph shows an E.P. Hayes bus that had been vandalized during the 1977 Connecticut Foundry strike. The company provided bus services to several towns in central Connecticut.

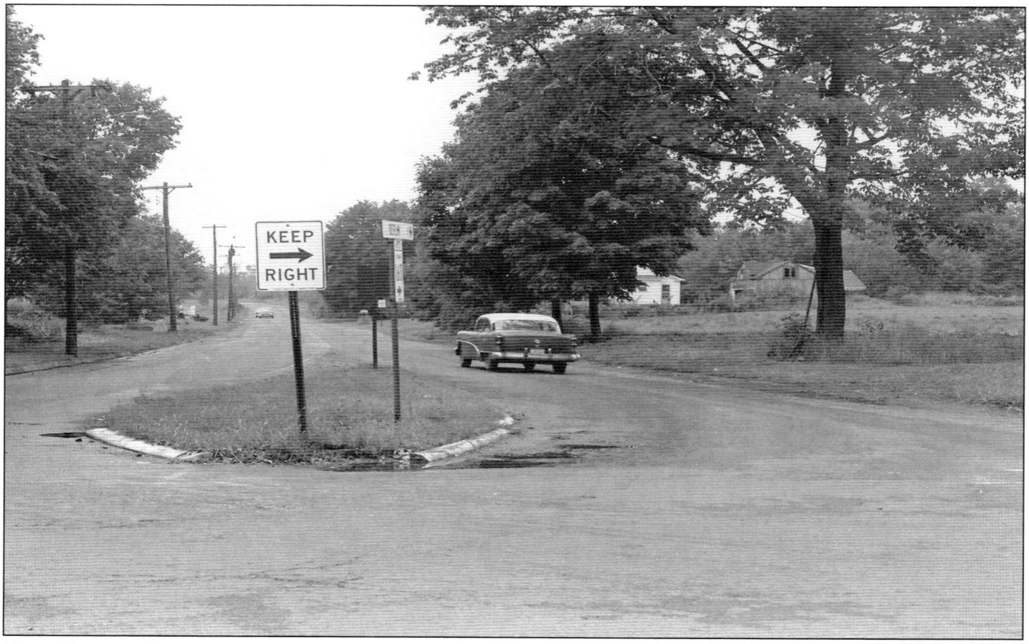

New Britain Avenue was once known as Beckley Road, since it ran to the Beckley Quarter of Rocky Hill and Berlin. It is part of Connecticut Route 160 and runs from the Berlin Turnpike (Connecticut Route 5/15) to Cromwell Avenue (Route 3). This photograph was taken in 1958 looking west from Cromwell Avenue. (Courtesy of Mike Martino.)

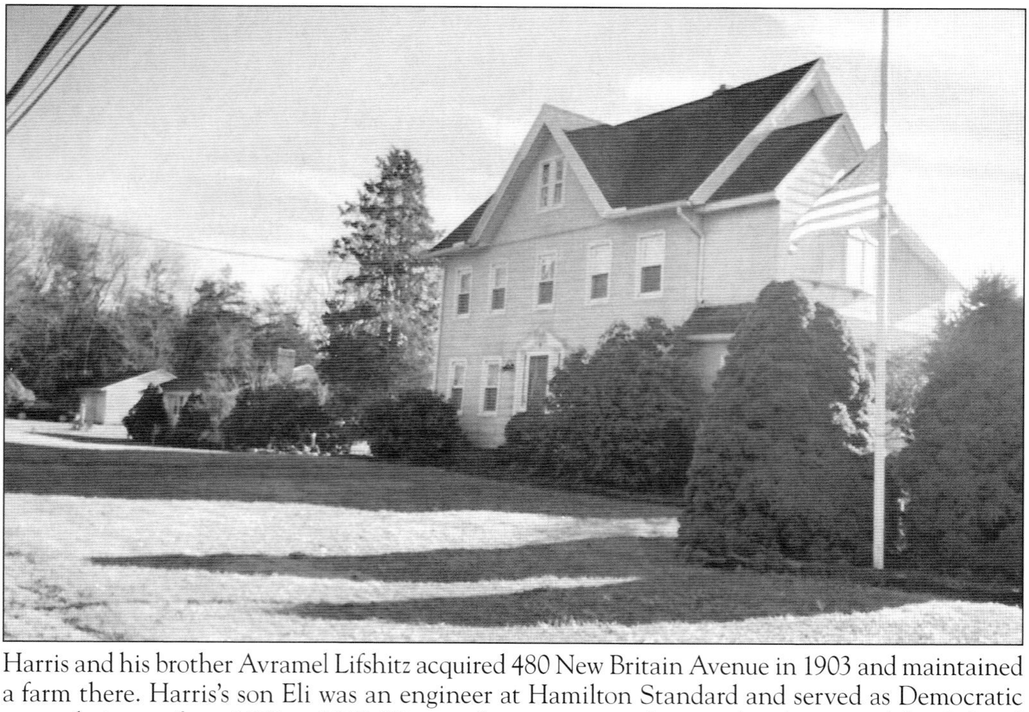

Harris and his brother Avramel Lifshitz acquired 480 New Britain Avenue in 1903 and maintained a farm there. Harris's son Eli was an engineer at Hamilton Standard and served as Democratic town chairman from 1957 to 1966. Eli served two terms in the state legislature and funded and mentored Richard Tulisano, another of Rocky Hill's prominent legislators. Eli's daughter Miriam currently serves on the town council.

Six

Rocky Hill Memories

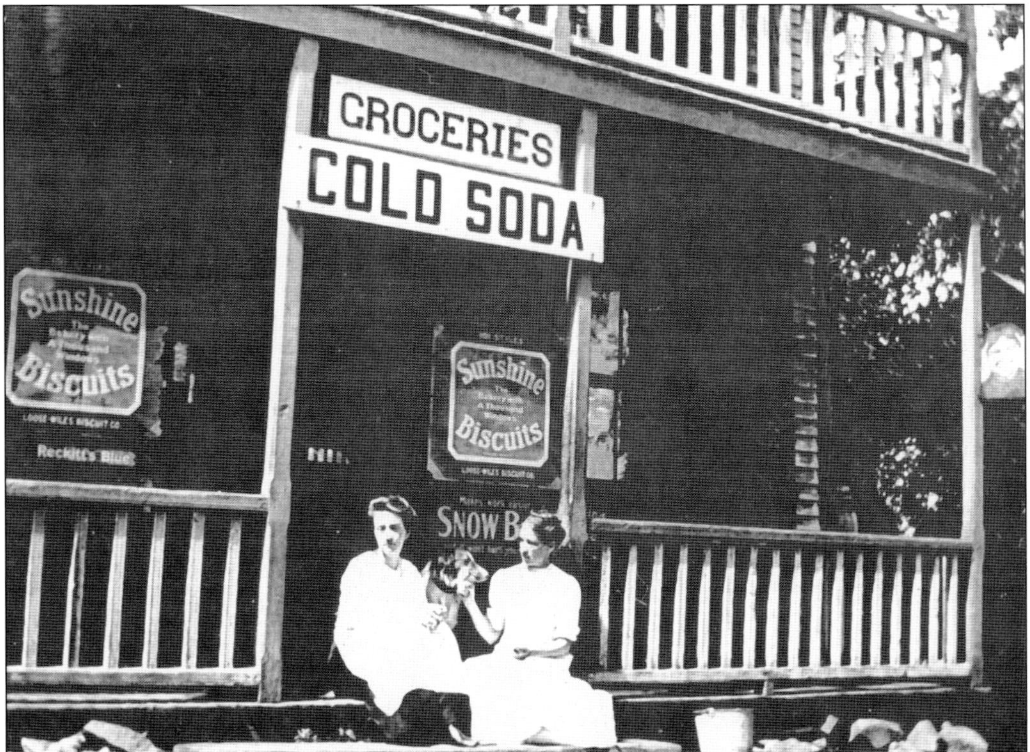

These women are sitting in front of the Sail Loft House at 276 Meadow Road in the 1890s. This building has undergone many changes. At one time, the facade was flat, and sails were hung to be worked on where the porch appears in this photograph. Today, the porch has been removed. (Courtesy of Mike Martino.)

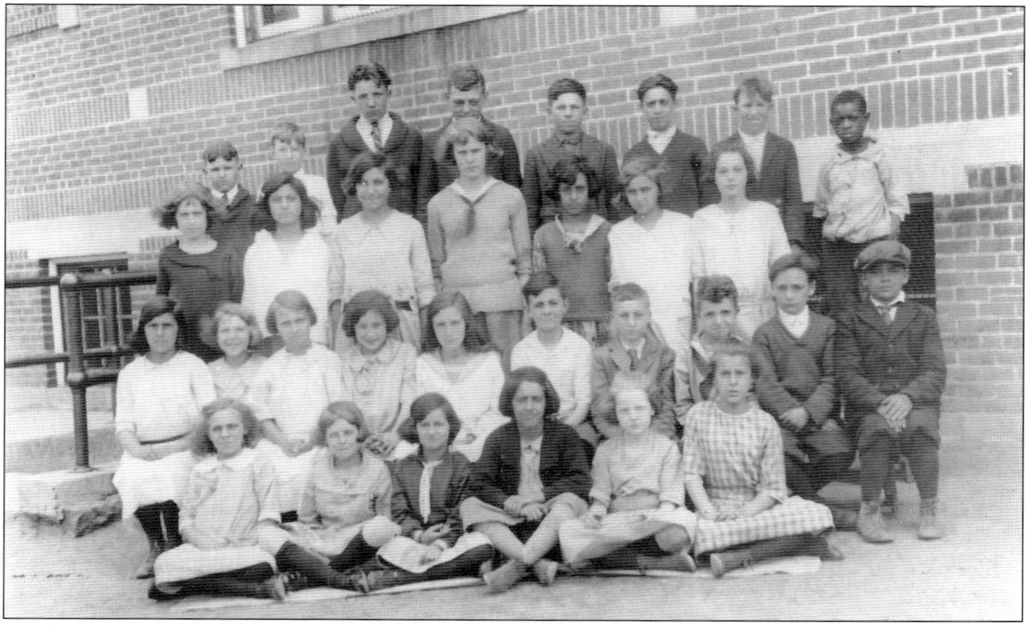

Students are pictured at Center School in the 1920s. From left to right are (first row) Ethel Butler, Frances Kelley, Ida Libera, Mary Cioto, Jennie Tuller, and Barbara Hunt; (second row) Lillian Martino, Viola Smith, Betty Woodward, Gladys Webber, June Soper, Winslow Avery, Darrel Atkin, Stewart Bidwell, Ernest Pawlich, and unidentified; (third row) Priscilla Hick, Mabel Markette, Clarinda Speno, Gertrude Ryder, unidentified, Carol French, and Gladys Medhurst; (fourth row) Dominic Sylvester, unidentified, Jimmy Dounouk, James Covey, Tony Carbonaro, and Arthur Klatt. (Courtesy of Mike Martino.)

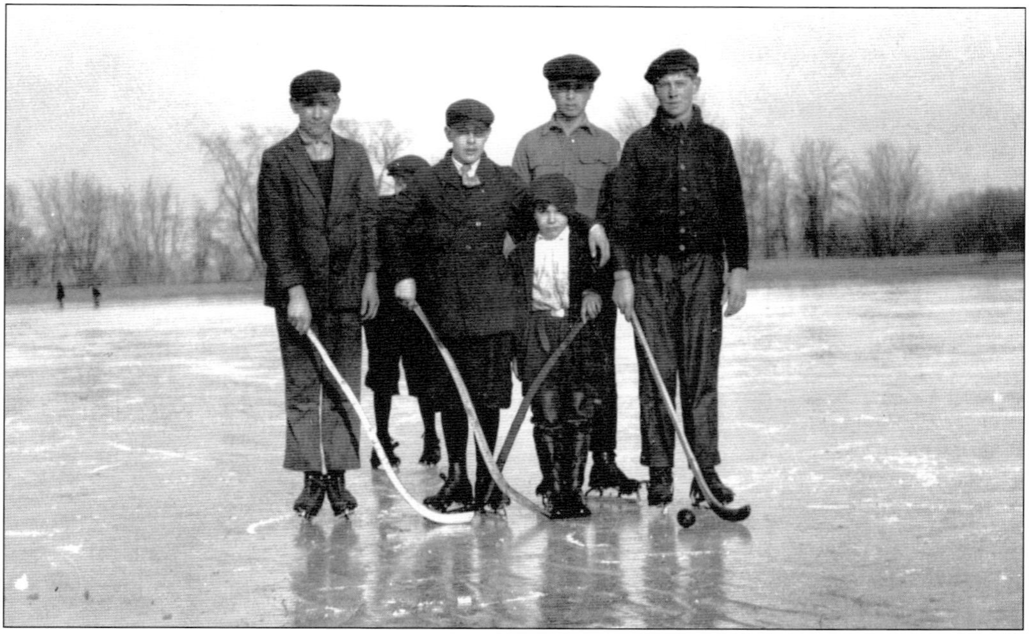

The Connecticut River provided a playground when it froze solid in the winter. Cold-weather pursuits included ice boating, skating, and hockey, as seen here in the 1920s. During warm weather, children would enjoy swimming and fishing. (Courtesy of Mike Martino.)

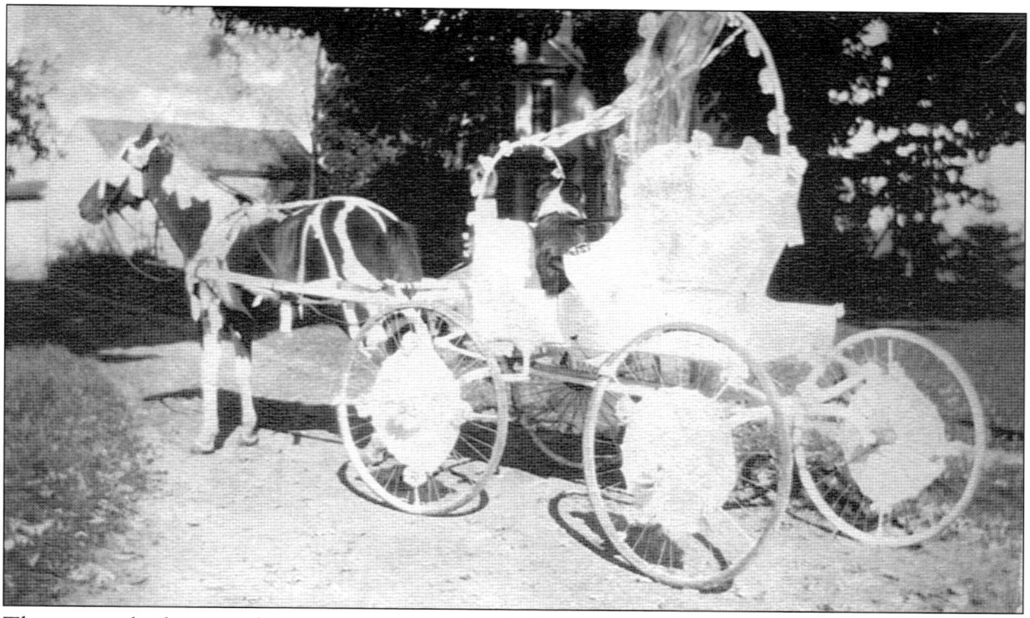

This ornately decorated wagon is outside the Gilbert farmhouse in the 1920s. There are more questions than answers concerning it. It was decorated for a parade but it is unclear which one. Is it the same wagon that is parked outside the Gilbert farmhouse being used as a planter in 2019?

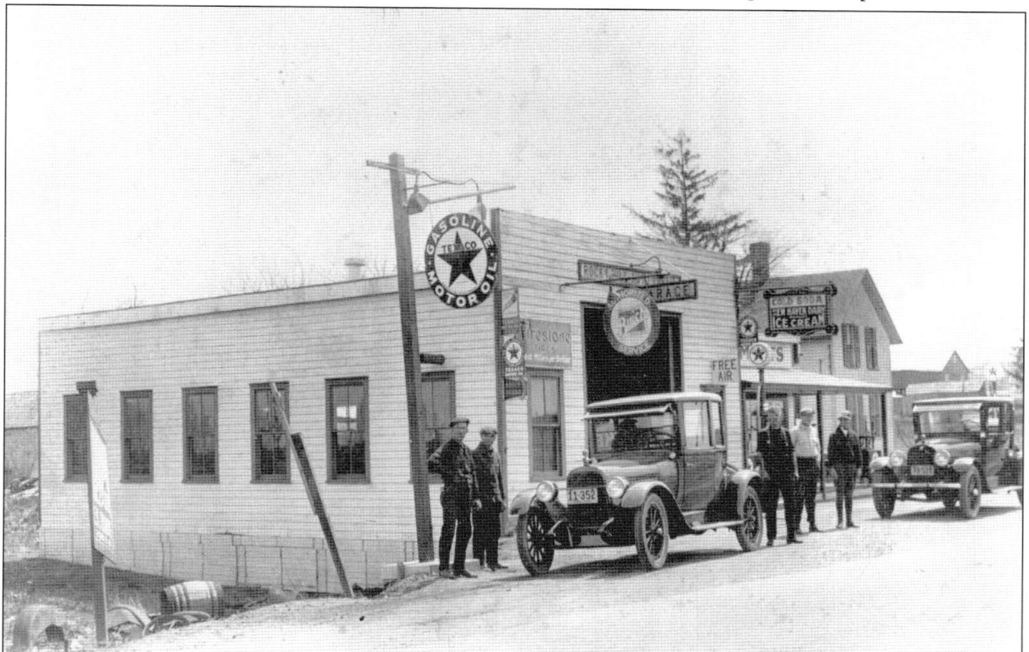

Before the Silas Deane Highway went through in 1930, Old Main Street was the primary thoroughfare through Rocky Hill. On the north end in the 1920s, Fred Helmstadt owned a garage and refreshment stop near the Wethersfield border. This was on the east side of the road a few hundred yards south of the Interstate 91 overpass. The garage is gone; the house still exists. (Courtesy of Mike Martino.)

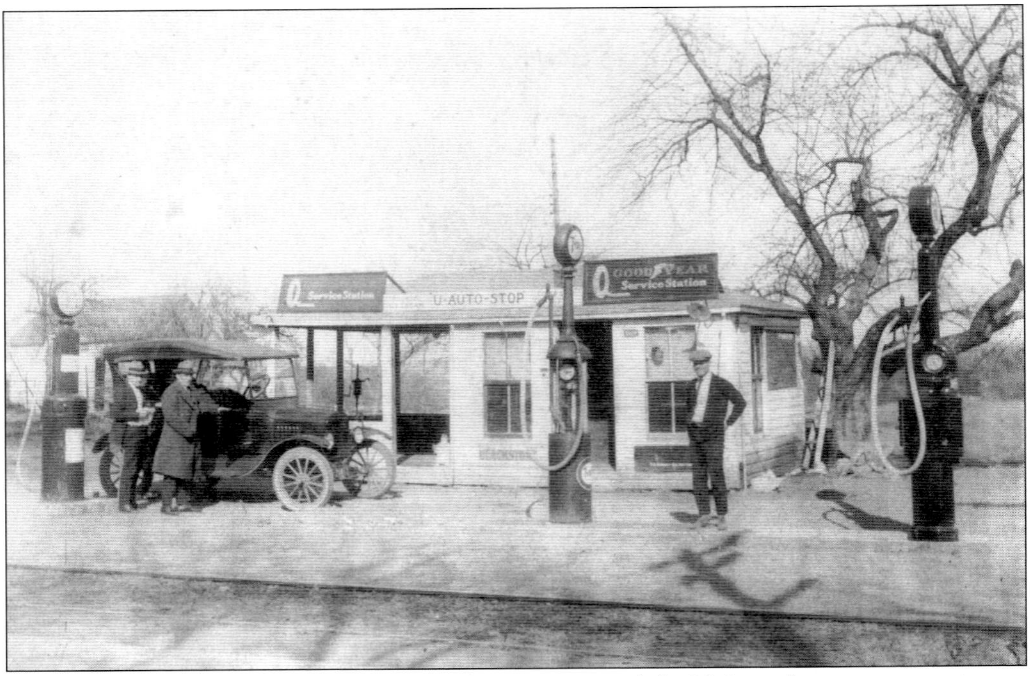

Entering Main Street from the south, travelers encountered the U-Auto-Stop service station on the east side of Main Street just over the Cromwell line. It sold four to five different brands of gasoline. The right side of the building was for the sale of gasoline, oil, and other automotive needs. The left side was porch-like and sold ice cream and candy. (Courtesy of Mike Martino.)

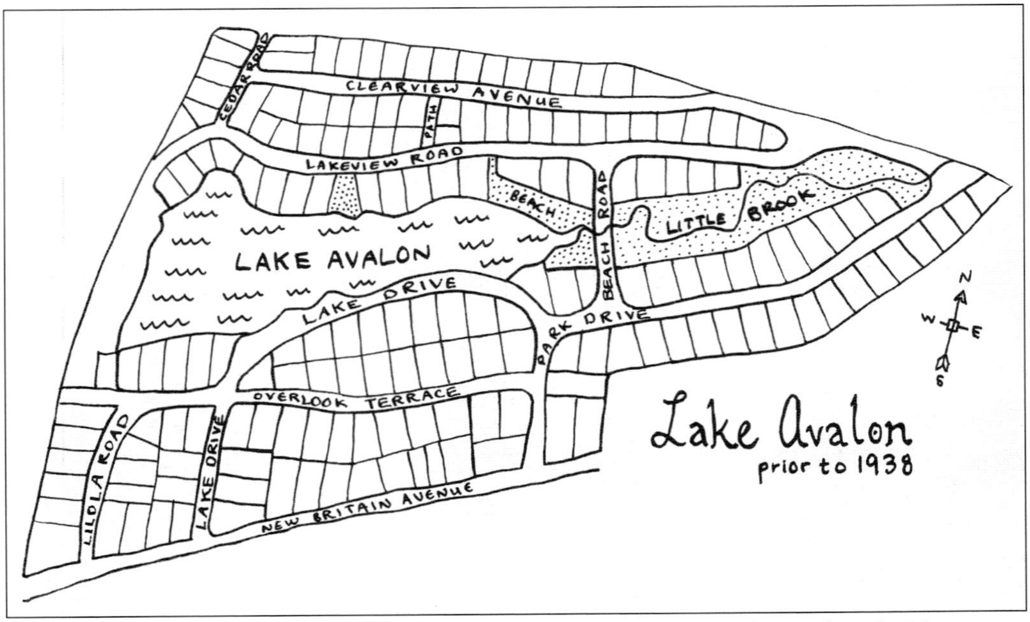

Lake Avalon, a resort development, began in the 1920s by damming Little Brook at the Newington town line. It was located off New Britain Avenue between Beach Road and modern Cobey Road. By 1933, the project was bankrupt, and water quality had become an issue. The 1938 hurricane broke the dam, flooding the lake into Berlin. Today it is a residential neighborhood. (Courtesy of Jennifer Duff Creations.)

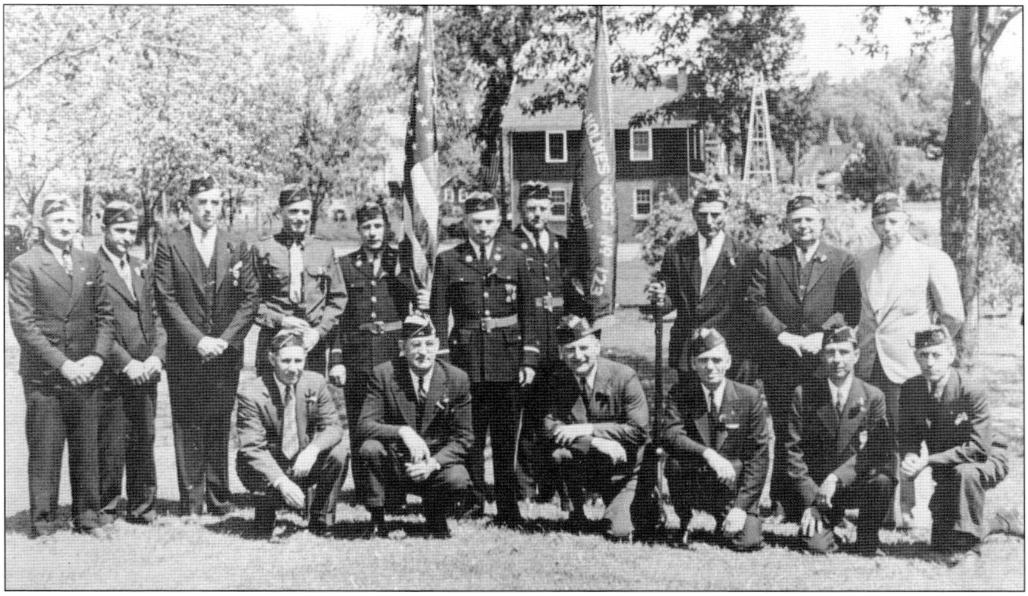

After World War I, the American Legion became important in public affairs and politics. Members of the Campilio-Holmes Post 123 are shown here in 1938. From left to right are (first row) Wally Peck, Roy Perkins, Robert Mason, Ray Evans, Alex Reduker, and Charles Gallager; (second row) Chester Steele, Sam Nazzaro, Harry Hick, Steve Grigley, Joe Gerritz, Joe McCarthy, Charles Yerrington, Dominick Spadaccaini, Bill Quinn, and Horace Hills. (Courtesy of Mike Martino.)

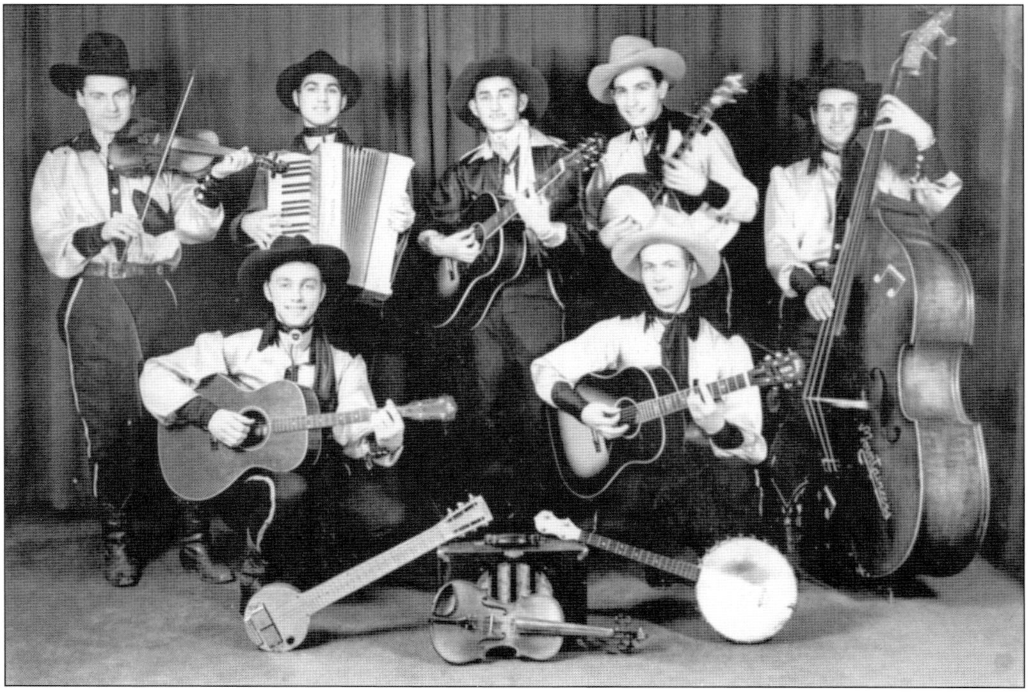

Home-grown country-western bands once played local events. The Rambling Mountaineers are, from left to right, (first row) Leonard Eurto and Pete Bogus; (second row) Chet Eurto, Horace "Corky" Bennino, John DeJohn (also known as Jed Summers), Orest Rigoletti, and Tony DeJohn. (Courtesy of Mike Martino.)

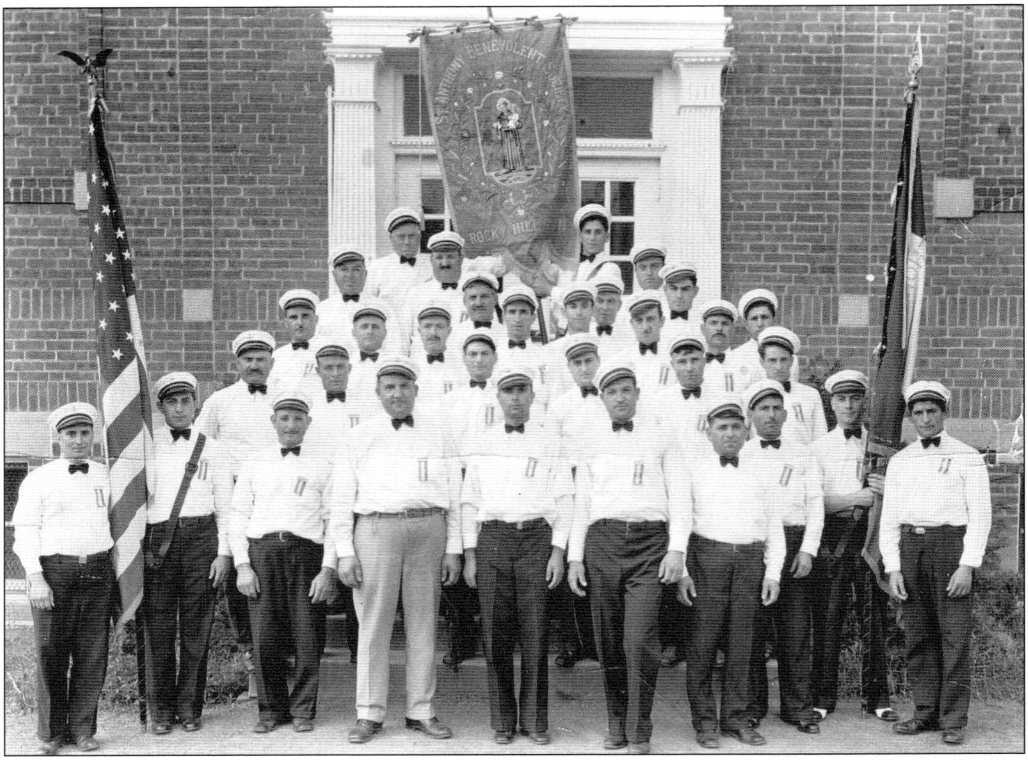

In 1898, there was one Italian American family in Rocky Hill. The quarry attracted many experienced Italian quarrymen, and suburbanization attracted many more Italian American developers and potential home owners. The Rocky Hill St. Anthony Benevolent Society was an Italian American social organization. Members in this photograph, taken at Center School about 1937, are not identified, although people often recognize relatives and friends. (Courtesy of Mike Martino.)

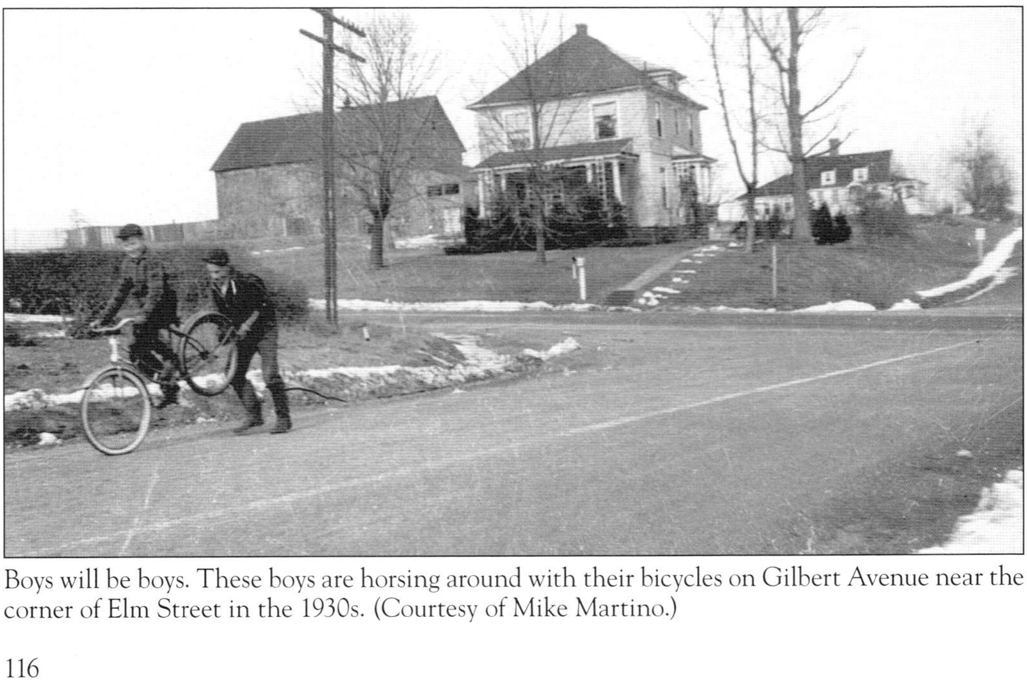

Boys will be boys. These boys are horsing around with their bicycles on Gilbert Avenue near the corner of Elm Street in the 1930s. (Courtesy of Mike Martino.)

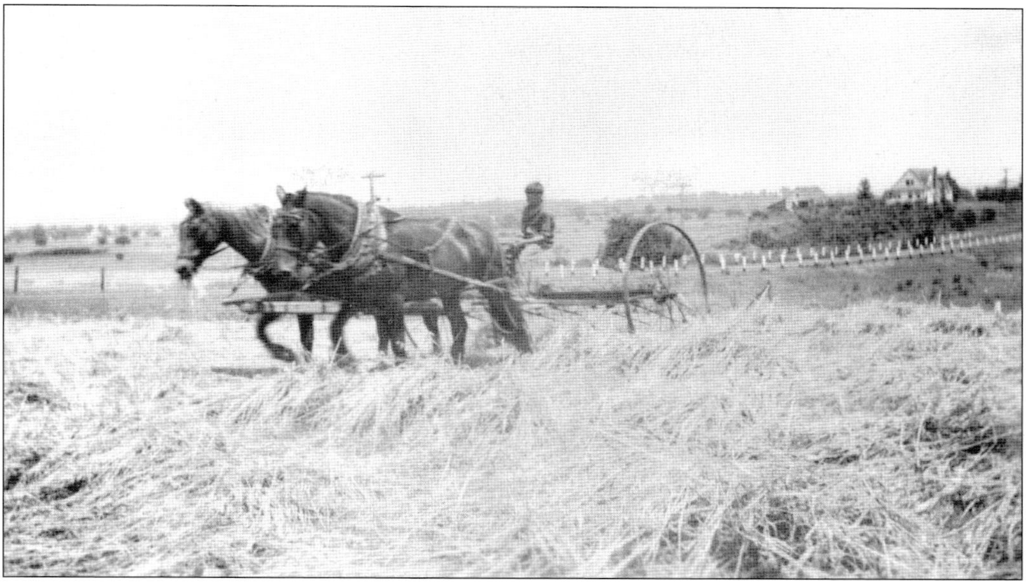

Leland Gilbert is shown mowing hay south of Elm Street and east of the Gilbert farmhouse at 730 Elm Street in 1937. The house across the road is 629 Elm Street. The fields have since been replaced with residences. (Courtesy of Mike Martino.)

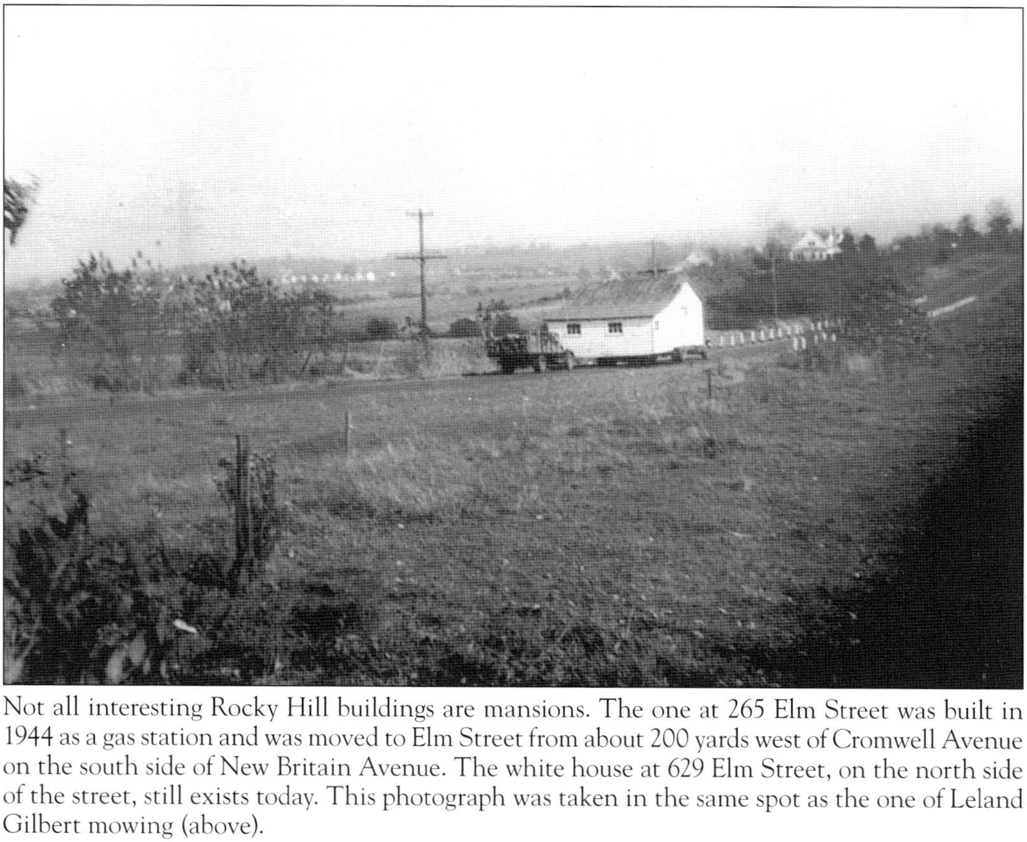

Not all interesting Rocky Hill buildings are mansions. The one at 265 Elm Street was built in 1944 as a gas station and was moved to Elm Street from about 200 yards west of Cromwell Avenue on the south side of New Britain Avenue. The white house at 629 Elm Street, on the north side of the street, still exists today. This photograph was taken in the same spot as the one of Leland Gilbert mowing (above).

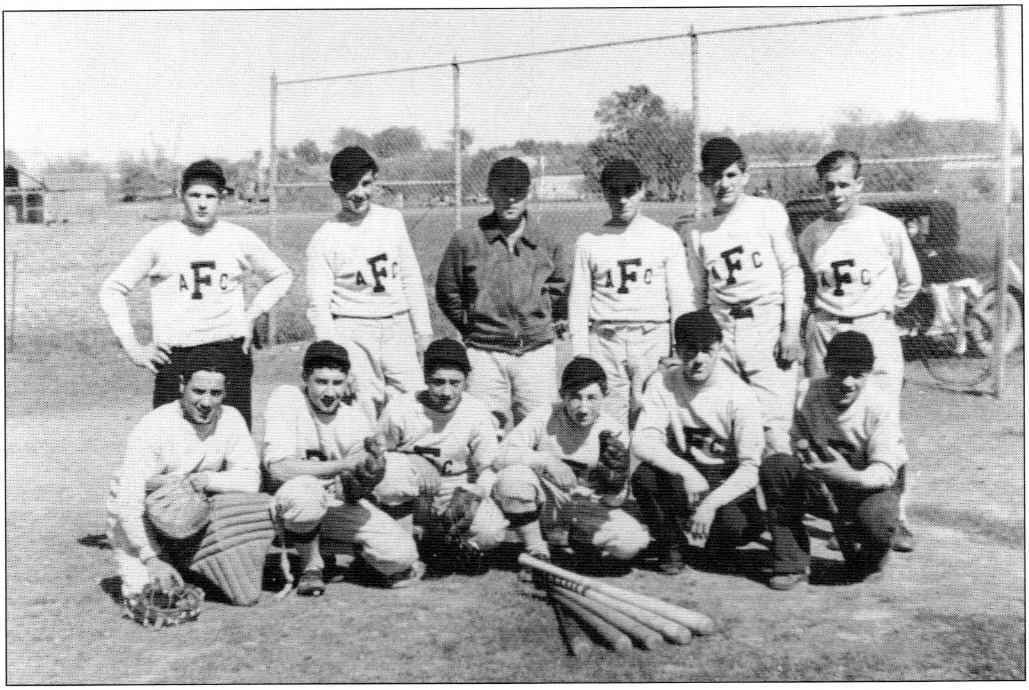

The Farmer's Athletic Club baseball team was from the west side of town. This photograph was taken at the West School baseball field on Elm Street in the 1930s. From left to right are (first row) John Allessio, John Mingo, Tony Allessio, Art Dorman, John Staron, and Mike Zdeb; (second row) Steve Klubko, Eddy Krol, Garson Goldberg, Nick Rago, Frank Tolli, and Mike Klubko. (Courtesy of Mike Martino.)

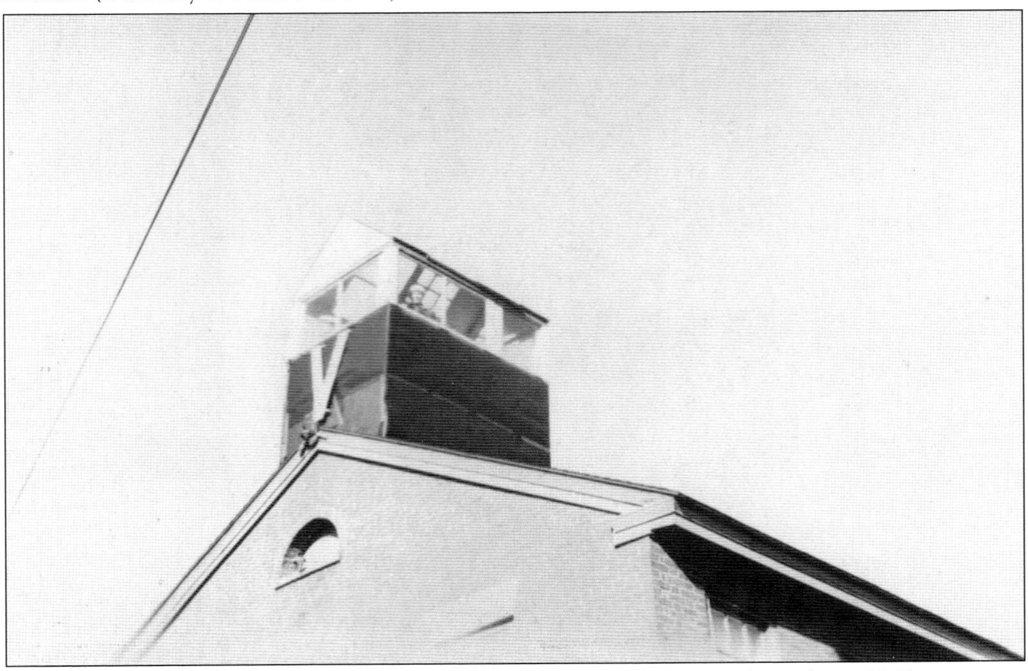

Early in World War II, a plane spotting tower was installed on top of Academy Hall to protect Colt, Pratt and Whitney, and other industrial sites. It was later moved to Quarry Hill.

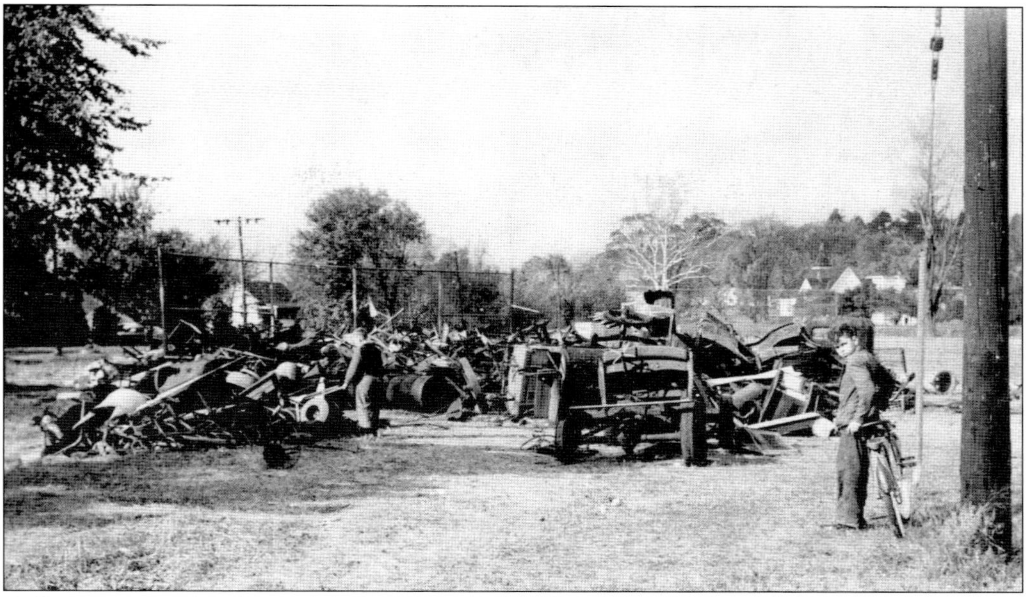

Collecting scrap metal to aid the war effort was a common activity during World War II. Here, Rocky Hill people contribute to that effort. (Courtesy of Mike Martino.)

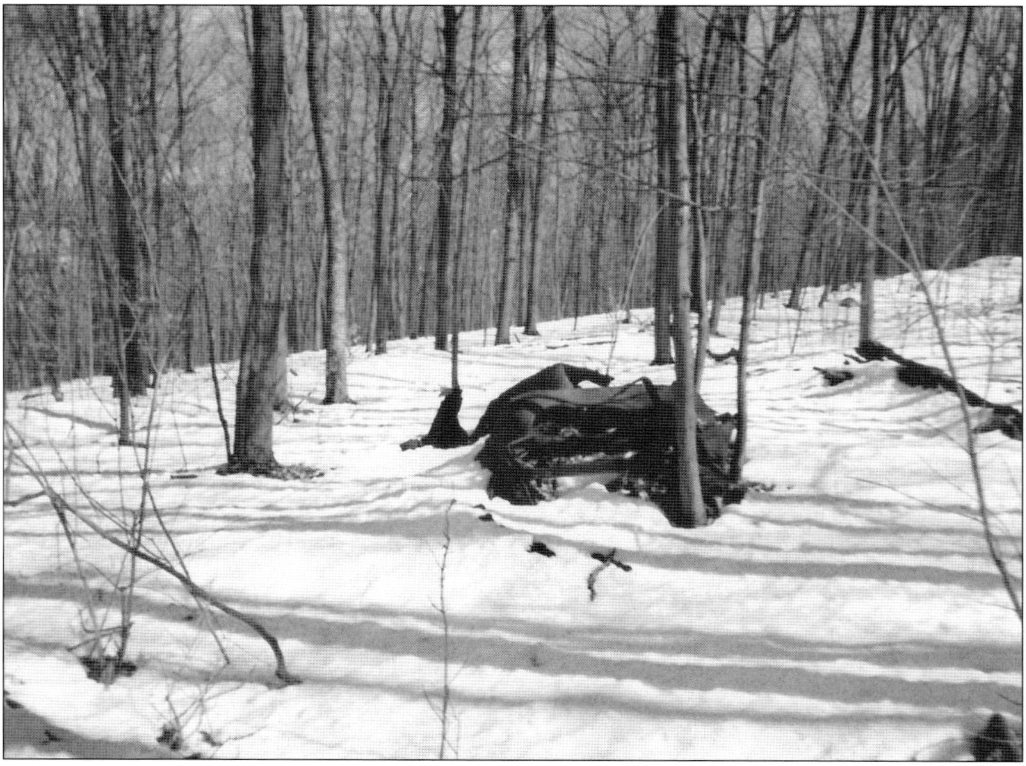

This was a 1936 Chevrolet that drove a rope tow for the Wethersfield Ski Club in 1949–1950. It was jacked up and the rope was wrapped around a rear wheel. The ski slope ran to the railroad tracks. For much of the town's history, the east slope of the rocky hill was clear-cut. The wreckage of the car is still there off Matteson Avenue on the quarry trail.

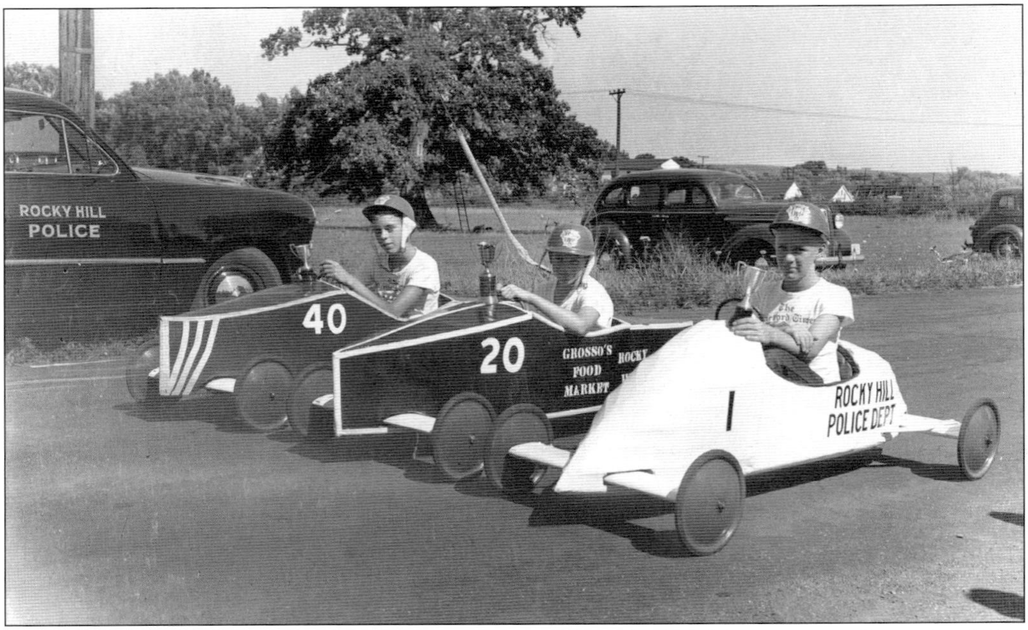

The Rocky Hill Soap Box Derby was an important event for local boys, especially in the 1940s and 1950s. These are the winners of the 1949 derby. No. 40 is the Connecticut Foundry racer, driven by Richard Starr. No. 20 is the Grosso grocery racer, driven by Gordon Jenning. No. 1 is the Rocky Hill Police Department racer, driven by Phillip Carpenter Jr. (Courtesy of Mike Martino.)

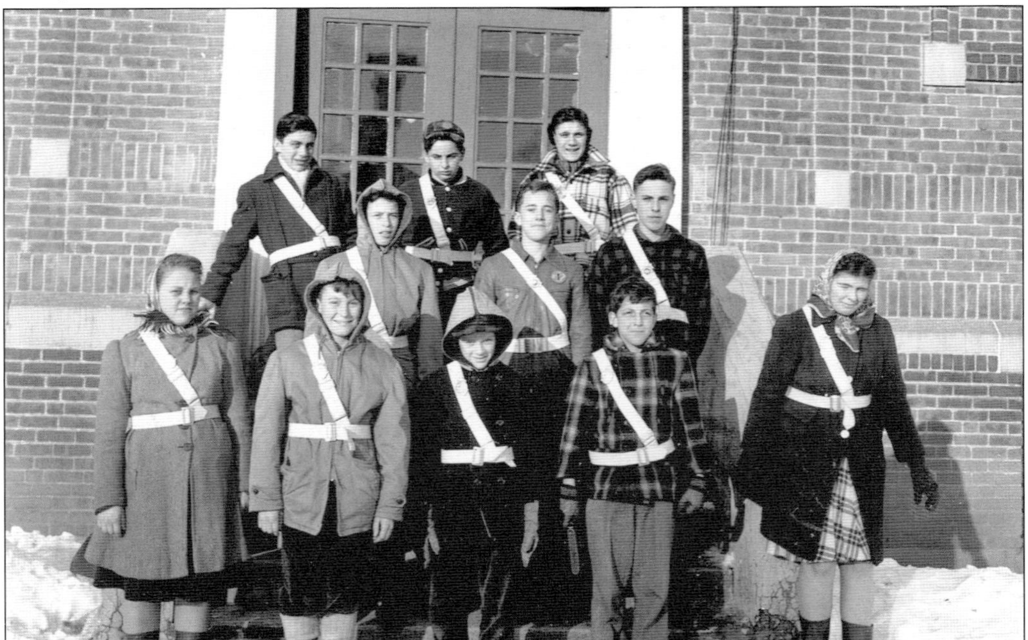

Safety patrol crossing guards pose at Center School in the 1940s. From left to right are (first row) Gertrude Eurto, Robert Hawkins, Phillip Warren Carpenter Jr., Peter Caruso, and Merece LeGeyt; (second row) Coe Hawkins, Art Brooks, and William Campbell; (third row) Henry Wilson, James A. Covey Jr., and Charles Tarum. (Courtesy of Mike Martino.)

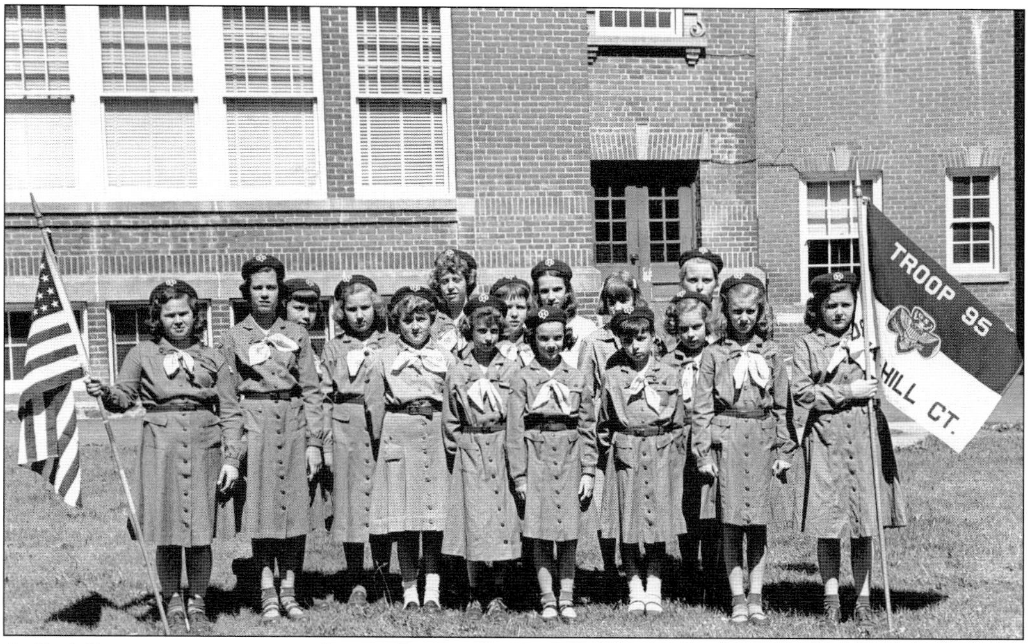

A Girl Scout troop poses in front of Center School in 1954. From left to right are (first row) Sandra Krasawa, Lelia McKinney, Janice Deresienski, Sandy Demma, Elaine Klewicki, Jane Morris, Patty Manning, and Peggy Hayes; (second row) Elaine Piolunek, Carol Coquette, Judy Ralston, Barbara McNeil, Peggy Morris, Jackie McCarsky, Mary Ellen Martin, and Mary Little. (Courtesy of Mike Martino.)

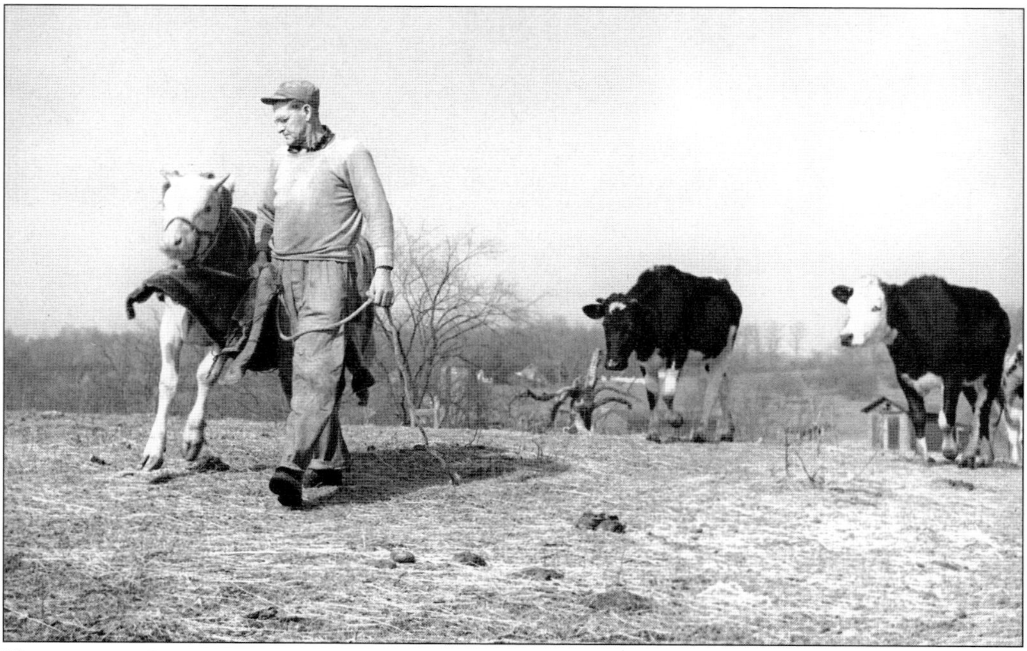
Hairyette, a Guernsey on Hayes Farm, gave birth to hairless calves. Hairyette's hairless calves became local celebrities in rural Rocky Hill. Her calf Pinky, a bull shown above who wasn't expected to live long, sired seven or eight full-furred calves and lived a long, happy life. Lerner Furriers of Hartford made a special coat for Pinky to keep him warm in the winter.

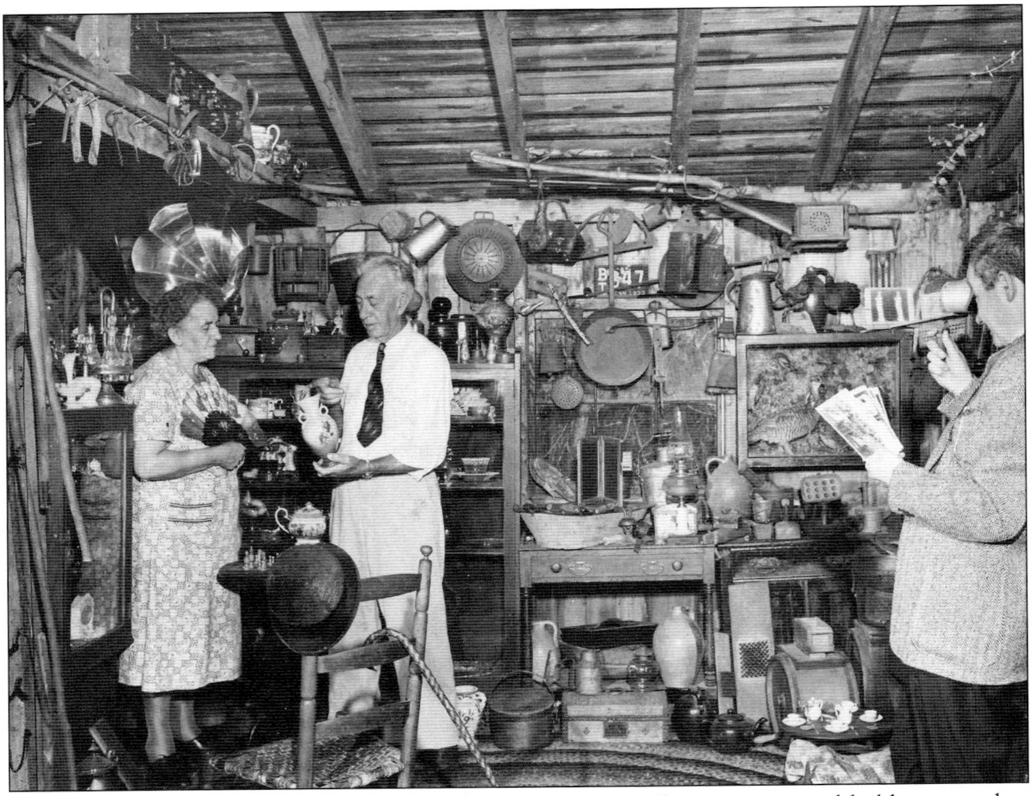

Charlie Yeager (middle) served as railroad stationmaster and postmaster and held many other responsible posts in Rocky Hill. He operated the Stepney Museum in his home at 1 Pratt Street from 1951 to 1959, when he died. The Friends of Cora J. Belden Library spun off the Rocky Hill Historical Society in 1960—a coincidence, or did Charlie seed the historical society?

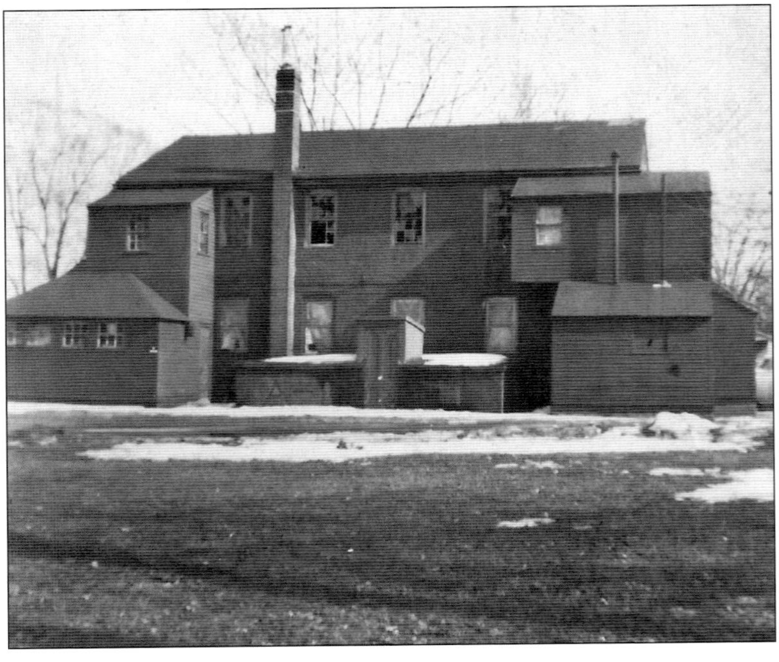

Academy Hall, in spite of its proud history, had fallen into disrepair and was scheduled for demolition by 1963. Peter Revill, a major figure in the development of the Rocky Hill Historical Society, obtained a grant from the State of Connecticut to restore the building. A substantial amount of sweat equity resulted in the beautiful piece of history enjoyed today.

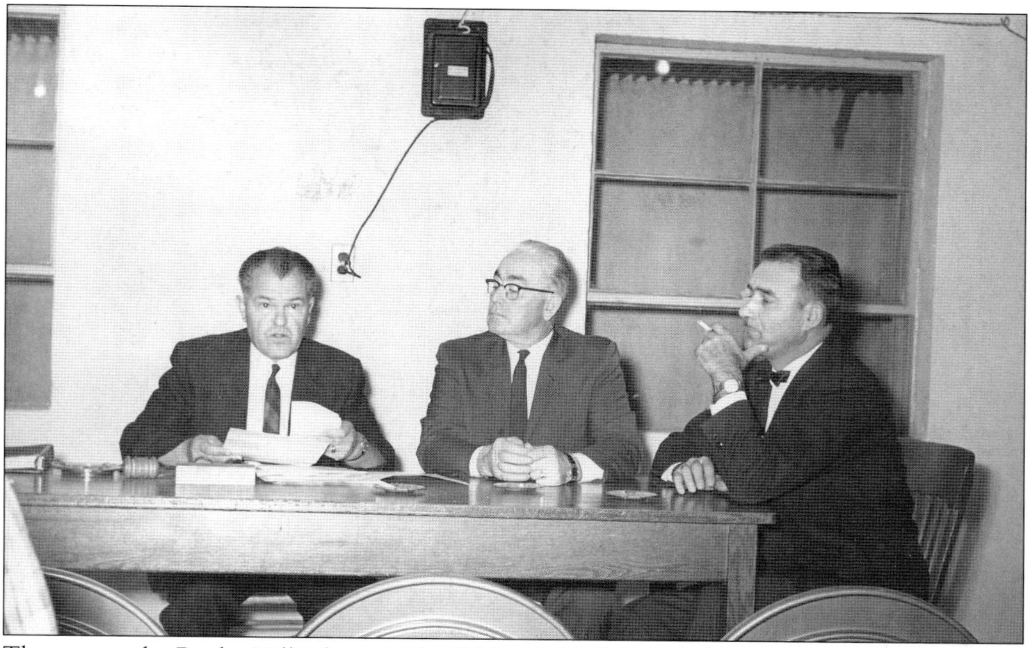

These were the Rocky Hill selectmen in 1964 and 1965. From left to right are First Selectman Domenic Sylvester, Second Selectman Edward P. Hayes, and Third Selectman Irmo Pia. Rocky Hill's form of government changed from selectmen to a mayor, town manager, town council, and specialized boards in 1967. (Courtesy of Mike Martino.)

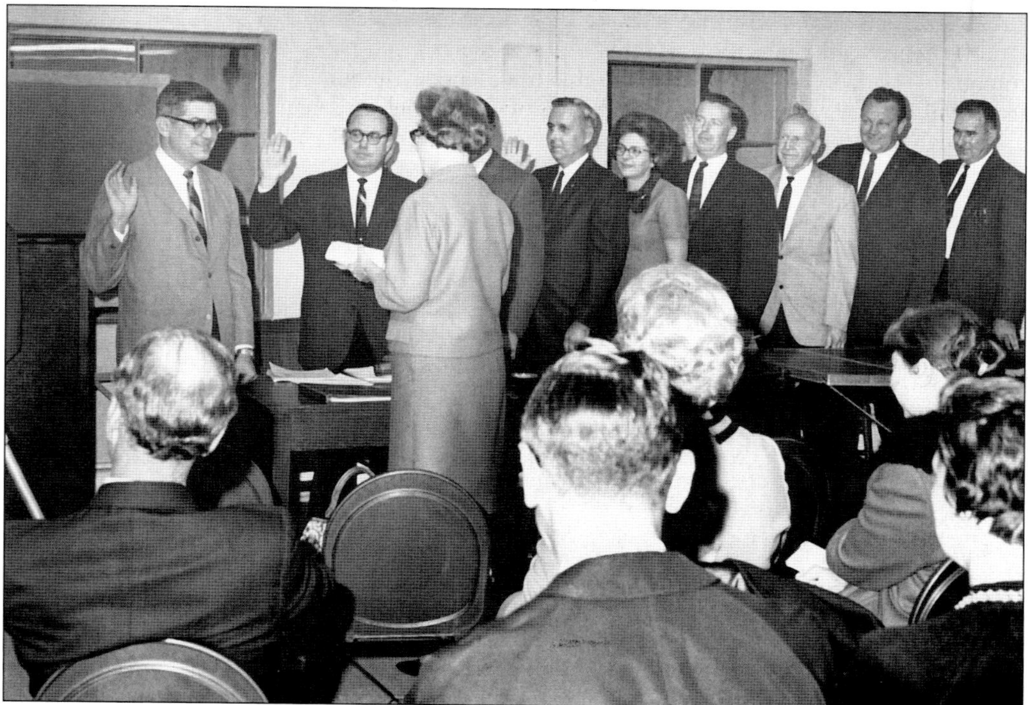

The first mayor and town council of Rocky Hill are sworn in on November 8, 1967. Members are Mayor David Moser, Richard Button, Nicholas A. Pizzella, Jesse M. Harrison, Barbara Pfeiffer, Richard J. Conway, William Harris, Howard Smith, and Irmo Pia. (Courtesy of Mike Martino.)

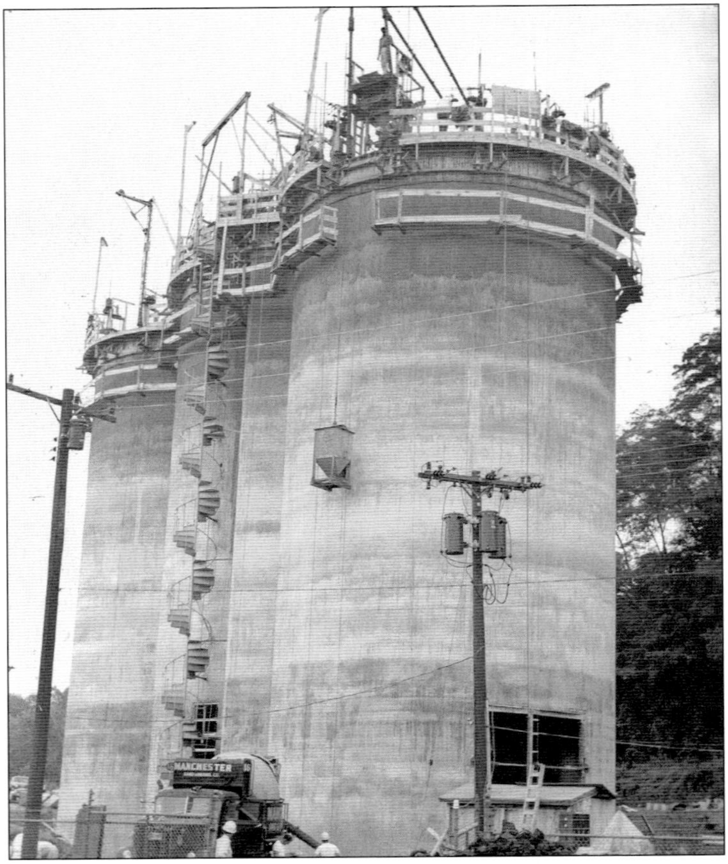

These are the Marquette Cement Company towers on Meadow Road. In the 1960s, cement was brought up the river and stored in here primarily for use on Interstate 91. As of 2019, they are scheduled to be razed.

The Neumann farmhouse (pictured) was burned in the early 1960s in a fire department drill to make way for Interstate 91. A similar fate befell the Anulewicz and Mingo farmhouses on the other side of Elm Street.

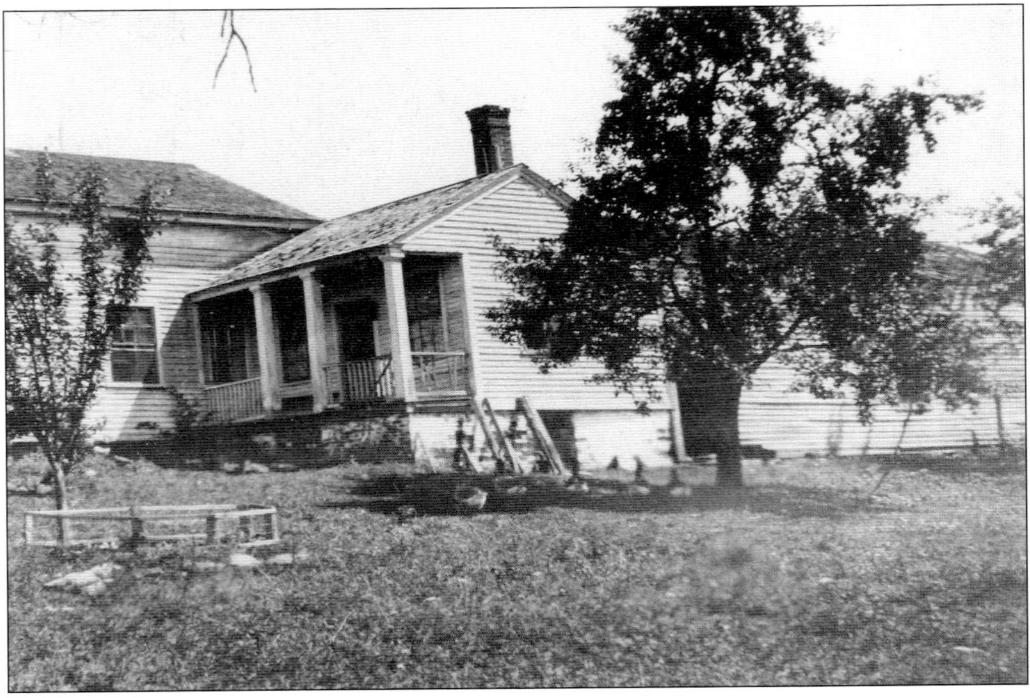

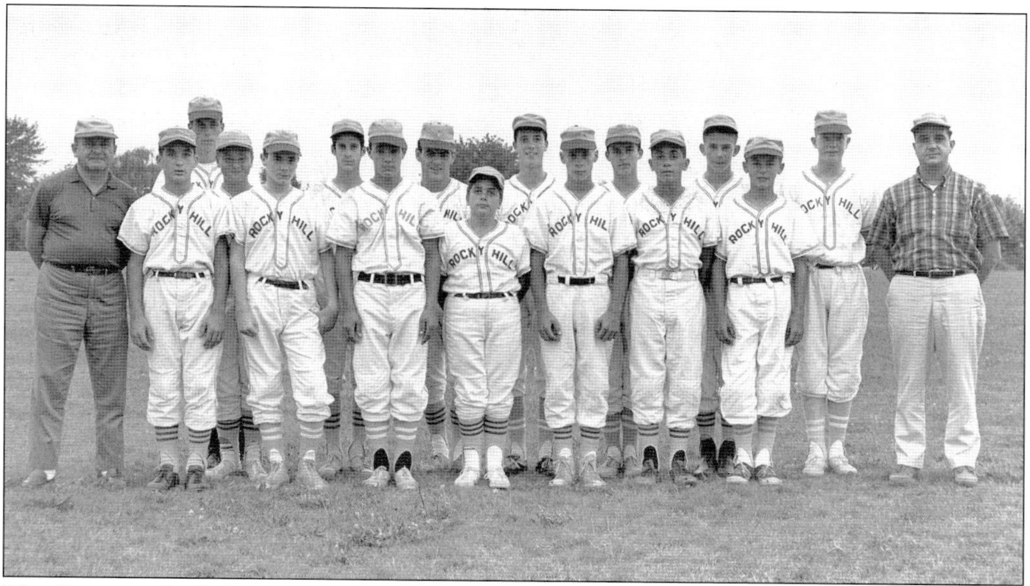

The Bennino-Beck Post 2138 Alumni League baseball team poses in the 1930s. From left to right are (first row) Michel Smith, Mark Deresienski, Edward O'Neill, Eddie Rogers, Richard Maraschiello, Hal Gilbert, Jon Cassarino, and Larry Aldridge; (second row) Pat Sullivan, Peter LeVasseur, John Burns, Larry Drake, Danny Flanagan, Michael Clen, and Bill McKenna Jr. Coach Richard Valenti is at left, and manager Paul Cassarino is at right. (Courtesy of Mike Martino.)

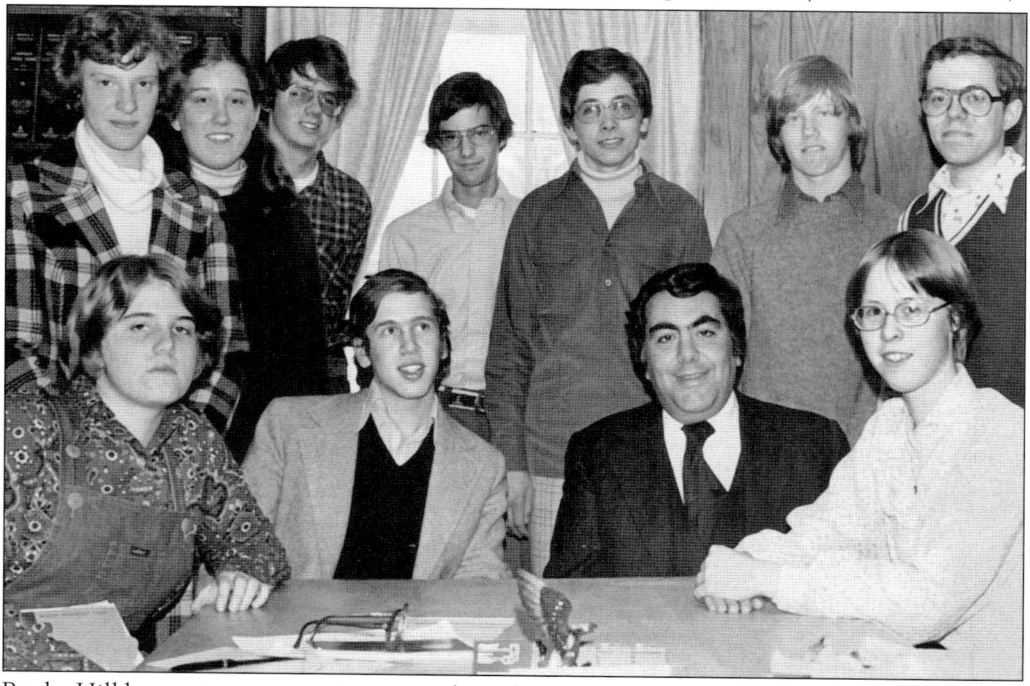

Rocky Hill has sent many prominent people to the state government. Richard Tulisano was one. He served in the Connecticut House of Representatives from 1974 until 2000, as house majority whip in 1995, and as chief of staff to House Speaker Moira Lyons in 2000. His "Italian Battalion" were protégés from Rocky Hill, Wethersfield, and West Hartford who provided intern services for him. None was Italian. (Courtesy of Beverly Tulisano.)

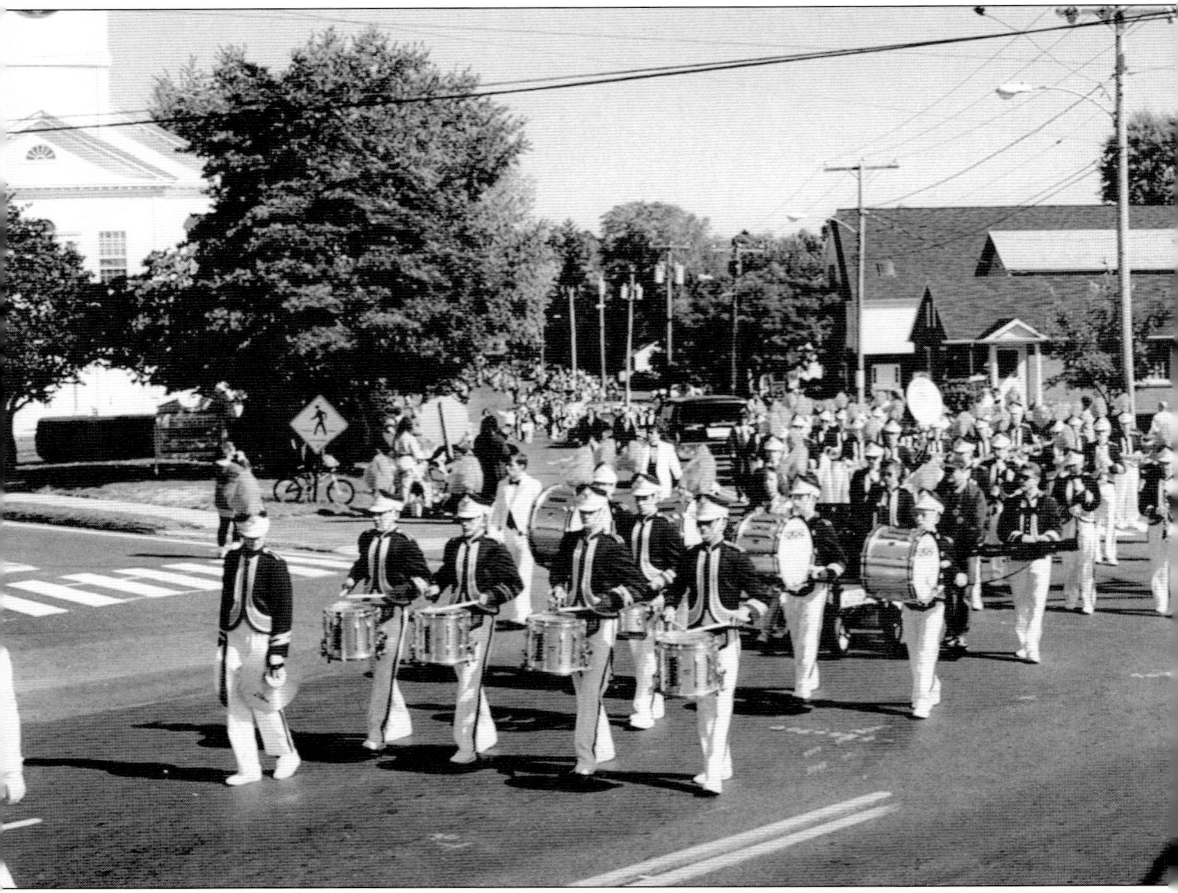

The Royal Blues, Rocky Hill High School's competition-winning marching band, changed their name from the Terriers in the mid-1970s. By 1993, when they marched in Rocky Hill's 150th anniversary parade, they were sporting the distinctive blue-and-white uniforms for which they are known. The band predates the football team by over 30 years and has long been a respected institution. (Courtesy of Mike Martino.)

About the Authors

Bob Herron has been the Rocky Hill town historian since 2017. He has served as a researcher for the Connecticut Historical Society, the Godfrey Memorial Library, and the Rocky Hill Historical Society. His writing credentials include a book on Rocky Hill in World War I and an article on the history of the Rocky Hill Veterans Home that appeared in the spring 2016 issue of *Connecticut Explored* magazine. Bob grew up in Hartford. He served four years in the US Air Force as an airfield firefighter and graduated from Central Connecticut State University in 1972. He has enjoyed a successful career in computer systems methodologies and data architecture. In addition to his career responsibilities, Bob taught courses in systems analysis and design at the Greater Hartford Community College and delivered guest lectures at the University of Michigan. He has published extensively and frequently presented papers at several professional computer forums, including GUIDE, COMDEX, and the Structured Development Forum. He retired in 2003.

One of the frustrations of being a historian is the occasional realization that, while you were digging for obscure historical facts, a historical treasure was right under your nose. Mike Martino is one of these treasures. Mike has developed such a fine reputation as a photographer and videographer that his vast store of historical information about his community tends to be overlooked. He has been photographing historic events in Rocky Hill for most of his adult life. He carried a scanner for many years and went to most important events to take pictures. Not only did Mike take pictures of current events, he also collected historically interesting photographs. He has written captions for these photographs, which form a treasure trove of historical information. Mike served as president of the Rocky Hill Historical Society from 1998 through 2016. He has produced videos that capture much of Rocky Hill's modern history and has written several history-related articles for *Rocky Hill Life*, the local newspaper.